Philip

The Poems

NICHOLAS MARSH

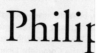

palgrave
macmillan

First published 2007 by
PALGRAVE MACMILLAN
Houndmills, Basingstoke, Hampshire RG21 6XS and
175 Fifth Avenue, New York, N.Y. 10010
Companies and representatives throughout the world

PALGRAVE MACMILLAN is the global academic imprint of the Palgrave
Macmillan division of St. Martin's Press, LLC and of Palgrave Macmillan Ltd.
Macmillan® is a registered trademark in the United States, United Kingdom
and other countries. Palgrave is a registered trademark in the European
Union and other countries.

ISBN-13: 978–1–4039–9267–3 hardback
ISBN-10: 1–4039–9267–3 hardback
ISBN-13: 978–1–4039–9269–7 paperback
ISBN-10: 1–4039–9269–X paperback

This book is printed on paper suitable for recycling and made from fully
managed and sustained forest sources. Logging, pulping and manufactur-
ing processes are expected to conform to the environmental regulations
of the country of origin.

A catalogue record for this book is available from the British Library.

A catalog record for this book is available from the Library of Congress.

10 9 8 7 6 5 4 3 2 1
16 15 14 13 12 11 10 09 08 07

Printed and bound in China

For Charles, Liz and Eva

Contents

General Editor's Preface

This series is dedicated to one clear belief: that we can all enjoy, understand and analyse literature for ourselves, provided we know how to do it. How can we build on close understanding of a short passage, and develop our insight into the whole work? What features do we expect to find in a text? Why do we study style in so much detail? In demystifying the study of literature, these are only some of the questions the *Analysing Texts* series addresses and answers.

The books in this series will not do all the work for you, but will provide you with the tools, and show you how to use them. Here, you will find samples of close, detailed analysis, with an explanation of the analytical techniques utilised. At the end of each chapter there are useful suggestions for further work you can do to practise, develop and hone the skills demonstrated and build confidence in your own analytical ability.

An author's individuality shows in the way they write: every work they produce bears the hallmark of that writer's personal 'style'. In the main part of each book we concentrate therefore on analysing the particular flavour and concerns of one author's work, and explain the features of their writing in connection with major themes. In Part II there are chapters about the author's life and work, assessing their contribution to developments in literature; and a sample of critics' views are summarised and discussed in comparison with each other. Some suggestions for further reading provide a bridge towards further critical research.

Analysing Texts is designed to stimulate and encourage your critical and analytic faculty, to develop your personal insight into the author's work and individual style, and to provide you with the skills and techniques to enjoy at first hand the excitement of discovering the richness of the text.

NICHOLAS MARSH

How to Use this Book

This book is designed to be used in close conjunction with the poems it discusses. Each chapter in Part I is built around detailed analysis of a selection of poems. The aim is to show how understanding of the poet's ideas and skill emerges from close study of each poem. The approach and techniques used are clearly demonstrated so as to help you to embark on independent study of further poems, with confidence.

You will gain most benefit from this book if you read each poem analysed for yourself, preferably more than once, before reading my analysis. This prepares you to read critically, with your own response to the poem already developing, and enables you to carry on a sort of internal debate with my analysis. Reading critically, you may think *No, I don't feel that: this poem gives me a slightly different feeling*, or, *I don't agree, I think the poem is more about such-and-such a theme*, or, *Oh, I see. I hadn't noticed that*. Reading the close analysis section after first reading the relevant poem, will increase your confidence and independence when it comes to pursuing your studies further on your own.

Then, you should have your copy of *Philip Larkin: Collected Poems*, ed. Anthony Thwaite (London, 1988) open at the relevant poem, next to you, as you read the analysis. In this way you will be able to refer back and forth between this book and the poem easily, so that you can follow the analysis, understand the phrase or the feature mentioned, and check whether your response agrees with mine.

Acknowledgements

The author and publisher wish to thank the following for use of copyright material: Faber and Faber, and Farrar, Straus and Giroux for 'Vers de Société', from *Collected Poems* by Philip Larkin; © 1988, 2003 by the Estate of Philip Larkin; reprinted by permission of Faber and Faber, and Farrar, Straus and Giroux, LLC.

Every effort has been made to trace the copyright-holders, but if any have been inadvertently overlooked the publishers will be pleased to make the necessary arrangement at the first opportunity.

Introduction

The Scope of this Book

The purpose of this book is to demonstrate how Philip Larkin's poems can be approached, by means of close analysis of a selection of poems. As we become familiar with Larkin's work, we will increasingly be able to discuss the poems' major themes, and at the end of Part I we will draw together tentative working conclusions. At the end of each chapter in Part I there is a summary of the methods we have employed when analysing the poems, and suggestions for further work, so that you can pursue your studies confidently and independently.

Nearly all of the poems selected for close analysis are drawn from the three mature collections published during Larkin's lifetime: *The Less Deceived* (1955), *The Whitsun Weddings* (1964) and *High Windows* (1974), as these three slim volumes made his reputation. As we find ourselves more and more able to compare poems and discern patterns, we will range more widely through the *Collected Poems*, referring to works we have not analysed in detail, to broaden our knowledge of a theme or find further examples of a particular effect.

Part II provides a range of contextual information useful to the student. There is an account of Larkin's life and a discussion of the literary context of the period in which he lived (Chapter 7); a discussion of the major political and historical events of his lifetime, and of social changes in England between the 1920s and 1980s (Chapter 8); and finally, in Chapter 9, you will find a brief account of the present state of Larkin criticism, and a sample of critical

1

arguments from four academic critics (Chapter 9). Finally, suggestions for Further Reading help set you off on pursuing your interest in Larkin further.

No poem is produced in a vacuum: poems are distilled out of the poet's experience within the culture and period of his lifetime. A very brief sketch of historical background is included in this Introduction, on the principle that it is helpful to have some points of contextual reference from the start. However, we will refer to aspects of Larkin's life, and discuss the background, or 'context', at appropriate times during Part I; and you are encouraged to read the contextual chapters in Part II, or refer to them using the index, at any time either before, during or after your reading of Part I.

Historical Background

Larkin lived between 1922 and 1985. He left secondary school and went to Oxford University in 1940, and took his degree in 1943. During his lifetime the Wall Street crash and the Great Depression devastated the country, and the rise of fascism and Nazism led to the Second World War. Larkin failed an army medical and remained a student during the war, but saw his home-town (Coventry) blitzed. Peace and atom bombs arrived in 1945, and in England Attlee's Labour government created the Welfare State. Tension between the NATO alliance countries, and the Soviet Union, turned into the Cold War and a nuclear arms race, ensuring that life could be wiped off the face of planet Earth in minutes. Confrontations between the superpowers persisted for the remainder of Larkin's lifetime.

Larkin was brought up without a religious belief. The Church was in decline, with congregation numbers falling fast: you could no longer imagine a community cemented by faith. However, twentieth-century intellectuals who rejected religion had to confront a newly empty universe. They sensed the potential futility of life: reason offered no substitute for religion.

The British empire was in decline. India and Pakistan became independent in 1948; and the Suez crisis of 1956 showed the decline of British influence in the world. In the 1960s and 1970s further colonies achieved independence. The postwar period marked Britain ceasing to be the centre of a far-flung empire, and becoming a second-rate power, a satellite of the superpower United States.

In the 1960s, however, Britain experienced glory of another kind: fashion design, pop music and culture, and the new 'permissive society' made its capital in London, and the Beatles led British pop music to world dominance. At the end of the sixties, the hippy movement coincided with political demonstrations and student unrest.

In 1979 Mrs Thatcher became Prime Minister leading a radical Conservative government, and Larkin lived to see a British victory in the Falklands war (1982), serious rioting in Liverpool, London, Manchester, Birmingham and Bristol, and defeat of the National Union of Mineworkers following the violent industrial conflict of the miners' strike (1983).

When Larkin was a toddler, radio broadcasts began; and during his lifetime the first scratchy records developed into hi-fi vinyl stereo 'LPs'. Television arrived after the war, and became ubiquitous before Larkin died. In the postwar years, the growth of consumerism filled the shops with cheap goods, and the country became saturated with advertising. Shopping was not the only aspect of society to expand and become a mass market: universities also expanded rapidly in the 1950s and 1960s. The number of students at Hull University, where Larkin worked, grew from around 700 to over 5,000.

This very brief sketch is enlarged in Chapters 7 and 8, but is already suggestive. We will meet poems which respond to the postwar state of England, and the loss of the empire; and because many of them begin with chatty anecdotes, or invitations to an everyday conversation, there will be much that reflects on ordinary life, the atmosphere of England at the time. There are also poems exploring the decline in religious faith, Larkin's own absence of faith and his confrontations with the demons of a rationalist century. The triumph of consumerism and other social changes, as attitudes became more liberal and behaviour more permissive, are also important themes. It is helpful to keep these suggestions in mind at the outset, because Larkin has long been celebrated for his 'Englishness': indeed, many have thought his public image and poems to be a caricature of 'Englishness'.

Analysis of Metre

We will make use of metrical analysis or 'scansion', when analysing Larkin's poems, and a short explanation will help. First, we should stress that 'metrical analysis' is a useful tool, a convenient way of labelling patterns and units of rhythm, and no more. Modern critics sometimes argue that 'scansion' was wrongly imported from classical poetry written in Greek and Latin, because English is a different language where sounds and emphases do not behave as a Roman thinks they should. On the other hand, Larkin was taught poetic scansion at school and made a point of continuing to write metrical poetry, rather than the 'free verse' popular with some Modernist poets such as Eliot, Pound and Lawrence. This introduction explains the technical terms we will use; but remember that you have to be flexible, and use common sense when applying classical scansion to English.

Metrical analysis relies on recognising that language is a string of syllables (complete sounds), some of which we say with more 'weight', 'emphasis' or 'stress' than others. So, in any phrase there are 'stressed' syllables and 'unstressed' syllables. Look at the first line of Larkin's 'First Sight' (*CP*, 112):

> **Lambs** that **learn** to **walk** in **snow**

The stressed syllables are emboldened. There is no real argument: everybody will naturally 'stress' these same syllables. To prove this, try to say the line aloud, stressing the wrong syllables, and you will hear something like this:

> Lms**thatl**en**toow**l**kin**sno

It hardly sounds like English, and a listener would not understand what you are saying. You can try this with everyday phrases – it is surprisingly difficult to talk in reversed stress, and it sounds like gobbledegook.

Now look back at the correct 'stress' pattern of Larkin's 'First Sight'. The first rhythmic unit in the line is made up of one stressed syllable followed by one unstressed syllable: '**Lambs** that'. Each unit of rhythm is called a **foot**. This kind of unit, which goes stressed–unstressed, is called a **trochee** or **trochaic foot**. You can remember what a trochaic foot sounds like by memorising the word '**dum**dy'.

We have not quite finished with the first line of 'First Sight'. There are three complete trochaic feet in the line, then there is one stressed syllable on its own: '**snow**'. This is quite common, because English poetic lines tend to end on a stressed syllable; and it has the effect of adding an involuntary pause at the end of the line – we unconsciously wait the split-second it would take to say the expected but missing unstressed syllable, before reading the next line. The point is that the end of the line is **irregular**. We hardly ever find pure, regular metre in an English poem; and if we did, the poem would sound terribly monotonous. The language, and poets, constantly adjust, deny or change the over-rigid pattern. So we must be ready to be flexible when deciding what kind of 'metre' a poem has, and make a reasonable judgement. We will often have to settle for finding the 'predominant' metre, despite frequent irregularities like the missing syllable at the end of our line from 'First Sight'.

This line introduced us to trochaic feet. There are three other metres. An **iambic foot** goes unstressed–stressed, and you can remember it by memorising the word 'de-**dum**'. Larkin's 'Essential Beauty' (*CP*, 144–5) begins in a regular **iambic metre**:

In **frames** / as **large** / as **rooms** / that **face** / all **ways**
And **block** / the **ends** / of **streets** / with **gi-** / -ant **loaves**,

An **anapaestic foot** goes unstressed–unstressed–stressed, and you can remember its sound by memorising the word 'diddy-**dum**'. Larkin hardly ever uses **anapaests** consistently, but one or two **anapaestic feet** crop up from time to time in poems, such as in the opening line of 'I have started to say' (*CP*, 185):

I have **star-** / -ted to **say**

and in these lines from the early poem 'Winter' (*CP*, 286–7):

In the **field**, / two **hors-** / -es,
Two **swans** / on the **riv-** / -er,
While a **wind** / blows **ov-** / -er

Here, there is an anapaest as the first foot of the first line, the second foot of the second line, and the first foot again in the third line. All lines end with a falling cadence, the final syllable unstressed. We can suggest that the alternating position of the anapaests provides a swaying effect to the poem, while the falling line-endings add a melancholy sound like a minor key in music, so the metrical form here enhances the feeling of 'Winter'. This is an example of Larkin's brilliance at manipulating metre.

The fourth and last kind of 'foot' is a **dactyllic foot**. This goes stressed–unstressed–unstressed, so it is a back-to-front anapaest. You can memorise the sound of a **dactyl** by memorising the word '**dum-diddy**'. This is a rare metre: Larkin only uses a **dactyllic foot** here and there. We could discern **dactyls** in these lines from 'Going, Going' (*CP*, 189–90), for example:

> I / **thought** it would / **last** my **time** –
> The / **sense** that, bey- / **ond** the **town**

However, to find these **dactyls** we have to cut off the first syllable, and the final three syllables, of the line. It makes more sense to think of these lines as **iambic**, and comment on the extra unstressed syllable in the middle, which gives a little extra bounce and speed, and creates the extra 'hanging' or 'ringing' lilt at the end of each line. Here is an example of regular dactyls, three lines from Alfred, Lord Tennyson's 'The Charge of the Light Brigade':

> **Can**non to / **right** of them,
> **Can**non to / **left** of them,
> **Can**non in / **front** of them

Notice that the four different 'metres' have different characters. Tennyson's dactyls are ideal for hinting at the rhythm of galloping horses. *Anapaests* give a lilt, and generally sound bouncy and light. *Iambs* are steady, and *iambic* is the most common and most flexible metre in English – it can be made to express almost any mood. *Trochees* tend to beat on the ear, with a heavy and immediate thump in the first sound (Larkin's 'First Sight' emphasises the bleakness of winter; the metre varies in lines 11 and 12, which hint at the miracle of spring).

This is the technical information needed to follow the metrical analyses found in the next five chapters. It only remains to remember that 'scansion' is a useful tool, a convenient way of labelling units of rhythm: it is not a 'thing' in its own right. So, why is it interesting?

We have mentioned the different 'characters' or 'moods' that different metres can evoke; but there are many other ways that metrical analysis can help us to understand how or why a particular effect is created, as we showed in our example from 'Winter', or can point us to the crucial part of the poem where the poet breaks his pattern. For these reasons, metrical analysis can be a very enlightening tool. Metrical analysis is no use at all if carried out for its own sake: it is helpful only when it helps us to understand how a poem works on us as we read.

PART I

ANALYSING THE POEMS

1

Hearing Larkin's Voices

Poems analysed: 'Wedding-Wind' (*CP*, 11); 'Poetry of Departures' (*CP*, 85–6); 'Next, Please' (*CP*, 52)

There is considerable biographical material about Philip Larkin, despite his reputation for being shy and reclusive. He wrote reviews of books and jazz, and numerous miscellaneous journalistic pieces or essays, many of which were collected in his *Required Writing* (London, 1983). He gave interviews to the press, broadcast on the radio, and appeared in programmes about himself, on television. He wrote novels in his youth. Several people who knew him well over a long period of time have either written or spoken about him. He was a canonical author before his death in 1985, so the literary industry lost no time in collecting impressions and opinions from people who knew him personally or met him in his professional capacity, either as a university librarian or on literary committees. Furthermore, we know a great deal about the times in which he lived. His contemporaries are now in their eighties: it is all within living memory.

We will consider Larkin's life in relation to his poems, and discuss the events and changes through which he lived: these are relevant to and can illuminate his poetry. How could one ignore, for example, that the background to his teenage years was the rise of Hitler and Nazi Germany; or that the war sits bang in the middle of his youth (he was 17 when war was declared – still a schoolboy – and 23, a graduate and already working as a librarian, when it ended). However, we

11

choose to start by looking at three poems, on their own merits. In this way we can begin developing approaches and analytical techniques that will help us to analyse our responses.

Because this chapter is our first encounter with Larkin's poetry, we have chosen poems from *The Less Deceived* (1955), the first published collection to establish Larkin's reputation. We begin with 'Wedding-Wind', which was composed in September 1946. In his introduction to the *Collected Poems*, Anthony Thwaite suggests that in this year Larkin wrote 'the earliest poems which strike his characteristic note and carry his own voice'.[1] We will investigate this 'characteristic note' and search for 'his own voice' in the present chapter, discovering that matters of tone and voice in Larkin's poems are a great deal more elusive than Thwaite's comment implies. 'Wedding-Wind' adopts the voice of a fictional bride.

'Wedding-Wind' (*CP*, 11)

There is no difficulty in reading the 'story' of this poem. The speaker is a bride, and on her wedding-night her husband has to rise from bed to shut a stable door and calm restless horses. He goes 'to look at the floods' on the first morning of their married life, and she sees to the poultry. So, we know that the speaker has married a farmer. The structure of the poem is equally apparent: wedding-night is described in the first section, the poem is divided at a half-line, and the following morning is described in the second section.

The form of this poem is much more difficult to pin down. On first reading, we have an impression of natural speech: neither metrical pattern nor rhyme obtrudes upon our notice, although there is a strong 'beat' and parts of the poem convey a sort of gusty energy. How is this done? Although a number of the lines conform to blank verse, and some even carry a natural iambic emphasis (for example, lines 4, 9, 19 and 21), the opening line is shorter, lines 2, 3 and 12 much longer, and the final three lines are six, eight and then thirteen syllables respectively; that is, the poem seems to grow again as it reaches its end. The nearest we can come to consistent pattern is to suggest that we can discern five beats in most of the lines, provided we regard lines 10 and 11 as a single broken line, and ignore lines 22–4, where it is hard to find more than three, four and four beats respectively. This rhythmic flexibility, which allows the language to beat repeatedly at one moment (as in 'the **wind blew all** my **wed**ding-**day**', l. 1) or contain a lengthy swoop between beats at another (as in '**und**er the **sun** by the **wind's blow**ing', l. 12), is reminiscent of Yeats, and gives the benefits of a convincing, natural tone, flexibility of pace, and the drive of an underlying beat.

The phrasing also contributes to the energetic naturalism of the poem. Several times phrases begin near the end of the line and carry over to the next, such as 'leaving me / Stupid in candlelight' (4–5) and 'When he came back / He said the horses were restless, and I was sad / That any man …' (7–9). Such enjambements occur a further five times in the second section. Leaving part of a phrase loose just at the end of a line has a wind-like effect: Larkin gives us another gust of language which blows us on through the poem.

No obtrusive rhymes hinder these natural rhythmic units from blowing us over the line-ends, yet the sound-patterning is intricate and often subtle. In the first section there are rhymes or half-rhymes between -*day* and *me*, *again* and *rain*, -*stick*, *back* and *lack*, and *sad* and *had*. The second section continues a complex pattern of rhyming, with some perfect rhymes (such as *thread/bed*), some half-rhymes (such as *sleep/up*) and most final sounds connected to others in some way (see, for example, the two open final sounds *day* and *I*). There are many other sound effects also, such as the blustery 'forests, thrashing', and the curious combination of alliteration with the open word in 'Set it down, and stare', which intensifies the bride's wonder and preoccupation, as if she forgets what she is doing.

We began by finding this poem easy to read in a natural manner, and easy to understand. Next, we have found that it is finely crafted, given energy, rhythm and sound effects in a dense but subtle manner. Now we can look more closely at the content, starting with the wind itself, which is not only the title and main statement of the poem but also – as we have seen from analysing rhythm – buffets the poem all the way through.

First, the title implies more than a literal statement. It is not just that the wedding day was windy, it is a hyphenated 'Wedding-Wind' and this links the bride's new experiences intimately to the unleashing of the wind's natural force. It is still ambiguous: does the wind blow because of the wedding, or does it blow the speaker into her wedding? This is metaphorical talk, of course, and such speculation may seem to go a stage too far, yet it is elaborated in the linked metaphors of the poem. Let us start to trace how these develop and feed into the poem.

The opening line is a clear and apparently literal statement. The second line elevates the weather to 'the night of the high wind' as if it was a famous event, with sonorous assonance. We are then told that 'a stable door was banging', and this introduces an anecdote with a range of new associations. The husband shutting the stable door 'after the horse has bolted' may make us smile; restless horses are another kind of elemental wildness not contained; and the bride is sad that 'any man or beast' lacks her happiness. Her husband is, archetypally, 'he', and perhaps both 'man' and 'beast'; or does she pity the horses' sexual frustrations? Should the horses be mating because she has discovered sex this night? This elemental imagery evokes the unleashing of passion on their wedding-night. Yet there are other contributions to the whole experience. When he leaves her she is 'Stupid', and seeing the reflection of her face, which is 'twisted', she is 'seeing nothing'. These are strong statements and not comfortable ones. Are we to think that marriage has 'twisted' her, or begun to nullify her, or that her dependence on a man leaves her 'Stupid'? These disturbing angles upon her 'wedding' experience are included, yet she does not acknowledge them. She sums up her state in conventional wedding-language: 'happiness', a vein of language reinforced by the later 'joy'. Equally, the suggestion of a brainless but animal existence, in her new sexual awareness, appeared in 'stupid' and the ambivalent reference to the horses, and is reinforced in the final line where she feels that she and her husband are 'cattle'.

There is much that is positive in the bride's experience, also. Her questions from line 18 onwards contain the evocative image that 'perpetual morning' shares her bed, and the astonishing image of her new married love defeating death – the ultimate absolute. At the same time, water has played an increasingly central role in the poem, from the 'rain' she heard in the night, to the 'floods' he went to see. There is no mistaking the use of water as a symbol of both arousal and fertility at the end, however: marriage has brought her 'new delighted lakes', and 'all-generous waters'.

But wait: in the second section we cannot pass over the traditional gender roles Larkin assigns to the couple. She carries a 'chipped pail' to see about the poultry, and her 'apron' and the 'hanging cloths' blow on the washing-line: these are the traditional contributions of the farmer's wife, while he is absent, out seeing about more powerful and masculine matters (he saw to the horses, we remember) such as the floods. Why is her pail 'chipped'? Is there a suggestion of roughness, or being worn out, about the female work that will occupy the rest of her life? We may also want to make sense of the enigmatic image in lines 18–20:

> this bodying-forth by wind
> Of joy my actions turn on, like a thread
> Carrying beads?

Joy is compared to a thread, and the wind is 'bodying-forth' joy; that is, the wind is a physical manifestation of her emotional state. In a secondary idea, she feels that joy is the origin and motive for all her 'actions', and she compares these to 'beads' on the joy-thread. The ideas behind this imagery are complex, and the expression is condensed as our focus has to shift from the wind down to her bead-actions. The effect is peculiar. To begin with joy, a powerful emotion, with the elemental power of wind as its metaphor, fits in with the elemental drama of the rest of the poem. But then Larkin warns us that another image is coming: 'like …', and to our surprise and disappointment it turns out to be trivial and related to domestic femininity: 'a thread / Carrying beads'. The second part of the image, in fact, belittles everything around it.

By this time, we have responded to most of the details that are yoked together into 'Wedding-Wind'; but we are still a long way from resolving the poem. Our paragraphs have tended to swing this way and that: we began by noticing the horses and the husband; but then her as 'Stupid' and 'nothing' with a 'twisted' face caught our eye, and this element seemed to complicate her simple assertion of 'happiness'. The same effects are still being produced by the image we have just discussed. It is as if the poem shows bold strokes (the wild wind as a metaphor for joy and passion, for example); but these are juxtaposed against other elements that are mean, questionable, or in some other way *less*. Less than we expect, or less than the bride realises, these niggly contributions to the poem seem to stain the grander ideas around the edges. So, when we finally arrive at the crucial question, 'Can even death dry up / These new delighted lakes, conclude / Our kneeling ...', we recognise that this poem is pitching the same romantic hope into the teeth of reality as did Romeo when he said 'There is no world without Verona walls', or Larkin's later and famous 'What will survive of us is love'. However, in this poem, the little beads, chipped pail, apron, twisted self and stupidity irritate the back of the reader's mind, and we feel tempted to answer the bride: 'Yes, I'm afraid death can, and will'.

In the end, then, there is no conclusion and our attempts to interpret and commentate the poem have been somewhat frustrating. With many poets' works, if they wrote a poem on an obvious theme such as this, you could more or less explain their attitude towards the theme, or their interest in the theme, from an analysis of the poem. For example, if you were to read Seamus Heaney's poem 'The Wife's Tale', which in some ways resembles 'Wedding-Wind' (it is a farmer's wife's dramatic monologue on a theme of rural gender roles and marriage duties), you could analyse the language, rhythm, tones of voice, imagery: all the time you would make progress and explore the poem's effects and your response. Heaney's is a complex poem, and contains numerous ambiguities and a great deal of suggestion, but when you study it in terms of its main theme – traditional gender roles in a farming marriage, power play between husband and wife – you would never feel the need to stop and wonder whether you are doing something appropriate. With 'Wedding-Wind', on the other hand, our attempt at interpretation raises the question: has this apparent theme – the wedding, the sexual awakening – got anything to do with the core of the poem, or not? Or, should we really be thinking in an entirely different frame? Let us try this, and look at Larkin's poem not from the point of view of what it is about, but only from the point of view that it is about a person. In other words, we will examine 'Wedding-Wind' as characterisation.

The character is the speaker of the poem, the wife. She talks to us, and the close analysis we have carried out has really been an exercise in listening to her voice. But it is not a single voice: she speaks in at least four different tones. First, she uses the vocabulary of a newly-wed, 'happiness', 'joy' and even 'delighted'. We sense that this is a social voice: she would use these words to a friend or relative, asserting the success of her decision to marry: 'Oh yes, I'm *so* happy'. Like any social account of personal feeling, this is a simplified discourse. This is a connected, dominating discourse that gives rise to whole structures in the poem, for example, her wish for her happiness to be shared by other people and animals, or her question about eclipsing the power of death.

Her second tone refers to natural forces and elements and acts as a reinforcement of the more socially conversational 'happiness'. The wife makes increasingly grandiose claims for natural forces, from their strength (the repetition 'again and again') to their scope ('all's ravelled under the sun') to their awe-inspiring benevolence ('by all-generous waters'). This vein in the wife's speech also contributes to a consistent discourse and fuels the ringing challenge of the final three lines.

The third and fourth parts of the wife's voice we have noticed appear only at isolated moments. Her shock and nihilism break through in the word 'Stupid', the image of her 'twisted' reflection and the thought of herself as 'nothing'. Then, her triviality appears when she tries to find an image for her happiness and settles rather lamely for a 'thread' and 'beads'. We said we could distinguish *at least* four parts to the wife's voice: there are undercurrents about masculine and feminine natures as well as marital roles, which are present in what she says by implication but do not quite reach the level of an act of speech.

We are looking at characterisation. So, instead of asking what the poet *means* by all that elemental imagery of wind, floods, cattle and waters, we should ask what role these ideas play in the wife's psychology. Why does she refer to the vague vastness of nature's powers? In our earlier analysis, we interpreted the wind and nature imagery as a metaphor for sexual awakening. Now, we can notice that the wife refers to nature rather loosely, bringing in wind, lakes, the sun, clouds and forests. She is either struggling to express emotions too powerful for her to describe, or being speciously grandiose, to reinforce her conventional assertion of 'happiness'. Does she use such sweeping imagery as a way of swamping her nihilism, her momentary feeling that she is 'Stupid' and 'nothing'?

Certainly, she seems to juxtapose the grand and the trivial in a questionable way: the wind is, at once, 'hunting through clouds and forests' and 'thrashing my apron'; and as we have remarked, it is 'bodying-forth ... joy' like 'a thread carrying beads'.

Once we turn our attention to the poem as a dramatic act of speech, some of our perplexity about its significance is resolved. We became frustrated by trying to decide what the poem is about, because we were thinking in terms of a theme – a subject, such as nature, marriage, gender roles or even death. Now that we accept the poem is about a character, we can appreciate it more naturally. The wife is both pathetic and sympathetic. She speaks in a complexity of assertive and nihilistic voices, and is unable intellectually to understand her experiences. She finds that 'All's ravelled [entangled or confused: *OED*] under the sun', and she finds it hard to imagine surviving ('can it be borne'), exhausting ('shall I be let to sleep'), and irreconcilable with the fact of death. All she can do is build a vague quasi-mythology out of nature and pseudo-religious language ('kneeling as cattle by all-generous waters'), while her mind struggles within the confines of beads, thread and aprons.

The poem, then, is about the wife who speaks it. She is an imagined, dramatic character in the first Larkin poem we have met, and her defining characteristic is a balance between discordant voices that cannot be resolved. In particular, she has assertive tones providing a discourse that bolsters or reassures her, and a tone that undercuts this dominant 'story'. It is now time to look at a second poem.

'Poetry of Departures' (*CP*, 85–6)

We are immediately struck by the difference between this poem and 'Wedding-Wind'. This is chatty, conversational, with colloquial phrases and an amused tone. The poet is explaining a minor thought to us, perhaps over a drink or a cup of tea. What is striking, after 'Wedding-Wind', is the apparent absence of passion, the absence of anything that could be called a crisis.

We can begin by taking note of the poet's technique. Despite the marked difference in style between the two poems, we find Larkin employing the same subtleties of technique to achieve an unforced, natural effect. 'Poetry of Departures' consists of four eight-line stanzas. The length of lines can vary, according to a syllable count, but there is a pattern to the number of stresses or 'beats': as in 'Wedding-Wind', Larkin has skilfully maintained the rhythmic pattern, but with sufficient flexibility to relegate pattern to a background, foregrounding an impression of natural conversation. Nearly half of the lines (twelve of them) are run-on, also; and stanzas 2 and 3 both begin new thoughts in the final line and run over to the next stanza. Finally, it is surprising to find that the whole poem is written to a complex ABCBADCD rhyme scheme, to which Larkin adheres throughout. On first reading, we are only likely to notice the rhymes between the sixth and eighth lines of each stanza (*approve ... move*; *bed ... said*, etc.). Nearly all of the other rhymes are half-rhymes (*hand ... sound*; *stirred ... bastard*; *if ... life*, for example), and are unobtrusive until studied. It is a measure of Larkin's technical skill that he should write to a complex form, adhere to it so consistently, and yet at the same time render it nearly inaudible by subtly muting its features.

Now to the poem, which hinges on the choice between an adventurous life, and a secure but humdrum existence. Again, there is no difficulty in grasping the poem's narrative: people talk admiringly of those who run off to lead romantic, adventurous lives. Are they right? The speaker answers 'And they are right, I think' in line 9. This seems like a straightforward proposition that is treated directly. There are other clear statements in 'Poetry of Departures', all of them related to the pivotal choice between adventurous and safe lives:

1 Going off on adventures is a social cliché we are all expected to admire.
2 'We all hate home' leads in to an expression of contempt for a safe and routine-dominated life 'in perfect order'.
3 Hearing about adventurers is thrilling and reassuring: knowing that he could run away if he chose to, helps the speaker to stay 'industrious'.
4 People who go adventuring are just following another predictable stereotype.

These insights are all explained, but not related to each other. We follow the turns of the subject through the poem, but there is no core of meaning as each part of the subject matter is oblique. Each statement almost undercuts another, but is not quite in conflict. For example, admiring clichés are parodied in the reported speech; yet contempt for a safe life seems real in stanza 2. These are not conflicting statements, yet they sit uneasily with each other.

Instead of trying to pursue the subject matter further, let us look at 'Poetry of Departures' as characterisation. In other words, we will analyse the voices, and the modulations of voice, that make up the character of the speaker. First, he reports the voices of others, who speak in clichés: they use phrases like '*chucked up everything*', '*just cleared off*' and '*walked out on the whole crowd*'. This language is energetic (the verbs 'chucked up', 'cleared off' and 'walked out') and dismissive of the 'everything' and 'whole crowd' that are jettisoned. The clichés are also colloquial and recognisable: we have heard conversations like these.

The speaker links these reported voices with two more clichés also in italics: the sensationalist clichés of pornography and violence, '*Then she undid her dress*' and '*Take that you bastard*'. The voice of pornography and violence is not the same as that heard in stanza 1, but has the same effect on the speaker. He becomes 'flushed and stirred'. So, these two slightly different forms of reported speech serve a dual purpose. They are both a parody of clichés in social and media language, and an opportunity for the speaker to offer some self-revelation.

The other voice in this poem is that of the speaker, and it is his ironic modulations of language that are so complex and suggestive. This speaker is analytical and intellectual: look, for example, at 'audacious, purifying, / Elemental' (ll. 7–8), 'industrious' (l. 23) or 'Reprehensibly' in the final line. These words are used precisely, in contrast to dismissive generalities like 'chucked up everything'; and our impression is of a pernickity, slightly fussy diction. This characteristic is reinforced by the speaker's caution. He gives his opinion, but then qualifies it with 'I think'. He places words in a careful order for added implication, such as '*always* the voice will sound' instead of 'the voice will always sound', to suggest that he is bored because the reported speakers are unoriginal. He can juxtapose the portmanteau 'specially-chosen' with the colloquial monosyllable 'junk', and use repetition in 'good books, good bed' to reverse the meaning of 'good', momentarily sharing the adventure cliché's contempt for his possessions. Then, asserting his freedom of action ('But I'd go today'), the speaker slips into parody, saying he would 'swagger the nut-strewn roads, / Crouch in the fo'c'sle / Stubbly with goodness', ridiculing the image of an adventurous hero by mixing metaphors absurdly.

In short, the speaker's voice shifts, constantly modulating to a new attitude, or loaded with a new implication. If, for example, we make notes describing our response to the three adjectives in lines 7 and 8, we might end up with something like this:

> *audacious*: this word suggests risk-taking. Its effect is largely positive and supports the idea of admiration. However, the word has a rather literary pedigree from stories of astonishing adventures. The Count of Monte Cristo and the Three Musketeers were 'audacious'. So, there is a slight overtone of irony, a sense of belonging in story-books rather than real life.
>
> *purifying*: this is a problematic word. It seems to imply that modern routine life, surrounded by possessions, is over-complicated and corrupting. There is a suggestion of spiritual 'purity' in a simpler life. The word associates with religion and there is an ironic overtone, and its overall effect is ambivalent.
>
> *elemental*: Back to nature? Getting in touch with your primitive self? In this word the irony is much stronger. It suggests a half-baked Lawrentian ideal: an escape from post-industrial society to rediscover the basic man in touch with raw nature. Later in the poem, and even more comically, the speaker parodies such primitivism in the phrase 'stubbly with goodness'.

So, in just three words, Larkin has touched on the vocabularies of adventure fiction, religion and quasi-Lawrentian primitivism. At the same time, the intensity of irony varies from a slight overtone (*audacious*) to sharply satirical (*elemental*), and the irony targets both the speaker and the reported speakers.

We have noticed numerous subtle shifts of attitude, socially defined language and ironic modulations in the speaker's voice.

There is one further feature to record: certain individual words stand out because they seem to carry more complicated implications than are justified by their tonal context. We are listening to a conversational voice, and on first reading we remarked that the poem sounds natural. Our speaker reports what others say, mimics sensationalist fiction, and mocks both others and himself, but we believe in the character we are listening to throughout the poem. However, just a few words still surprise us: they carry implications well beyond the ostensible conversational level of discourse. They do not 'jar' against the chatty voice of the speaker. The best way to describe their effect is that they 'ping' like a sudden bell ringing a different note. In 'Poetry of Departures', the word 'epitaph' (l. 2) and the repeated 'perfect' (lines 15 and 32) seem to do this. Possibly the word 'Reprehensibly' (l. 32) also does – although this word is so deliberately highlighted by its unusual length and its placing as the poem's penultimate word, that its prominence seems too obvious.

An 'epitaph' is for the dead. Suddenly, the word suggests parity between ditching normality for an adventurous life, and dying. In what sense was the adventurer's departure a 'death'? Does this imply that, once they are out of sight, they turn into a simple romantic stereotype and, in that sense, cease to live? Therefore, are *both* the lives we can choose, the safe and the adventurous, merely kinds of death because they are fixed and predictable? So, 'epitaph' helps to highlight the ambiguous connotations of the poem's title: 'departures' are both partings and deaths.

'Perfect' is repeated as the final word, and its significance therefore grows. In line 15 it means little more than 'well-organised', although even there it stands out as a superlative. By the time it is repeated, however, 'perfect', like 'epitaph', applies to both choices of life. This implies that perfection is like death: does the speaker mean that only imperfect things are truly 'alive'? Only the uncertain, incomplete, shifting, unfinished and unresolved is 'alive'. That which is perfect will never change; it has reached its final form, and is now fixed, 'dead'.

This sounds very fine: rather philosophical and 'thematic'. It almost amounts to an 'interpretation of the poem'. Remember, however, the glee with which the speaker turns from his vain boast 'I'd go today', to a riotous satire of 'nut-strewn roads' and a hero 'stubbly with goodness'. Remember also the almost whining complaint 'if / It weren't so artificial'. Is the speaker really brilliant and wise, equating death and perfection? Or, is this voice driven by something else less admirable. Is the speaker's rejection of adventure a craven rationalisation, envious and inventing clever excuses for avoiding adventure's challenge?

This is a lesson for us. We should be alert to any interpretation that sounds clever and gives an impression of brilliance or nobility. There may be other evidence in the poem as well, hinting at the speaker's more sordid motive. The result is a stand-off: the brilliance is there, and so is the craven self-excuse. We cannot say that one is the *real* speaker rather than the other, and we are left unable to give ourselves wholeheartedly to the contemplation of our preferred solution.

To return to our few outstanding words: 'Reprehensibly' is a word of censure. It associates with schoolteacher authority. The final line therefore has an oxymoronic effect: *You naughty child, you are perfect!* The poet is clearly mocking himself, but in a very complex way which reflects on numerous normative social assumptions. We assume that obedient children become good, responsible adults: they have steady jobs and well-organised lives, and do not cause trouble. Naughty children become rebellious adults: they do 'audacious' things and rebel against convention. Now, the speaker and his friends have grown up to have rebellious attitudes (they admire rebels, they 'hate home'), which they regard as good. It is 'naughty' to seek 'perfection', that is, to settle into a fixed stereotype. The joke is that this adult's subversive attitudes are still expressed in the language of the schoolroom: his new opinions exist within a childish concept of 'good' and 'naughty', a hangover he cannot outgrow. The further joke, as we have seen, is that both 'good' and 'naughty' lives are equally 'perfect' and therefore dead.

We remain bemused by the multiplicity of different and shifting tones in which this speaker characterises himself. From listening to, and following, the polyphony of voices, we have found him contemptuous, uncertain, bored, arrogant, angry, self-mocking, confessing squalid reactions, and vainglorious. In the process of being all these things, the speaker has knocked down everything the poem sets up. The original choice between safe and adventurous lives is not really a choice at all (both are comic clichés). Indeed, there is no possibility of choice while this speaker is so uncertain, his attitudes so laughably influenced by cheap thrills, social clichés or childhood training. He cannot possibly decide anything; and, the poem implies, would be best advised not to try.

The character created in 'Poetry of Departures' in 1954, is already recognisable as the ironic and self-mocking narrator we come to know in the main body of Larkin's poetic output. He speaks to us in 'Mr Bleaney', 'Toads' and 'Toads Revisited', and we will meet him again. Before we move on, however, we should record how the different voices of 'Poetry of Departures', in cancelling each other out, are the dominant structure of the work.

The poem sets up a choice between conventional and adventurous lives. The main, ostensible argument of the poem cancels out that impression: there is no choice between stereotypes, which are both dead. Then, this argument is mocked because the speaker has not grown out of his adolescent response to pornography and violence, and his ethics are still couched in schoolroom terms. We are left with nothing. The art of the poem is that it leaves us with a nothing that is pleasingly neat, even symmetrical, in the way that it cancels itself out; is complex and filled with shifts, puzzles and changes; and is unfinishable.

'Next, Please' (*CP*, 52)

'Next, Please' is a simpler and more direct poem than 'Poetry of Departures'. We look at it now because it declares a theme of death and is different again from both of the poems we have looked at so far. In studying 'Wedding-Wind' and 'Poetry of Departures', we have been made to consider them as dramatic creations made up of different voices which undercut each other. In both cases, it has proved very difficult to isolate any communication from the poet himself because of the overlying layers of characterisation. Both the wife of 'Wedding-Wind' and the speaker of 'Poetry of Departures' are complex and unresolved personalities. Now, in 'Next, Please', we seem to be given a coherent idea developed to a declaratory conclusion, all in the uncharacterised tones of a generalisation covering 'us' – the poet, his readers, the rest of humanity. The argument of the poem is: we live for the future, never experience the present, always hope and are always disappointed. The only certainty is death, the 'black-sailed unfamiliar' towing a 'huge and birdless silence'.

The technical features of 'Next, Please' provide a more confident and assertive tone than in either of the other poems. Four of the six stanzas open on a firmly stressed beat ('**Al**ways', '**Watch**ing', '**Flagged**', '**On**ly') and the AABB rhyme scheme is consistently strong, even down to the funny, contrived rhyming of 'tits' and 'it's'. The poet uses sentences to structure his argument, also. The opening two stanzas, for example, are three sentences: the theme of 'expectancy' is stated in lines 1 and 2, elaborated in lines 3 to 6; then a frustrated exclamation, lines 7 and 8, rounds off the poem's opening phase. In the fourth and fifth stanzas, a sentence ends with the third line, so that the short final line begins the next sentence and carries over to the next stanza. This clearly imitates the pattern of 'expectancy': each time, a sentence ends too soon, and is over, but we immediately begin building up our expectation for the next in our 'armada of promises' to arrive: we start to hope again straight after each full stop. In the final stanza this hopeful impetus is brought up short by two groups of stresses which act as a brake: 'Only **one ship** is seeking us, a **black-sailed un**familiar'. This halts the flow of the poem as death halts the flow of living, and coincides with the arrival of the sinister black-sailed ship. The final sentence is shorter than any others and the only one broken by a line-ending. Thus cracked and abrupt, it mimics the suddenness of death, in contrast to the poem's long build-up of expectancy in the central sentence (lines 9 to 15). The short final line of each stanza has a similar effect, surprising us because we expected more, and in this way creating a silence: the absent second half of the line.

The poet's skill in modulating his voice is present here as well. Although language is less varied in this poem than in 'Poetry of Departures', we recognise some familiar features. The colloquial 'pick up bad habits', for example, contrasts with the more literary and conceptual 'expectancy'. Exasperation is emphasised by placing 'Refusing' at the start of the line. Alliteration of '**b**alks / Each **b**ig approach' adds a heavy, dull beat in sinister contrast to the pretty ringing rhymes 'prinked' and 'distinct' with which approaching ships are 'sparkling'. The stylistic oxymoron 'golden [romance, riches, myth] tits [schoolboy vulgarity]' is a characteristic Larkin moment like 'specially-collected junk' from 'Poetry of Departures'. Somehow the dreadful rhyme 'it's', stuck on its own at the end of the next line, seems to emphasise linguistic oafishness, underscoring the deflationary effect. A similar yoking together of lower and higher dictions occurs in the fifth stanza: 'unload [a rough industrial word, with connotations of 'dump'] / All good [moral and spiritual values]', this effect is repeated in the idea of waiting 'devoutly' (religiously) for what we are 'owed' (crass commerce).

All these features show that the 'we' of the poem, its speakers, are being subtly characterised in a similar manner to the speaker of 'Poetry of Departures'. The unspoken implication here is that our deluded 'expectancy' is, at root, only adolescent sexuality and material greed, garnished with a resentful sulk about what we deserve. The poem, in fact, is ambiguous about the nature of our hopes. Do we really want a 'sparkling armada' to bring us 'all good'; or are we excited by the figurehead's 'golden tits' and ready to grab what is 'owed'? In 'Poetry of Departures', the relation between 'audacious, purifying' and '*then she undid her dress*' is never explored, yet both are present. In 'Wedding-Wind', the wife is 'Stupid ... nothing' and filled with 'happiness'. Here, our 'expectancy' is romantically a 'sparkling armada', as well as lustful greed. What is striking about all three poems is the silence we find in between these poles. By setting up such disparate interpretations of experience, the poems force us to look in between. We hope to discover how they are linked, looking for their relationship. What we find is a gap: the poems do not allow us to posit cause and effect. We cannot say that fine ideals are a pretence and what we *really* seek is 'golden tits', for example. Simply: both are present, and there is emptiness in between. With 'Poetry of Departures' we were left with a similar non-answer to the question: is the speaker's rejection of adventure wisdom, or envious rationalisation, self-excuse?

'Next, Please' does not have quite the straightforward effect it promised on first reading, then. The bulk of the poem is a complex satire on 'expectancy'. As we have found, it is an exploration of our unresolved self-deceptions and our determination to avoid or suppress unpleasant truths. Like 'Poetry of Departures', this poem also leaves us with nothing. The difference is that it does so explicitly. It leaves us with the broken abrupt sentence, black colouring and harsh 'k'-ending rhymes of the final stanza, together with the echoing phrase 'a huge and birdless silence', and the sinister '*un*familiar' (a 'familiar' is a witch's companion, an evil spirit). The final stanza does, nonetheless, undercut the previous five: our 'expectancy', hypocrisy, avoidance and denial, and our uncomfortable blend of noble and soiled motives – the entire subject matter of living and life – are rendered foolishly irrelevant.

We have studied three poems from *The Less Deceived*, the first of Larkin's mature collections. They were written in 1946, 1954 and 1951 respectively, that is, before Larkin was 32 years old. Already, we are aware that this is a poet capable of producing quite astonishing effects by the manipulation of utterance and silence. We will highlight one further example of his poetic power, just to remind ourselves how extraordinary a talent he possessed, before considering how far this chapter has taken us, and what analytical techniques we have employed.

In 'Next, Please', Larkin develops an extended metaphor in which we stand 'Watching from a bluff', scanning the open sea that starts below us and stretches away to the horizon. As the metaphor proceeds, some visual details are touched in naturalistically: the 'sparkling' armada suggests a bright sunny day, and ships approach vividly, seen in increasing detail and with such evocative touches as 'leaning' (there is no mention of sails, but these must be sailing ships heeling in the wind – and the historical word 'armada' suggests square-riggers). By the time we reach the final stanza of the poem, the poet has created a vivid metaphor. Most of us have stood on a cliff overlooking the sea, and seen films and pictures of cliffs, sea and square-rigged sailing vessels. Our imagination of the scene Larkin touches in is filled out by reference to these memories. However, it may only be when we reach the word 'birdless', that we suddenly realise *we have been hearing the crying of gulls*. The poet has not mentioned birds at all, yet it is quite natural to propose that they are there, and their cries are there, for most readers. One astonishing word, 'birdless', deprives us of this wordlessly provoked aural experience. In our experience of reading the poem, therefore, the sound of gulls may be taken from us before we realise we are hearing it. It is an astonishing poetic achievement, contributing to the desolation and suddenness of the final stanza. Notice that Larkin achieves this by manipulating both utterance and reticence: the word 'birdless' follows the absence of any mention of gulls. Both word and silence are necessary to the effect. We will find this to be typical of Larkin.

Concluding Discussion

What Triggered these Poems?

When 'Wedding-Wind' was written in September 1946, Larkin was working in the library of University College, Leicester, and living in a rented furnished room in the town. He was in a relationship with Ruth Bowman whom he had met when she was still at school, and he was the librarian of a small local library, in Wellington. By 1946 she was at college in London and they met most weekends, but Larkin was increasingly unable to commit himself to the relationship. Here is what he wrote fourteen years later, explaining why he wrote poems:

> I write poems to preserve things I have seen / thought / felt (if I may so indicate a composite and complex experience) both for myself and for others, though I feel that my prime responsibility is to the experience itself, which I am trying to keep from oblivion for its own sake. Why I should do this I have no idea, but I think the impulse to preserve lies at the bottom of all art. Generally my poems are related, therefore, to my personal life, but by no means always, since I can imagine horses I have never seen [in 'At Grass'] or the emotions of a bride [in 'Wedding-Wind'] without ever having been a woman or married.[2]

It is beyond our ability to guess what 'thought' or 'experience' Larkin sought to preserve in 'Wedding-Wind'. There is nothing in his life to suggest why 'the emotions of a bride', particularly a farmer's bride, should come to the mind of an unmarried young man who had always lived in towns. Charitably, we could agree with Larkin's next remark, 'I believe that every poem must be its own sole freshly created universe', and chalk up 'Wedding-Wind' as just that. More cynically, we may see a debt to Yeats in the technique, as well as the possible influences of both D. H. Lawrence and Edwin Muir (where the suggestion of elemental wild horses may have originated). In other words, it is possible to read 'Wedding-Wind' as a poem in which Larkin was struggling to find his 'voice', struggling to integrate the influence of the poets he admired, such as Hardy, Auden and Yeats. As a non-biographical dramatic monologue, it strikes us as an experiment, a *tour de force* for a shy, inexperienced young man.

For 'Poetry of Departures' it is easier to theorise an origin in Larkin's life. It was written in January 1954, in Belfast. Two women with whom Larkin had been involved, Winifred Arnott and Patsy Strang, had both moved out of his life the preceding year; and we can theorise that he felt in a rut and left behind by the exciting travels and changes other people were undertaking, while he continued to work in the university library. On the other hand, this poem also seems to be on a long-cogitated theme. Andrew Motion records that in 1944 Larkin 'debated with Sutton whether they might both leave England when the war ended, and swagger the nut-strewn roads in America. Even as he considered this, he knew he would never allow the idea to become a reality'.[3] In the case of 'Poetry of Departures', then, there are some events that may have triggered the poem; but again, nothing definite except that Larkin regularly complains about his cautious way of life. We certainly cannot trace the poem to any single experience, with confidence.

The same applies to 'Next, Please', which was written in 1951. Larkin's father Sydney died in 1948, and the poem may be a delayed response to this most significant of deaths. In one sense, Sydney's death could hardly *not* be relevant. On the other hand, 'Next, Please' is a long-postponed reaction if it records the 'experience' of losing his father; and Larkin had long manifested a preoccupation with death. Again, biography may help us to imagine the man who wrote these poems, but it tells us little about their origins.

In the case of 'Wedding-Wind', then, the poem may be an experiment, a blending of youthful influences as the poet tries out his skill. In the case of the other two poems, the nearest we come to explaining their origin is to say that they hinge on subjects that occupied Larkin throughout his life: choices and decisions about how to live; and death. We come no closer than this by matching composition to biography. It is possible that Larkin was less than frank when he suggested that a poem might 'preserve ... an experience ... from oblivion'. He may have enjoyed portraying himself as the poet who captures the moment, but it is not true. These poems are the result of prolonged meditation on dilemmas that constantly occupied Larkin's mind; and all three are deliberate literary acts. Larkin had decided to be a writer when he was young. These are crafted poems.

There is a consequence to realising this. Once we know that Larkin set out to 'be a writer' and, later, to 'be a poet', we understand that he thought about how to develop an original voice. He deliberately chose those he admired, from among his predecessors; and he consciously learned from them. In other words, Larkin set out to be an artistic maker, and this involved making two artefacts: first, he made poems; and secondly, he made a poet; and this is the reason why we have found it fruitful to focus on the speaker's characterisation in our first three studies. We have met a farmer's wife, a confident philosopher, and a timid, self-doubting man. Clearly, Larkin was still casting around for his poetic persona. Which one of these three characters will become 'the poet' when Larkin's voice stabilises?

Conclusions to Chapter 1

From studying three poems, we are able to draw some tentative conclusions. We will treat these conclusions as hypotheses because we are at an early stage: they may prove useful as we meet other poems and gain a fuller understanding, but they need to be tested. If some of them lead nowhere, so be it.

1   Larkin writes in a dramatic mode. This means that his poems are spoken by characters, such as the self-doubting man of 'Poetry of Departures' or the wife of 'Wedding-Wind'. This is true even of the most direct poem, 'Next, Please', which purports to be no more than the poet's own view.

2   We have tried interpretation, looking at imagery and themes and seeking the meaning of these poems. This method has not worked. The theme may be apparent, but is not resolved in the poem (for example, gender roles in 'Wedding-Wind'). Even where there is an apparent conclusion the resolution may not be central to the poem (as in 'Poetry of Departures' and 'Next, Please').

3   We have found it helpful to think of the character(s) who speak the poems. In 'Wedding-Wind' and 'Poetry of Departures', the unresolved themes can be understood as unresolved elements of the speaker's character.

4   The characters are complex: they appear to contradict themselves, and their motives are often ambiguous. For example, the speaker of 'Poetry of Departures' rejects adventure either (*a*) from perception and wisdom, or (*b*) from jealousy and fear. We should beware of conclusions that present themselves as single and clear, or logical. They are likely to be undercut by another element of the speaker's character.

5   Many of the poems have a story, but the internal structure consists of layers of different tones poised against each other like a house of cards: more three-dimensional than linear. The different tones cancel each other out, so the final effect of the poem is both pleasing (because of the complexity and exactness of the structure, which is made up of attitudes and feelings poised against each other) and reductive. Another analogy to explain this 'structure of attitudes' is that it resembles a mathematical equation: the halves are different, but equal.

6   Larkin uses silence as well as words. In this chapter, we found that inconsistent attitudes are not explained: there is a gap, or 'silence', where we expect to find a cause-and-effect analysis of the character (for example, idealism and lust in 'expectancy', in 'Next, Please'). We also found that Larkin used an absence of words to prepare a powerful poetic effect (the effect of 'birdless' in 'Next, Please'). We should pay close attention to these 'silences': places where we expect more but it is not there.

7   Recurrent themes are already apparent. Death is a theme that has appeared in all three poems, from its dominance of 'Next, Please',

to its subtle suggestion in the word 'epitaph', in 'Poetry of Departures'. Additionally, there seems to be an abiding interest in how we choose to live our lives; or, how the choices we make define us. In 'Wedding-Wind', for example, the wife's choice of marriage determines her future of 'chipped pail' and domestic chores; 'Poetry of Departures' is overtly about choice, and the speaker's decision to be 'sober and industrious'. From 'Next, Please', we could say that we *choose* to live in 'expectancy', ignoring the approach of death.

8   Finally, Larkin alludes to or borrows from other writers. For example, we speculated that the reference to wild and restless horses in 'Wedding-Wind' may have been suggested by D. H. Lawrence or Edwin Muir . Similarly, the black-sailed ship of death in 'Next Please' is a version of the skeleton-ship from Coleridge's *The Rime of the Ancient Mariner*, which passes in front of the sun. Also, the word 'elemental' in 'Poetry of Departures' suggests a fashionable admiration for basic nature, derived from D. H. Lawrence.

Methods of Analysis

We have used a variety of analytical techniques in this chapter, but some have proved much more effective than others.

1   It has been useful to analyse *metre, rhythm and rhyme*. This helps to explain how Larkin achieves naturalness of tone, and reveals his painstaking technique. For example, the contrast between 'Poetry of Departures', which is mostly *half-rhymed*, and 'Next, Please', where all the rhymes are perfect, helps explain the difference between the two poems' uncertain and confident voices.

2   We have noticed *other technical features* which contribute to a poem's effect. Among these have been:

   (*a*)   *Alliteration*, as in 'nothing **b**alks each **b**ig approach', in 'Next, Please'.

   (*b*)   *Onomatapoeic effects*, as in 'forests, thrashing' in 'Wedding-Wind'.

(c) *Stanza-form*. For example, we noticed the short final line of each stanza in 'Next, Please', which creates an abrupt effect and a silence.

(d) *Repetition*. In each case we have noticed, repetition renders ironic, or enlarges, the meaning of the word. We noticed 'good books, good bed' in 'Poetry of Departures', and the growth of the word 'perfect' in the same poem.

(e) *Sentence structure*. We noticed a contrast between long and short sentences in 'Next, Please', and sentence breaks before the final line of the stanza, in the same poem.

(f) *Imagery*. We have interpreted images in the poems, and responded to imagery. For example, we interpreted the 'chipped pail' in 'Wedding-Wind' as representative of the wife's subservient role, her married future; and we suggested that water signifies fertility, in the same poem. We both interpreted and imaginatively followed the imagery of sea, cliff and ships in 'Next, Please'.

We could have noticed many other examples of these features, and other features; but these are the ones that caught our eye in the three poems studied.

3   We have been open to other effects which do not have a 'technical' name. For example, the effect of 'birdless' in 'Next, Please' or of 'Reprehensibly' and 'epitaph' in 'Poetry of Departures'. In these cases we have (a) *noticed our response*, then (b) *investigated how the poem evoked our response*. This involves being willing to describe your own responses in close detail, using connotations and associations open-mindedly, and following these up by thinking about where they lead. For example, we followed an imaginative response to the seashore metaphor in 'Next, Please', to explain why we experienced a sudden feeling of loss at the word 'birdless'. Also, we suggested that the word 'Reprehensibly' is associated with the world of school discipline, and developed our insights from there.

4   The three points above all contribute to *hearing the voices in the poems*. We have paid particular attention to this. Pay special attention to changes in the style of language (for example, the contrasting dictions in 'specially-chosen junk' from 'Poetry of

Departures', or the descent to vulgarity in 'golden tits', from 'Next, Please') and references to other language styles (such as the neo-biblical 'kneeling as cattle by all-generous waters' of 'Wedding-Wind', or the sensational-novel-style *'Then she undid her dress'* and *'Take that you bastard'* from 'Poetry of Departures'). It is important to follow the changes and modulations in Larkin's voices very closely, throughout a poem. Different kinds of language, different tones of voice, may suggest *literary comparisons* (the Psalms or the Song of Songs, at the end of 'Wedding-Wind'), *social class* and *social attitudes*, or *emotion* (such as the resentful complaint in 'so artificial', from 'Poetry of Departures').

5   Hearing the voices in the poems leads naturally into *considering the poems as dramatic characterisation*. When you have developed your analysis by trying the approaches listed above, this is the next thing to do. To consider the poem as dramatic characterisation:

  (*a*) *ask questions about the voices* that speak in the poem:
      What sort of person am I listening to?
      What different feelings does he or she express?
      What contradictions are there in the character?
      What are the relationships between the character's different thoughts, or their different feelings? (In some instances in this chapter, we were surprised to find no relationship between a character's potentially conflicting attitudes.)

  (*b*) *notice the silences in the poem*. This means, pay attention to what the characters do not say, as well as to what they say; what the poem excludes, which is implied by what it includes. You will find yourself naturally directed towards these 'silences', because there will be something you expect to find that is not there.

6   We have *considered the structure of a poem in a conceptual way*. This means that we find 'structure' in the 'shape' of different ideas in the poem, not in its organisation into stanzas, or a beginning, middle and end, on the page. Focus on how different ideas and attitudes in the poem contrast, conflict, undercut or cancel out each other. This will give a sense of the 'structure of ideas' we have found most illuminating.

Suggested Work

At this stage, it is beneficial simply to practise reading and analysing some of Larkin's poems. Doing so will familiarise you with using the approaches demonstrated in this chapter, and you will naturally develop a surer judgement about which approaches yield the most fruitful results with different poems. The more you practise, the more quickly you will recognise features, and save yourself from a lot of unrewarding, plodding work. At the same time, of course, you are broadening your knowledge of Larkin's poetry with each poem studied.

I suggest that you begin by trying out the analytical techniques we have used in this chapter, on two more of the poems from *The Less Deceived*: 'Deceptions' (*CP*, 32); 'If, My Darling' (*CP*, 41). In both of these poems, you will find our method of looking at dramatic characterisation particularly rewarding. In 'Deceptions', the dramatisation lies in the intricate relation between past and present, and between Mayhew, the victim, the rapist and the poet. This poem has provoked virulent debate, particularly between feminist and other critics. Ask yourself why the speaker feels compelled to respond to this anecdote? In 'If, My Darling', the crowded references carry multiple domestic, social and period allusions. At the same time the poem's speaking voice modulates with many sudden changes of attitude. Follow the speaker's twists and turns of thought and mood, and appreciate the humour.

2

'Solitaire, Solidaire'

Poems analysed: 'Self's the Man' (*CP*, 117–18); 'Dockery and Son'
(*CP*, 152–3); 'Vers de Société' (*CP*, 181–2); 'Wild Oats' (*CP*, 143)

In the previous chapter we suggested that Larkin has a recurrent
interest in the choices we make: our decisions about how we live our
lives, particularly the dilemma between living alone, and forming
relationships or joining in social activities. This chapter studies four
out of the many poems that explore a 'Solitaire, Solidaire' dilemma,[1]
beginning with one from the collection *The Whitsun Weddings*.

'Self's the Man' (*CP*, 117–18)

'Self's the Man' contrasts the lives of the bachelor poet and his married
friend Arnold. The first five stanzas are framed by the repetition (in
lines 1–2 and 19–20) of:

> Oh, no one can deny
> That Arnold is less selfish than I

and support this assertion by describing Arnold's married life. The
final three stanzas cast doubt by suggesting that Arnold is, at base,
just as selfish as the poet.

The poem sounds like poor doggerel when we read it. We are already
admirers of Larkin's technical skill, so 'Self's the Man' immediately

raises the question: why would he write a poem so jerky in its rhythm, so pitter-patter and sometimes grotesquely forced in its rhyming? And why would he use such ugly, clumsy expression? Frankly, 'Self's the Man' is a Bad Poem, and we must conclude that Larkin is having a laugh.

The four-line stanzas have an AABB rhyme scheme. The phrasing sticks rigidly to the lines as in a child's first attempt at verse, with no genuine enjambement. The result is that we sense the line awkwardly trying to reach the rhyme, which then lands like an elephant's foot. This is particularly true of the longer lines (line length varies arbitrarily, without a pattern to the stanzas), where the effect becomes funny:

> And when he finishes supper
> Planning to have a read at the evening paper

We hear the speaker's clumsy construction 'have a read at' and the unnecessary 'evening', and sense the poor blighter's relief when he finally reaches his chosen, awful, rhyme: 'paper'. The line cries out for redrafting: 'Planning to read the paper' would be far more elegant. Other awkward rhymes are *houses/trousers* and *mother/summer*. These jar: they are not subtle half-rhymes, but the work of somebody who has no facility with language; and the same effect of bumbling awkwardness we notice in 'Planning to have a read at the evening paper' occurs several times with varying degrees of obviousness, for example as the speaker lollops towards 'sake' to rhyme with 'mistake' (ll. 25–6).

As is consistent with an unskilled poet, some lines seem to be added just because there should be another line. 'And the electric fire' and 'Not just pleasing his friends' may strike us as fill-in lines of this kind. This is particularly true of 'Not just pleasing his friends', because friends have not been mentioned (Arnold married 'to stop her getting away'). We guess that the poet put this line in merely to finish the stanza, and only decided to use 'friends' because it rhymes with 'ends'. One of the funniest words in the poem is its first word, 'Oh'. It is there only because this speaker thinks that poems ought to begin with 'Oh': an inspired poet's romantic cliché utterly at odds with the domestic whinge that follows.

In terms of technique, then, 'Self's the Man' is a comically bad poem. Why? The answer is obvious: because it was not written by Philip Larkin, Oxford English graduate and accomplished poetic technician. Instead, it was written by the speaker, a brash and unrefined man, and if we now listen to his voice we will hear it distinctly.

The vocabulary is lower middle class. The speaker says that Arnold married 'a woman' (what else would he marry?), and uses 'gets', 'perk', 'clobber'. It is very likely that Larkin was taught at school – as I was – never to use 'get': there is always a more elegant alternative (in line 5, 'earns' would replace 'gets'). The evening meal is 'supper', rather than the middle-class 'dinner'. The children are 'kiddies' and then 'nippers'. There is, however, a slight change in the speaker's voice in the final three stanzas. There are still colloquial expressions such as 'out for his own ends', 'playing his own game', 'I'm a better hand' and 'them sending a van'; but the lines are more uniform in length, and these expressions define the speaker's social class less narrowly. The voice, in fact, seems to be toned down when the speaker has finished describing Arnold's marriage, and begins to compare it with his own life. He still lacks some poetic skill in the final three stanzas; but he is less aggressive, and the poem is less uneven, less out of control. For example, would the person who wrote 'Planning to have a read at the evening paper' have been able to frame the couplet:

> But wait, not so fast:
> Is there such a contrast?

Unlikely. That speaker might have written 'But wait, don't go so fast: / Do Arnold's life and my life make such a big contrast?' or something equally clumsy.

Why would the speaker calm down, and be in better control of himself, in the final three stanzas? The answer must lie in his feelings about Arnold's marriage. The opening couplet might suggest guilt, since 'selfish' is a derogatory term. However, the speaker's cynicism quickly cuts against this theory. Since Arnold married 'to stop her getting away', he clearly does not believe that Arnold is unselfish: Arnold is possessive, and that is why he married. The model is a crass one: the man catches and then owns the woman, with a comic suggestion of hooking a fish

in to 'stop her getting away'. The speaker continues to describe
marriage in cynical terms. When we hear that his wife takes Arnold's
money as her 'perk', for example, we expect to hear that she spends it
on having her hair done, or on fancy clothes. In fact, she spends it on
the children and the house, not on herself at all. The speaker gives
himself away here: clearly, he thinks the children and the home are her
business, and Arnold should not be responsible for them. In describing
Arnold's marriage, then, the speaker reveals himself. We cannot trust
this narrator, because of his blatant misogyny. We quickly realise that
we are reading an ugly revelation of the speaker's attitudes, not a true
description of Arnold's life at all.

Clearly, the speaker hates women and children, and believes that
they sponge on men. None of this suggests that the speaker feels guilty
about his selfishness. When, later, he says that he 'feels a swine' in
comparison to poor Arnold, this cannot be true: the feeling we sense
is much more like smug self-satisfaction, and sure enough, he soon
argues himself around to that point of view.

What do we hear about Arnold in the last part of the poem? Just that
he had selfish reasons for marrying. This seems to refer back to 'to stop
her getting away', and is apparently part of Arnold 'playing his own
game'. The speaker finally believes that they are both 'selfish', and the
only difference between them is that he is better at selfishness than
Arnold. In other words, from his supposedly self-critical beginning, the
speaker has finally managed to justify feeling superior. Morally – in
selfishness – they are the same; but he is the cleverer of the two. The
image used for how we play our lives is typically crass: that of a card
game with Arnold cast as the loser. If we now compare this with the
change in voice we heard around stanza 5, it fits an understanding of
the speaker's character: he is agitated for as long as he feels that Arnold
is in some way better than himself. He becomes calmer, and speaks
more confidently, as he rationalises his own superiority. It also makes
sense that he expends so much aggression on the awfulness of Arnold's
marriage: he is so aggressive because he has to persuade himself, not us.

What has Larkin given us, then? The speaker of this poem is an
unpleasant character. He hates and distrusts women and children, and
has antediluvian attitudes towards them. However, the prospect of
marriage drives him so far out of control (seen in the poem's clumsy

voice, and the blatant injustice of his case) that there is an implication
of bluster and panic. He sees relationships with other people in terms
of hunting and fishing, catching and owning; and in terms of commercial bargains and card games. Finally, the whole poem is driven by
his need to feel superior, which he finally, smugly, achieves.

Is this what the poem is about? Is the 'message' of this poem that
there are cynical, misogynist men about, and this is what they are like?
Partly, but not wholly, because two elements of the final stanza undercut the entire portrait. First, the speaker acknowledges that life can
drive you insane, and he has to know 'what I can stand / Without them
sending a van'; then, in the final line, he doubts the entire construction
of winning and losing that he has fashioned: 'Or I suppose I can'.

The speaker does not tell us that his aggression and arrogance is a
defence against insecurity, although this would be a reasonable infer-
ence. The final line resonates for more than one reason. Not only
does it cast doubt on the speaker's superior confidence; it also brings
into play the whole question of what it is like to be single. This opens
up the possibility that the driving emotion at the start of the poem
was neither guilt nor mere insecurity: it was envy. Perhaps the speaker
is lonely in his single existence. The technique is similar to that we
noticed in Chapter 1, in the word 'birdless' from 'Next, Please',
because it has been prepared by a carefully created silence.

Much of the poem, and the speaker's overbearing personality, have
begged the question: Well then, what is it like to be single? The poem
has not provided any answer, and as we read we become naggingly
aware of this gap, this omission. Here is a man comparing his life
with another's, but we hear nothing of his life at all. It is as if we are
looking at a butterfly with one wing – the rest of the pattern an empty
space. Then, in the final line, the whole of the other side comes into
view suddenly. Being single is equally untenable: perhaps he cannot
stand it, and like marriage, it will drive him mad. The effect of this
silence is revisionist: when we return to 'He has no time at all', we
now wonder how slowly time passes for a solitary man, as well as
recognising Arnold's busy, but full, life.

In 'Self's the Man', then, the choice between being single, or
having a family, is the topic. Misogyny, bluster, self-aggrandisement,
insecurity, smugness and cynicism are all there. The character's

instability is portrayed by the out-of-control voice, and Larkin has much fun at the expense of his poetic ineptness. However, the possibility of loneliness is also present. Then the final line undercuts the entire poem in a sudden and unexpected flash of insight. As in 'Poetry of Departures', the choice is no choice at all: single or married, life is hard to stand, and it may drive you mad. This man is not 'happier' than Arnold, however hard he rationalises and however aggressively he compensates for his panic. The poem, then, provides an intricate set of layers, each rendered null by the succeeding implication, and each ambiguous or incomplete. No resolution of the dilemma is offered, but the dilemma itself is acutely presented and experienced. The outcome is a focus on evasion and self-deception, with universal misery as a sudden, final backdrop.

Our conclusions about 'Self's the Man' are in danger of sounding too fine. We should remind ourselves that the seriousness of the poem is undercut by its comic treatment. Even being driven insane by life is comically reduced to 'them sending a van'.

'Dockery and Son' (*CP*, 152–3)

'Dockery and Son' is a simple story which sets off a far from simple meditation in the poem's speaker. Visiting his old college, the speaker learns that one of the current students is the son of Dockery, who was a year younger than he is. As he travels home by train, the speaker meditates about Dockery, about his own childless, wifeless state, and how time has passed since he was an undergraduate.

The poem opens in a conversation with the Dean, and the speaker's voice is natural throughout. Sentence lengths vary, there is a great deal of enjambement, and rhymes, although mostly perfect, are chosen and placed in such a way as to seem unforced. Many of the rhyme words, for example, are casual parts of conversation, such as 'good Lord' (l. 12) or 'now' (l. 29). The rhymes also seem less obtrusive because the rhyme scheme changes. So, in the first stanza there is the clear alternating pattern ABABCDCD; but already in the second stanza this is altered to ABABCDDC. The four remaining stanzas have: ABBACDCD, ABCADCBD and ABBCADDC in both the final two. Notice that the pattern adopted for the fourth stanza ensures that all rhymes are separated by at least two lines (the B rhyme is separated by four); and the pattern adopted in the final two stanzas ensures that the A and C rhymes are separated by three lines. This complexity and evolution of rhyming patterns prevents us from predicting sounds and reduces our awareness of their harmonies because they are more widely spaced, particularly in the second half of the poem. Rhyming remains close and regular until the fourth stanza, the stanza which records the speaker's 'shock' on realising 'how much had gone of life, / How widely from the others'.

Metrically, 'Dockery and Son' is in iambic pentameter, but Larkin uses the form loosely. The opening line has only four feet, for example, and the aphoristic 'Life is first boredom, then fear' (l. 45) is only seven syllables. Several other lines are missing a syllable, and most of them are irregular: we cannot force them into the 'de-dum de-dum' of iambic metre. Within this technique, Larkin has the freedom to dramatise his speaker's voice as he travels through several changes of thoughts and mood. See, for example, how easily the speaker's sleepy meditations on the train are presented, crossing stanza and line endings at will, and leading to the unfinished half-thoughts, separated by dots, as he falls asleep:

> Was he that withdrawn
>
> High-collared public-schoolboy, sharing rooms
> With Cartwright who was killed? Well, it just shows
> How much ... How little ... yawning, I suppose
> I fell asleep ...

This meandering, sleepy voice is different from the sharp-edged, rather desperate short sentences that chronicle how he leaves Oxford. The word 'Locked' is cut off at the start of stanza 2, then there are two vivid impressions: the lawn 'spread dazzlingly' and a bell onomatopoeically 'chimes', each in its own short sentence. The speaker's sense of disconnection and loss is sharp and short: 'I catch my train, ignored'.

The poem, then, records the speaker's slow reaction to the news that Dockery's son is now a student. First, he attempts to contact his previous life by trying 'the door of where I used to live', but is shut out not only by the lock but by the indifference of lawn and bell: he no longer belongs in this place. Then, he thinks about Dockery, trying to remember him and idly calculating his age and his son's probable age. This leads him to begin a philosophical meditation 'How much … how little …', at which point he falls asleep. This part of the story does not acknowledge how deeply the news has affected him: the speaker seems to think about it idly. On the other hand, there are signs that the shock is already growing, under the surface. The locked door, and 'Cartwright who was killed', prefigure the negativity of the poem's end where hopes and ideals 'warp tight-shut, like doors', and death is 'the only end of age'.

Finally, when he stands at the end of the platform in Sheffield, looking at tracks 'joining and parting', he acknowledges the shock as 'a numbness' and begins to think more seriously about Dockery and himself. Larkin portrays his speaker as a man who reacts to emotion after a delay: he is unaware of his emotions until they force themselves through, much later. From here, the speaker's meditation follows two tracks, only one of which is completed.

First, he imagines that Dockery must have been very purposeful, 'must have taken stock / Of what he wanted', with the implication that he himself lacks this decisiveness. This line of thought is interrupted, however, and he begins the second line of thought, asking why Dockery was the kind of person who would have a son, while he was not. The speaker rephrases the question: 'Where do these / Innate assumptions come from?' Remember to focus on dramatic characterisation. Here, we should notice what the speaker has done for himself by shifting his meditation from the first track to the second.

He has moved from active to passive concepts of living. Lines 30 and 31 sound energetic and active, with 'taken stock' and 'capable'. Dockery is less active, but still deciding his life, as he 'is convinced' and 'thinks' in lines 33 and 34. Now that the question is rephrased, Dockery is completely passive and his actions are what move, as they 'come from' somewhere else. Secondly, notice how the form of expression has changed. There is a theory ('must have taken stock'), then an interruption as the speaker corrects himself. Then there is an exclamation, followed by a question ('How convinced he was …' and

'Why did he think ...'). When the question is rephrased, it is no longer a question: it has become a rhetorical question, one that contains the answer in itself. If these assumptions are 'innate', you have them at birth: that is where they 'come from', and there is nothing you can do about them.

It is at this crucial point in the poem, when he interrupts his own thoughts and changes their direction, that Larkin subtly provokes our suspicion of the speaker. We may still partly accept the negative philosophy developed from this point to the end of the poem; but the questionable process of the speaker's thoughts does suggest that we should question his motives. Why did it take so long for him to recognise his own shock? Why does he turn away from an active concept of living, and towards helpless hopelessness?

There seems to be an element here of the same mental process we found in 'Self's the Man', where the speaker rationalises, constructing an argument in order to feel superior to Arnold. Here, the process is much more subtle. This speaker does not feel superior to Dockery, but he allocates responsibility for the differences between them to 'innate assumptions' neither of them can influence. It is not that Dockery is more decisive. Dockery is not in control of his life. It is just that he was born different. This speaker, then, has eventually achieved what the speaker of 'Self's the Man' managed: just as that speaker and Arnold are equally selfish, this speaker and Dockery are equally helpless.

This time, however, there is a painful cost. When he concludes that neither of them has any control over his life, that their innate assumptions have hardened 'into all we've got', he has pushed himself into an acutely painful outlook. Looking back, his determining character rears 'Like sand-clouds, thick and close' bringing him 'nothing'. Life will leave only this predetermined miserable outcome, then 'age, and then the only end of age'. The speaker's crumb of comfort comes from the fact that this applies to Dockery – patronised by his son – as well as to himself. Nonetheless, it is a desolate and painful outlook.

This is what we are left with. We do not know whether the speaker's pessimism is right or wrong. We understand how and why he reaches that conclusion, to protect himself from the other one: that you can take charge of your life. Either way, the structure of the speaker's character gives no way out. The different elements that are poised against each other and form the structure of moods and ideas in 'Dockery and Son', none of them certain yet none of them dismissable, leave no escape from misery – for this character. We will return to 'Dockery and Son' in later chapters, particularly in connection with the poet's portrayal of journeys. For the present, we have again seen a contrast between lone and gregarious existences melt away, to the point where there appears to be no real contrast, or choice, at all.

'Vers de Société' (*CP*, 181–2)

We are becoming familiar with Larkin's fluid, flexible conversational style, and we understand the technical means by which he achieves this extraordinarily natural impression. Here again, the rhyming patterns of the stanzas evolve as the poem proceeds. This time, the regular, noticeable rhyming marker set down in stanza 1 (three couplets: AABBCC) returns in the final stanza; but in between, there are four variations. Phrasing runs across the ends of lines and stanzas with ease, beginning with 'perhaps / You'd care to join us?' in the second line. The impression of the speaker talking to himself, and passing from mood to mood, comes from natural colloquial expressions seamlessly woven into the form. As in 'Dockery and Son' and 'Self's the Man', we hear him change his mind as if debating with himself: 'Too subtle, that. Too decent, too. Oh hell'.

Here is a poem filled with voices. We hear Warlock-Williams's invitation; two versions of the reply; the voice of social mores ('*All solitude is selfish*' and '*Virtue is social*'); and a variety of language from the speaker, including profanity, as his moods and thoughts change. It is obvious on first reading that 'Vers de Société' hinges on the dilemma presented by the invitation: to accept (socialise, join in) or decline (withdraw, be alone); and the poem's speaker debates this issue throughout. As we might expect from our previous studies, a complex, dazzling array of thoughts and moods is deployed in the poem before he reverses his decision and considers accepting the invitation, in the final line.

It is time to make use of what we have learned about Larkin's poems. This time, we will try a systematic approach, based on the central dilemma Solitaire, Solidaire, and see where we arrive from trying to formalise the forces in the poem. Which parts of the poem push the speaker away from society, and which parts draw him towards it? Let us begin by dividing the poem into these two forces. Here is 'Vers de Société', with the parts that urge rejecting the invitation underlined. In carrying out this task, it is inevitable that some phrases will defy allocation to either force. These are in bold type:

> My wife and I have asked a crowd of <u>craps</u>
> To come and <u>waste their time and ours</u>: perhaps
> You'd care to join us? <u>In a pig's arse, friend.</u>
> **Day comes to an end.**
> **The gas fire breathes, the trees are darkly swayed.**
> <u>And so *Dear Warlock-Williams: I'm afraid* –</u>
>
> Funny how hard it is to be alone.
> <u>I could spend half my evenings, if I wanted,</u>
> <u>Holding a glass of washing sherry, canted</u>
> <u>Over to catch the drivel of some bitch</u>
> <u>Who's read nothing but *Which*;</u>
> <u>Just think of all the</u> spare time <u>that has flown</u>
>
> <u>Straight into nothingness by being filled</u>
> <u>With forks and faces, rather than repaid</u>
> <u>Under a lamp, hearing the noise of wind,</u>
> <u>And looking out to see</u> **the moon thinned**
> **To an air-sharpened blade.**
> <u>A life</u>, and yet how sternly it's instilled
>
> *All solitude is selfish.* No one now
> Believes the hermit with his gown and dish
> Talking to God (who's gone too); the big wish
> Is to have people nice to you, which means
> Doing it back somehow.
> *Virtue is social.* <u>Are, then, these routines</u>
>
> <u>Playing at goodness, like going to church?</u>
> <u>Something that bores us, something we don't do well</u>
> <u>(Asking that ass about his fool research)</u>
> But try to feel, because, however crudely,
> It shows us what should be?
> <u>Too subtle, that. Too decent, too.</u> **Oh hell,**

Only the young can be alone freely.
The time is shorter now for company,
And sitting by a lamp more often brings
Not peace, but other things.
Beyond the light stand failure and remorse
Whispering *Dear Warlock-Williams: Why, of course –*

This division of the poem into two sides of an argument is, inevitably, crude. We have had to ignore a number of shades of mood and ambiguity, when deciding to allocate a word or phrase to one side or the other. Some parts of the poem challenged us to make a personal judgement. For example, we felt comfortable that time 'repaid / Under a lamp, hearing the noise of wind, / And looking out to see' are all aspects of staying at home that attract the speaker. However, what he sees, 'the moon thinned / To an air-sharpened blade' struck us as a hostile image of isolation and distance, almost sinister. Certainly 'thinned' associates with emptiness and loss, and 'blade' associates with hostility. It would be possible to read this as an image conveying fear of loneliness, but we were not sure and therefore put it in bold, as an ambivalent phrase. A similar problem occurred with 'spare time' (l. 12). We sensed that this does stand out from the surrounding argument against going to the party. It is an acknowledgement that the time will not be used, anyway; and is a spondee that slows the iambic line: two longer stressed vowels that make the poem 'hang' for a moment.

The exercise has, however, shown clearly how the poem sways from one tendency to the other; or, how the speaker is caught between two contrary forces. We now examine the result, to gain more detailed information. What are the forces pushing him in two directions? Starting at the beginning of the poem, we will attempt to construct a list:

1 The invitation itself urges him to *accept*.
2 'Craps': his contempt for the people who will be there makes him recoil from the proffered party, and *reject*. He clearly hates them and feels degraded having to socialise with them. This hatred and contempt surfaces in the form of profanity and abuse: it is there again in 'In a pig's arse, friend', 'washing sherry', 'the drivel of some

bitch / Who's read nothing but *Which*' and 'that ass' and 'his fool research'. The spluttering alliteration of 'filled / With forks and faces' also expresses this anger; and his contempt is expressed by the comic invention of the host's name: double-barrelled, pretentiously unlikely, and a comic combination of the historical / absurd 'Warlock' with the common 'Williams', the name is a satire of the aspiring-to-middle-class. Perhaps his contempt for the socially 'nice' appears again when he finds his own thoughts 'Too decent'.

3   '*Waste their time and ours*' urges him to *reject*. The waste and pass- ing of time returns in lines 12 to 14.

4   Peaceful comfort at home urges him to *reject*. Darkness outside the circle of the lamp, and intimations of natural surroundings outside, attract him. This surfaces again when he hears 'the noise of wind' and looks out at the sky.

5   Fear of loneliness urges him to *accept*. This fear may begin to obtrude again in the rather beautiful, but threatening image of the moon 'thinned / to an air-sharpened blade'. Fear of loneliness surfaces again in the final stanza from 'Only the young …' to 'failure and remorse / Whispering …' (ll. 31–6).

6   Mores instilled by society, such as '*All solitude is selfish*' and '*Virtue is social*', exert pressure on him to *accept*. This social pres- sure returns in two other, closely related forms: first, he would like to have society's approval, but 'No one now / Believes the hermit', so he will be censured for solitariness. Secondly, he feels that human society and social relationships are intrinsically worthwhile, and morally better: they are 'what should be', despite the fact that they remain crude and boring.

Again, we are aware that such a list oversimplifies the poem. For example, there are references to the wasting of time ('flown / Straight into nothingness'), the speaker's regrets ('failure and remorse') and the approach of death ('The time is shorter now'), which we have touched on under numbers 3 and 5 above. Arguably, this note in the poem would merit its own place in the list. Then, there are numer- ous shades of mood, where the prevailing urge slackens as we read one more ambiguous word. For example, 'filled' in line 13 almost chimes with the speaker's fear of emptiness. It comes in a very anti-social context, yet after '*spare* time' (my italics) it hints at the opposite argument. Most of the poem is shaded in one way or another: the speaker rarely has a single mood. However, at the risk of oversimplifying, let us see where our list can take us. We will make notes on each item, trying to identify what lies behind the pressures we have found.

1   The invitation is simply that. However, there are supplementary indications in the poem. Clearly, the speaker has experience of these parties – he has accepted invitations in the past, and people do seek his company. In other words, whatever his private feelings, he is socially involved. When he describes socialising, the most prominent feature is his viciously expressed hatred and contempt. However, we also notice that he behaves himself: he is 'canted / Over', and listens politely. He does ask 'that ass' about his research. His note rejecting the invitation is apologetic: '*I'm afraid* ——'.

2   His profanities and abuse, on the surface, fit the boredom he feels. However, these words and phrases are so violent that they stick out of their context like spikes. See, for example, how shockingly the word 'craps' falls into the polite invitation. 'In a pig's arse' is very coarse, and 'bitch' seems too violent for a person for whom he merely feels contempt. The suggestion is that self-hatred fuels such violent anger. He could and should have stayed at home, and hates himself for giving in to social pressures. Clearly, he also hates himself for two further reasons: for his weakness in being unable to bear loneliness, and for 'failure and remorse' in his empty life.

3   Not wanting to waste time is also, ironically, a social pressure. The surface reason for this is that hosts and guests are boring – so he will gain no value from the time he spends with them. However, the concept of time 'wasted' comes from a work ethic that is part of Protestant culture. We are brought up to frown on 'wasted' time. We should 'use' our time, gain some profit from it.

4   The attraction of staying at home is associated with comfort (the lamp, the gas fire) and nature. Referring back to number 3 above, the speaker believes that noticing nature is a profitable use of time: he gains a value from noticing that 'the trees are darkly swayed' or 'hearing the noise of wind'. It is typical of the Protestant/capitalist

work ethic that he thinks of time in commercial terms: it will be 'repaid', even though this value lies in nature rather than profit.

5   Fear of loneliness grows throughout the poem, beginning with the casual 'Funny' that introduces his remark in line 7. Notice that 'sitting by the lamp' has a changing background. At first, we hear of the gas fire, 'trees', 'wind' and 'looking out'. The moon image is pivotal: ambivalently beautiful and frightening. At the end of the poem, the natural background has vanished: sinister 'other things' have taken its place, and 'failure and remorse' whisper to him in place of the wind.

6   Social pressures, the belief that human relationships are intrinsically good and morally desirable, comes from the speaker's upbringing and background. 'Selfish' is a word that echoes from 'Self's the Man'. For this speaker these pressures are associated with a past culture (God and the church, both of which are 'gone' in his modern milieu). There is a hint of regret at the decline of religion, and a sense of obligation to bestir himself, to take part in keeping the lights of civilisation moving forward towards 'what should be'.

These notes are not necessarily those another reader might make: you may well pick up on different implications from those described above. However, it is likely that all readers' responses will follow a similar pattern: that the genesis of the pressures acting on the poem's speaker will spread out into (a) the social, cultural and historical context; (b) the speaker's deeper and less resolved emotions; and (c) philosophical questions regarding our existence as conscious individuals facing death.

As our enquiry spreads, it will peter out and we will find ourselves in one of the silences the poem leaves. It is becoming a familiar experience in interpreting Larkin's poems: as we try to construct meaning, the poem pulls the rug out from under us, for these are poems 'double-yolked with meaning and meaning's rebuttal'.[2] For example, the poem does not tell us about the decline of the church in twentieth-century middle England, and its effect on social mores. It tells us what *this speaker* speculates and then rejects as 'Too subtle ... Too decent'.

Having expanded our response into increasingly uncertain areas of implication, we should now try to reduce it by summarising what we have found. We have compared the Larkin poems we have studied with a house of cards: different elements built up to a 'shape' by leaning against each other, but with empty spaces around them. Here is an attempt to summarise the forces acting (or, the cards poised) in 'Vers de Société', and therefore its structure.

> Pushing the speaker towards *accepting* the invitation are: fear of emptiness, fear of nature, failure, remorse, habit (personal); moral and social obligation (social); nostalgia for the church-going past (cultural).

> Pushing the speaker towards *rejecting* the invitation are: hatred and contempt for others, self-hatred, love of nature (personal); anticipated boredom and futility (social); reluctance to waste time unprofitably (cultural).

To summarise in this way is, of course, a gross oversimplification; but it is helpful as it can enable us to see the poem's shape. The summary also helps us to identify the gaps which we have called 'silences' in the poem. Here, for example, our attention is directed towards nature. In the poem, the wind and trees, peace and the speaker's openness to his surroundings figure as love of nature. The moon is ambivalent, but then the passing of time, advancing age and death induce fear of nature. The poem is silent, refusing to relate or resolve the two. Similarly, the social pressure of '*All solitude is selfish*' and the cultural exhortation not to waste time act in opposed directions. Both contribute to environmental pressure on the speaker, yet they are not related to each other. Again, the speaker is vividly conscious of superiority to the 'crowd of craps', and of his own 'failure and remorse'.

Finally, notice that the poem does not even resolve the simple practical dilemma that set it off. At the end, 'failure and remorse' are whispering to him the words of a note accepting the invitation. The poem does not tell us which reply the speaker eventually wrote and sent, the one in the first stanza or that in the last. He remains vacillating, caught in the unresolved dilemma between the social and isolated passing of time. Both ways of passing time are, anyway, overshadowed by the terrifying 'other things' he fears – increasing age, the approach of death, 'failure and remorse' (both of these words assume that active life is over). Line 32, 'The time is shorter now for company', has an exquisite ambiguity. It can be paraphrased in three ways:

> The time remaining is too short to be wasted on company, or There is only a short time left for me to enjoy company, or There is so little time left it won't matter if I spend it in company.

This is a group of words that pushes the speaker in every direction. It is a perfect example of Larkin's insoluble irony.

'Wild Oats' (*CP*, 143)

Rhyme in this poem is reminiscent of 'Poetry of Departures': the poet adheres to a strict rhyme scheme (ABCABDCD), but it is not obtrusive because there are only two perfect rhymes (*doubt/out, snaps/perhaps*) and all the rest are half-rhymes (such as '*ago/to*' or '*rose/hers*' in the first stanza). Rhythm is again flexible, relying on beats rather than metre, and the majority of line endings are run-on. There are some very ordinary, everyday expressions ('Two girls *came in where I worked*', for example, 'snaps' instead of 'photographs', the casualness of '*About* twenty years ago', and 'in those days'). The over-all effect is to characterise the speaker's voice: we are hearing a conversational anecdote from a friend, in a casual register.

As with most of Larkin's poems, the story is simple. The speaker met two girls, had a seven-year affair with the less attractive of them, which finally ended by mutual agreement. He keeps photographs of the more attractive girl. We can focus on the character straight away, because this simple story provokes a question that cries out to be investigated: why? Why on earth does the speaker behave in such an irrational manner?

The initial moment of the poem – when the two girls come in, and the speaker chooses – occurs in the first stanza. First, notice that four lines are devoted to 'bosomy' and two to the 'friend'. Lines 3 and 4 set up a contrast of sound and rhythm, also. 'A **bos**omy **Eng**lish **Rose**' has a lilting beat, while 'And her **friend in specs** I could **talk to**' sounds clumsy in comparison (as well as the clumsy style of a preposition at the end of the sentence). Line 3 also sounds soft and lush, while line 4 has shorter and harder sounds in 'specs' and 'talk to'. The lilt of 'A **bos**omy **Eng**lish **Rose**' is echoed in 'If **ever** one **had** like **hers**' (line 7). In between, Larkin has referred to the permissive revolution he celebrates elsewhere in 'Annus Mirabilis': twenty years ago, girls were more demurely dressed, so 'Faces … sparked / The whole shooting-match off'. 'The whole shooting-match' is a revealing euphemism. It stands for sexual excitement, and at the same time characterises the speaker. The fact that he uses a euphemism implies that he is self-conscious and embarrassed, from his out-of-date upbringing; and his choice of a weapon metaphor ('shooting-match') indicates a macho attitude to sexuality. Does this language reveal his response to 'bosomy' as an embarrassed youth; or does he still respond to women in this way, twenty years later?

The stanza remains silent on the question of why the speaker goes out with the 'friend in specs'. We are simply given different elements: his sexual excitement about 'bosomy', the social constraints of that era, his ability to talk to the friend. We are also given several statements which hold up implied blanks to our view. He could talk to the friend: can we assume that he could not talk to 'bosomy'? If so, was this the fault of his acute embarrassment, or her lack of conversation? Girls' 'Faces' excited him in those days, and line 7 tells us that 'bosomy's' face was really exciting. But the only thing he has mentioned about her is her bosoms. Can we assume that her bosoms did not excite him, then? Is he being honest? If 'bosomy' was sexually attractive, can we assume that her friend was not? These silences give an impression of symmetry: what is missing is the correlative statement to the one given; and the questions raised but not answered suggest how irrationally he behaved. He chose the 'friend' *because* she was not sexually exciting. He ran away from attraction.

The second stanza describes his seven-year relationship with the friend. It is a relationship carried on at a distance: the poem emphasises letters, and meetings in 'cathedral cities'. The suggestions here remain very uncertain. For example, we could speculate that they made up reasons for meeting – to visit 'cathedral cities' – implying that they needed excuses to meet. Does 'ten-guinea ring' imply that he knew it was cheap when he bought it, or is his contemptuous tone more recent? Why were their visits 'unknown to the clergy'? Does this imply that he never intended to marry? Or is it a hangover from his upbringing, the feeling that their sexual relationship has to be clandestine?

There is a current of numbers and arithmetic running through this stanza, as if remembering the relationship is a matter of adding things up. It lasted 'seven' years, with 'four hundred' letters, a 'ten-guinea' ring and 'numerous' cities, during which time he met the other girl 'twice'. Again, the overtone of this motif is difficult to judge. It is as if the sheer volume of time and letters and money will, in some way, make the relationship itself more important. At the end of the stanza, we are reminded that he has no understanding of the other girl: she tried 'so I thought' not to laugh.

The third stanza deals with the end of the relationship. He and the 'friend' discussed breaking up six times. Eventually, they reached an 'agreement' which appears to lay the blame on him: he is 'selfish', 'withdrawn' and 'too easily bored'. Even this, however, is not entirely straightforward. 'Selfish' is a fault. 'Withdrawn' may be a misfortune if you wish to form relationships (and if *'All Virtue is social'*[3] could be called a fault). 'Easily bored' can cut both ways: he is clever, which boosts his ego; she is boring, which is an attack on her. 'To love' is also ambiguous. Does it mean that nobody could love him, or that he cannot love anybody? Either way, it damns him. It is not just this relationship that has failed, all his relationships are doomed.

What is the tone of his comment, 'Well, useful to get that learnt'? Possibly relief, now that the futile relationship is finally over; possibly amusement, because it took seven years to arrive at this assessment, which is a lie anyway; possibly bitterness, because he has shouldered all the blame for seven wasted years. Any or all of these possible feelings may inform the speaker's ironic remark. When we consider the story as a whole, with its various questionable moments, there is a further possible ironic meaning in this line.

We strongly suspect that he took out the 'friend' only because she was not attractive or exciting, in order to run away from attraction. We do not know why he needed to suppress the attraction he felt for 'bosomy', but there are strong hints about this. First, that he was embarrassed by his sexual arousal (called by the self-conscious euphemism 'the whole shooting-match'). Secondly, that he expected and feared rejection (he thought she was 'trying ... not to laugh' at him). It is likely, then, that he found the strength of his own sensations distressing and threatening. In this crisis, he sought out an insipid relationship with the 'friend' as a refuge from emotional turmoil. Next, he made sure that he invested a lot of time and letters in this relationship. Perhaps this was so that he could say, afterwards, that they had really tried to make it work. In the end, they agreed that he was incapable of a love relationship. This could be 'useful' to learn, because it lets him off the hook for life. He ran away from a powerful and disturbing attraction twenty years ago. Now, in the present, he still runs away from sexual sensations, or a risk of rejection. Now, however, he has the ready-made excuse that he is 'too selfish, withdrawn, / And easily bored to love'. He tried it once. Oh, how he tried (imagine: over 400 letters!). There is no point in trying it all again, is there? In this sense, it may be 'useful' for him to learn such a convenient lesson.

This does not give a pleasant picture of the speaker. He used the 'friend in specs' merely as a diversion. He wasted seven years of her life, and showered her with letters, merely as weight of evidence to bolster him against any further threats to his equanimity. Finally, he broke up with her, happily shouldering the blame for selfish reasons!

The speaker seems to be aware, or at least half-aware, of his own dishonesty and self-deceptions. He still runs away from relationships. In the final three lines he reveals another, rather sordid aspect of his character: he still keeps 'snaps' of 'bosomy' in his wallet. They must have been there throughout his seven-year affair with the other girl, which underlines the extent of his dishonesty. It also suggests that he deals with sexual excitement in an unhealthy way: the girl herself is too disturbing and threatening, but when reduced to a photograph, she can be kept for titillation. 'Unlucky', in the final line, is disingenuous. This speaker's actions had nothing to do with luck, and everything to do with a consistent, compulsive self-interest driven by embarrassment and fear.

The last two paragraphs have been critical of the poem's speaker, but it is worth considering more widely: who is the villain of the piece? It is quite believable that a self-conscious, shy young man would behave in exactly this way, overwhelmed by embarrassment and to avoid the horror of rejection. This would be particularly true in the early 1940s when these events are supposed to have taken place. As he says, 'Faces in those days sparked / The whole shooting-match', because women dressed demurely, society was much more strait-laced, and sex was a taboo. In 'Annus Mirabilis', Larkin's speaker explains that until 1963:

> there'd only been
> A sort of bargaining,
> A wrangle for a ring,
> A shame that started at sixteen
> And spread to everything.

(CP, 167)

In 1962, in 'Wild Oats', Larkin writes for a much more liberal and permissive society than had existed in the early 1940s. Perhaps the character of the speaker in this poem shows how a repressive, strait-laced upbringing turns a shy boy into a twisted and selfish misogynist. Perhaps the villains of the piece are the same post-Victorian attitudes to sex against which D. H. Lawrence inveighed earlier in the century.

This remains a poem full of silences. Simple statements, and fertile implications, are placed side by side in such a way as to provoke questions and withhold answers. Now that we have explored the poem, we can appreciate the truly complex irony of the title. The speaker never sowed his 'Wild Oats'. Instead, terrified by the prospect of powerful sexual excitement, he ran away from the situation and spent the next seven years suppressing the urge to do so. The fact that he did not sow his 'Wild Oats' determined much about his character and life.

In this chapter we have explored the dilemma between joining in with other people, participating in society; and remaining withdrawn. We have looked at 'Self's the Man', where the speaker compares the lives of a family man and a bachelor; 'Dockery and Son', which treats a similar theme but focuses on what the speaker and Dockery have acquired by the age of 40 (in the speaker's case, 'nothing'); and 'Vers de Société', which explores the choice between social involvement and a withdrawn, 'hermit' existence. In all of these poems, the blend of motives, attitudes and moods has been an uneasy, unstable mix; and the poems' speakers have revealed a need to feel superior, lack of confidence, and a tendency to rationalise, either to dismiss the dilemma as artificial, or to deny any responsibility for their lives. We included 'Wild Oats' in this selection of poems on the Solitaire, Solidaire question, on the basis that its speaker is faced with a similar choice: to join and participate, or to keep his distance. When he chooses the 'friend in specs' *because* she is unattractive, devotes seven years of his life to an affair carried on through letters and brief meetings, and concludes that he is incapable of a love affair, the speaker of 'Wild Oats' is, effectively, keeping himself separate. He is rejecting the temptations, and the invasion of his inviolate self, offered by the attraction he felt towards 'bosomy'.

In 'Dockery and Son', the villains that have turned him into a lonely adult with the 'harsh patronage' of 'nothing' are – ostensibly – those 'innate assumptions' that always have made people different from each other. In 'Wild Oats', the speaker is more specific in referring to the prudish era of 'About twenty years ago', which is partly responsible for his embarrassment, fears and subsequent actions. In all of the poems, there is a blend of contributing emotions, some laudable, many not, surrounding a speaker who rationalises and agonises over decisions about whether or not to participate in a social life.

In all of the poems we have studied, the central dilemma is insoluble. In 'Self's the Man', either there is no real difference in motive, as they are both 'selfish', or no difference in outcome, as both of their lives may drive them mad. In 'Dockery and Son' their motives are not their own, but proceed from an accident of birth; while the outcome subjects both of them to equivalent 'harsh patronage' before they face 'the only end of age'. In 'Vers de Société', it does not matter whether he accepts or rejects the invitation: he will be miserable, bored and angry if he goes to the party, and frightened, lonely, and haunted by 'failure and remorse' if he stays at home. In 'Wild Oats', he does not know whether 'bosomy' was laughing at him or not. Could he have sown his 'Wild Oats'? Probably not, in 'those days', and the poem says nothing of an alternative story. This speaker has reached an accommodation with the insoluble dilemma. He keeps 'snaps' for titillation, and avoids love out of prolonged, now proven, fear and embarrassment which he calls 'selfish … withdrawn … easily bored'.

This chapter's concluding discussion will refer in passing to a number of other poems which explore the Solitaire, Solidaire dilemma: it was a topic ideally suited to Larkin's presentation of the complex, self-revelatory and helpless persona we are beginning to recognise as the 'speaker' of these poems. The next chapter will further investigate Larkin's interest in social interactions and rituals, but approaching the theme from a different angle.

Concluding Discussion

Background to the Poems

As in the previous chapter, we will glance at the events in Larkin's life to which these poems may refer.

'Self's the Man' is dated November 1958. Larkin finally finished 'The Whitsun Weddings',[4] after three years and multiple drafts, on 18 October, and by 5 November had written 'Self's the Man'. He had been Chief Librarian at Hull University Library for three years, higher education was going through a period of rapid expansion and Larkin was deeply involved in designing and planning for a new, much bigger library. Andrew Motion tells us that Arnold is modelled on Arthur Wood, Larkin's deputy librarian at Hull,[5] and the poem arises from Larkin's wish to 'deride' his married colleague. This may be so; but it is equally possible to speculate that Larkin created this comically 'bad' poem to balance the extraordinary delicacy of poise he had so arduously achieved in 'The Whitsun Weddings', on the principle that, as he always sought to combine 'meaning' with 'meaning's rebuttal',[6] so now he sought to balance style with style's rebuttal. Equally, we could speculate that Larkin felt more settled and satisfied in Hull than ever before: *The Less Deceived* was a success, and he could look forward to an expanding future in both his literary and work lives. This may have brought other forms of 'settling down' and 'domestic happiness' to mind, and tempted him enough to provoke this cynical poem as a defence. These are speculations, however.

'Dockery and Son' is dated March 1963. The anecdotal opening refers to a visit Larkin paid to his old college in Oxford, in 1962, on his way back to Hull from attending a funeral. This information elucidates the phrase 'death-suited', in a literal sense. However, the phrase echoes with extra meaning in the poem, prefiguring the increasingly bleak ending dominated by the expectation of death. Larkin's readers do not know about the funeral he had attended: he must have kept the phrase for its wider implications, not as an isolated, unexplained circumstantial allusion. As we have found with other poems, the event in Larkin's life the poem refers to may have occurred some time before. 'Dockery and Son' was written a full year after the event. Significantly, the speaker of the poem also takes time to digest and mull over his experience: his 'shock' is delayed, which may be a comment on the gestation of the poem.

'Vers de Société' was completed on 19 May, 1971. We have no information about a particular invitation, or any acquaintance who was the original of 'Warlock-Williams'; but the situation is ordinary and believable, and must have happened to Larkin repeatedly. His biographer argues that the poem really proceeds from Larkin's obligations to his mother and Monica Jones,[7] but in the absence of any evidence there seems no reason to make such a leap. In any case, it is plain that Larkin continually returned to the theme of solitude versus social involvement in his poems.

In the case of 'Wild Oats' (composed in May 1962) we have a solid biographical basis to go on. The two girls who came into Wellington Public Library when Larkin began to work there in December 1943, were called Jane Exall ('bosomy English rose') and Ruth Bowman ('her friend in specs'). Larkin and Ruth Bowman became engaged in May 1948. During the months before leaving England to take up his new job in Belfast, in 1950, Larkin rather half-heartedly and sporadically proposed marriage to her. Ruth eventually wrote to break off the relationship in September. The story of their love affair fits the narrative of 'Wild Oats' closely, then: we can even hear 'too selfish, withdrawn, / And easily bored to love' in Ruth's breaking-up letter:

I hope that you will be happy in Ireland and that you will, in a new environment, be able to come to better terms with life and with yourself.[8]

So, there is a clear genesis for 'Wild Oats' in Larkin's life. On the other hand, the story has been fictionalised. Larkin did, in fact, take out Jane Exall – once; and by the time he proposed to and broke up with Ruth, he had begun the affair with Monica Jones that would continue for the rest of his life.

The most interesting point that arises from comparing 'Wild Oats' with what we can learn of Larkin's life is that the poem tells us nothing about either girl. Like any poem, it has its subject; and the subject of 'Wild Oats' is the arrested adolescent character of the speaker – with implications about the background of 'those days' that was partly responsible. Larkin's life provides some interesting anecdotal information, then, but in most cases this tells us nothing new about the significance of the poem. However, in this chapter we have taken notice of some cultural and historical allusions. What follows is a brief introductory discussion of these, before we give fuller consideration to the poems' context in the next chapter.

How do these poems allude to the social and historical background? 'Self's the Man' paints a 1950s picture of family life, in an unmistakably half-educated and provincial voice. We commented that the speaker's background is probably lower middle class. In 'Dockery and Son', there is a tension between the idyllic college past of naughtiness, authority and a 'dazzlingly wide' lawn, and the war background that briefly obtrudes in 'Cartwright who was killed'. The picture of Dockery as a 'high-collared public-schoolboy' is of the period, reminding us that there was a class divide between ex-public-school and ex-grammar-school students at a 1940s university: one could be told from the other instantly by accent, clothes and manners. Larkin came from a grammar school. In 'Vers de Société' there are a number of contemporary allusions: to pretentiousness (the name 'Warlock-Williams'; drinking cheap sherry); to a rising consumer culture combined with educational decline ('some bitch / Who's read nothing but *Which*'); to the decline of religion, and to the social imperative insisting that it is virtuous to be a good mixer. In 'Wild Oats' a broad change in courtship behaviour, sexual mores and female dress is implied between the 1940s when he chose the 'friend in specs', and the 1960s when the poem was written.

What can we learn from these references? Perhaps grouping them into past and present would help. The past appears in the formal authority of the Dean, and formal attire of the students ('Black-gowned'). The world was well ordered where 'a known bell chimes' and there were 'routines / Playing at goodness, like going to church' in the old days before God was 'gone too'. On the other hand, this same fixed and authoritarian society did not allow women to dress revealingly, and swamped a young man's sexual feelings with shame and embarrassment. In the present, Arnold lives a life of domestic drudgery, struggling to afford improvements like the 'drier / And the electric fire'; and the new middle class apes the behaviour of its predecessors but with inferior 'washing-sherry', artificial names, a preoccupation with consumer goods and prices and no education.

There are elements of the past that appear attractively reassuring, then, such as Oxford's dazzling lawns and the 'known bell's chime'. Certainly it was a time when people felt safer, and the authority of Dean and church would tell you how to be good. The Dean in particular seems to have been a reassuring boundary against which students could rebel in safety. On the other hand, society has become a great deal more liberal by the 'present'. A stifling moral code could cause personal misery and distortion of character ('Wild Oats'), and the chaos of war and death lay behind Oxford's superficially orderly calm. The present has brought greater freedom and equality, then; but at the same time the reassurance of religious observances and moral authority has gone. People are without depth or true values, dominated by knowing the price of everything and the value of nothing, and are ignorantly pretentious.

For the moment, we can observe that Larkin *almost* refers to an idealised past of solid values and social cohesion; and decries a shallow, ignorant present of cheap pretentiousness. At the same time, each of these pictures is undercut by contrary feelings: hatred of the past's prudish taboos, and recognition of the new freedoms society allows. The picture of people deserted by their religion, blindly striving towards 'what should be', however 'crudely', provokes some sympathy for those struggling in the formless, boundary-less modern world.

The Theme of 'Solitaire, Solidaire'

The four poems we have studied in this chapter were chosen from many that treat this theme. In some, such as 'Reasons for Attendance' (*CP*, 80), the dilemma of remaining solitary or joining others is central. Others, such as 'The View' (*CP*, 195) foreground the speaker's 'Unchilded and unwifed' isolation. Yet others, such as 'This be the Verse' (*CP*, 180), focus on family relationships. In 'Reasons for Attendance', the speaker sets up a conflict between his dedication to the 'rough-tongued bell / (Art, if you like)' and the attractions of a party with 'the wonderful feel of girls'. The poem's dilemma is, typically, dismissed by the uncertainty of the final line: 'If no one has misjudged himself. Or lied'. 'This be the Verse' gives a cynical appraisal of family relationships in which 'They fuck you up, your mum and dad' and advises the reader to 'Get out as early as you can, / And don't have any kids yourself'. However, the exaggerated negativity of this creates an undercutting irony: it is so bitter as to satirise itself.

'The View' comments on the speaker's single state; and self-consciously suggests that he is socially inept or unconfident ('Overweight and shifty'); In the final stanza the focus shifts, however, from his fruitless singleness to that which it enables him to see: death, 'So final. So near'. Increasingly in Larkin's later poems, being alone becomes associated with being flooded by thoughts of death; and there is a counterpoint set up between busy people and busy lives, and an intolerably frightening emptiness. Even as early as 'Next, Please', the picture of people too busy to notice the approach of death is clear. We have met this in 'Vers de Société', when 'sitting by a lamp' brings terrifying 'other things'; and in the progression of ideas that finishes 'Dockery and Son'. In 'Ambulances', there is the sense that recognition of death lies just beneath the surface at every moment, as women coming from the shops are suddenly jolted out of their everyday preoccupations by seeing an ambulance. They

> sense the solving emptiness
> That lies just under all we do,
> And for a second get it whole,
> So permanent and blank and true.

(*CP*, 132)

Death is 'emptiness', 'permanent' and 'blank', but these are predictable. The word here that encapsulates what we have found from exploring the Solitaire, Solidaire dilemma, is 'solving'. Each dilemma we have examined is insoluble: either perceptions are so uncertain that we doubt the reality of the dilemma in the first place; or the honesty of the speaker is questionable, 'double-yolked ... with meaning and meaning's rebuttal'. In most of the poems, death arrives as an overwhelming reality. Fear of death prolongs the dilemma by rendering solitude unbearable; death itself will be the only effective solution.

Returning to the Solitaire, Solidaire dilemma: why is it insoluble? The answers we have come across again and again, are that the poems express pessimism about human relationships and social relationships; express pessimism about life alone; and are pessimistic about self-knowledge.

The caricature of life with a wife and family presented in 'Self's the Man' is bitterly endorsed by the speaker of 'This be the Verse' and quietly echoed by the more tentative speaker of 'Dockery and Son' who believes 'addition' is not 'increase' but 'dilution', and assumes that Dockery's son subjects him to 'harsh patronage'. In 'Vers de Société', the speaker expresses his contempt for wasting time with a drivelling 'bitch' and an 'ass', in other words a 'crowd of craps', with some viciousness. This estimate of socialising appears again in 'Reasons for Attendance'. The suggestion that those dancing inside are not quite in their right minds is present as light irony in 'Shifting intently, face to flushed face', and the speaker suggests that they appear absurd, remarking that they perform this sex ritual 'solemnly'. Later in the poem, his contempt appears more clearly: they 'maul to and fro'. In 'Wild Oats', the relationship was doomed from the start, as the one he could 'talk to' was not the one who set 'the whole shooting-match off'. We have found a pessimistic assessment of human relationships and the value of social involvement, then.

There are signs that Larkin's speakers accord a higher value to staying 'outside', alone. In 'Reasons for Attendance' he believes that 'Art, if you like' proves to him that 'I too am individual'. This asserts a wish to preserve himself intact from being worn away by others, and is present in the idea that having a son would be 'dilution'. In 'Vers de Société' there is an implicit claim that separateness enables him to appreciate natural beauty. However, each of these claims is undercut within its poem, and each speaker, sooner or later, recognises that with peace and silence come thoughts of death, and pessimism about himself, accompanied by unbearable pain. Even the speaker of 'Self's the Man' only *supposes* that he will manage not to go mad. The thought from 'Vers de Société', 'Funny how hard it is to be alone', occurs to each poem's speaker sooner or later. We have found, then, a pessimistic assessment of living alone.

On the other hand, terrifying emptiness is sometimes presented in such transcendent and lyrical language that it evokes fascination as well as fear. The final lines of 'Here', which end at empty sky and sea 'Facing the sun, untalkative, out of reach' (*CP*, 137); and of 'High Windows', which reaches 'the deep blue air, that shows / Nothing, and is nowhere, and is endless' (*CP*, 165), are examples of this effect. This suggests a powerful attraction towards nothingness, and is expressed in a tone of wonder.

Finally, the speakers fall into two groups: those who are charac-terised as lacking self-knowledge, and those who are fundamentally suspicious of themselves. The first group is typified by the speaker of 'Wild Oats', whose fear of his own sexual excitement drove him, probably subconsciously, to invest enormous time and energy in a doomed love-affair, and to accept his own isolation afterwards with ironic smugness: 'Well, useful to get that learnt'. Perhaps he of 'Dockery and Son' also belongs to this group, as the poem's voice and rhythms reveal his thoughts changing tack when he rejects the possi-bility of purposeful life, and a smug and melodramatic tone can be detected in the aphoristic, gloomy ending. The second group includes most of the rest. He of 'Vers de Société' catches out his own rationalisations with a brusque 'Oh hell', and has no trust in his own 'failure and remorse'. In 'Self's the Man' the speaker does not know whether he is fooling himself, and 'Reasons for Attendance' ends sug-gesting that the speaker may have 'misjudged himself. Or lied'. Both groups of speakers, then, may be driven by unconscious urges; and they cannot know what these are. They are either unsuspecting, or suspicious, characters. What is constant is that they are unable to assess the value of their ideas, because they cannot trust themselves. All of the poems, then, convey pessimism about self-knowledge.

The Solitaire, Solidaire dilemma is therefore hopeless. All the speakers of these poems will remain caught within it: pessimistic about relationships, pessimistic about isolation, and rendered helpless by suspicion of themselves, until the 'solving emptiness' of death settles the matter.

In *High Windows*, Larkin's third and last collection, the poem 'Livings II' describes a lighthouse-keeper exulting in his solitude. This poem has often been taken as unequivocal evidence that Larkin exults in a solitary existence.[9] The final stanza is:

> Guarded by brilliance
> I set plate and spoon,
> And after, divining-cards.
> Lit shelved liners
> Grope like mad worlds westward.

> (*CP*, 188)

The poem is unusual for Larkin in showering the reader with metaphors, and highlighting the symbolism of the tower in a waste of sea. This final stanza, however, returns to a metonymic manner with the exception of the 'mad worlds' simile. I would contend that 'Livings II' does not 'exult': like the poems we have studied in this chapter, it defies resolution. The critical ambivalence lies in the line 'Guarded by brilliance'. First, and literally, the keeper guards the light, not vice versa, but this line suggests the contrary: that solitude is a defence. Secondly, the double meaning of 'brilliance' suggests intellectual vanity and reminds us of the speaker's pompous devotion to 'Art, if you like' from 'Reasons for Attendance'. This vanity is further mocked: how brilliant do you need to be to put out a plate and spoon, or to indulge in a superstitious game?

In this chapter, then, we have found that the Solitaire, Solidaire dilemma is insoluble, and that Larkin refuses to resolve it. At the same time, this aspect of choice in life provokes powerful energies and emotions: wonder, desire for escape, terror, regret, and even smugness are all a part of the knot Larkin has tied around this choice. The speakers are shown unable to cope with such a dilemma, and so unable to make a choice.

Methods of Analysis

Developments from Chapter 1

In this chapter, we have made use of the techniques and approaches listed at the end of Chapter 1. However, we have learned from the first chapter. We have:

1 moved much more quickly to considering a poem as 'characterisation'; and
2 studied a group of poems treating a common theme, with that theme in mind.

The first of these has saved us from fruitless efforts to 'interpret' a poem as a whole: from becoming too lost among contradictions as Larkin's voices change, modulate and shift. The second development has helped us a great deal. We noticed in Chapter 1 that certain concerns about life recur in many poems. Having a particular theme in mind is useful, because it enables us to *frame relevant questions* as our analysis proceeds. The simplest way to frame an analytical question is to ask: *What does this tell us about [such and such a] theme?* For example, in 'Vers de Société' we noticed that there are several spikes of abusive language referring to the proposed party. *What does this tell us about the Solitaire, Solidaire dilemma?* It tells us that the speaker's feelings are disturbed and immoderate: his language is excessive, too strong to be explained by the boredom in prospect. Asking and answering this question led us to speculate about his self-disgust, because he knows his own weakness and suspects that he will eventually go to the party.

The disadvantage of having a particular theme in mind is that you may miss other elements of the poem. For example, in 'Dockery and Son', we did not comment on the speaker's railway journey, and the significance of the 'ranged / Joining and parting lines' he sees from the end of the platform.[10] However, all this shows is that poetry can be immensely rich, and we should return to each poem again and again.

Discussing the 'shape' or Structure of a Larkin Poem

In this chapter, we attempted to use a more formalised method to analyse the 'shape' of 'Vers de Société'. Here is a summary of how we did this:

1 Choose a central dilemma explored in the poem.
2 Go through the poem, separating the words and phrases that exert energy towards one side of the issue, from those exerting force towards the other side.
3 Remember that you will need a third form of notation, to mark parts of the poem that are ambiguous, or apparently neutral.
4 Collect and summarise the forces acting in each direction. While you are doing this, reread the poem and make notes on each of your items in the context of the poem. Do this open-mindedly, and allow yourself to explore connotations and associations.
5 List those places where you might expect a relationship between different items to be explained, but where the poem gives nothing: these are the 'silences', many of which are powerful elements in the poem's effect.

This process, followed step by step, will help you to appreciate the structure of ideas, emotions and attitudes Larkin has built across and against each other, like a house of cards, so that his poem has an unresolvable intellectual 'shape' that seems to be perfect and unfinished at the same time.

The method we applied to 'Vers de Société' may appear unnaturally long-winded, but is worth practising and applying to other poems by Larkin. As you become more familiar with the poems and the method, you will see the poem's shape more quickly, and be able to take short-cuts.

Suggested Work

1 The poem 'Here' (*CP*, 136–7) was written about Hull, in 1961, when Larkin had been more than six years in the town. There are

elements of attraction, revulsion, amusement, contempt, and so on, in the complex relationship between the speaker and the place. It will be a useful exercise to attempt to go through the poem, using the method we applied to 'Vers de Société' in this chapter. Try to divide the poem into parts that are charged with a positive emotion towards Hull, and parts that are negative.

This will be a sensitive and difficult exercise, and your solution may well differ from that of others: it will depend on the tone of voice you 'hear' in each word or phrase, and the attitude you consequently ascribe to each part. The benefit will be that the exercise will put you in a position where you have to think about, and attempt to define, the many different attitudes you find, and you will face the challenge of recognising ambiguities.

2   The poem 'Annus Mirabilis' was written in 1967 about the year 1963. Its subject is a new liberal permissiveness in society, what journalists have called 'the swinging sixties'. You will quickly notice, however, that this poem is related to 'Wild Oats', studied in this chapter: it refers to an apparent change in society, and the speaker's continuing difficulties about sex and girls.

Apply the approaches we have demonstrated in the first two chapters to this poem. In particular, go through the poem and attempt to separate the parts that refer to the past from those referring to the present. What are the speaker's tones in his references to social change? Does the poem make a comment on history, and if so, how confident can we be that the comment is Larkin's?

3   You may and should, of course, read more of Larkin's poetry; and you are encouraged to try our developing analytical methods as widely and often as you feel is helpful.

3

Weddings and Work

Poems analysed: 'The Whitsun Weddings' (*CP*, 114–16); 'Toads' (*CP*, 89–90); 'Going, Going' (*CP*, 189–90); 'The Building' (*CP*, 191–3); 'A Study of Reading Habits' (*CP*, 131)

This chapter explores the picture of contemporary life that is portrayed in Larkin's poems. We will begin by focusing on social rituals, such as weddings, and on work; but it is the intention of the chapter to discuss wider issues as we proceed, attempting to appreciate Larkin's insights into society and the time in which he lived. The first poem we study in this chapter is complex, long and famous.

'The Whitsun Weddings' (*CP*, 114–16)

Larkin has created an unusual stanza form for this poem. The rhyme scheme is consistent throughout the eight stanzas: ABABCDECDE. This scheme begins with an alternating quatrain (ABAB), which gives a sense of clear form, and then moves into the sestet (CDECDE) where rhymes are less noticeable because more distant from each other. The alternating rhymes of the quatrain are partly hidden, however, because the shortness of the four-syllable second line cuts against the poem's iambic beat so strongly: when reading, we do not accept it as a full line, but take a breath before returning to iambic pentameter for the third and remaining lines of the stanza. We 'hear' a natural conversational voice through most of the poem: believable

69

and unforced like the voice in 'Poetry of Departures', so we may be surprised to notice that nearly all of the rhymes in 'The Whitsun Weddings' are perfect, and only one line ('We hurried towards London, shuffling gouts of steam') is irregular in length.

Metrically, the stanzas are regular, but the second line of each stanza cuts against the five-foot length of all other lines: either we wait before restarting pentameter rhythm in the third line, and a lengthy pause is generated; or we read on, and become disoriented because our internal sense of rhythm finishes at the sixth syllable of line 3. The opening stanza sets up this effect. We read, 'That **Whit**sun, **I** was **late get**ting a**way**'. There is a minor irregularity in the stress on 'get-' but we remain comfortable, and recognise this as quite a standard line of iambic pentameter. It is therefore natural, according to our internal expectation of the metre, to read on thus:

> Not **till** ab**out** One-**twen**ty **on** the **sun**

and at that point all our internal sense of metre tumbles into disarray, because we have stopped halfway through a word and not reached the end of the line. The enjambement at 'about / One-twenty' encourages this effect. Alternatively, we may read:

> **Not** till ab**out** [de-dum de-dum de-dum]
> One-**twen**ty **on** the **sun**lit **Satur**day

This way of reading enables us to re-configure our internal rhythm for the remaining eight lines of the stanza, but causes an unnatural and lengthy silence to break the sense between 'about' and 'One-twenty'. Either way, the second line disorients our internal expectations of rhythm. A large proportion of enjambements (44 out of 80 lines) acts further to obscure the regularity of metre and rhyme. Several of these run-on line endings begin a phrase with only one word at the end of the line, as in 'and / Canals' (ll. 14–15) and 'girls / In parodies of fashion' (ll. 28–9), and five of the stanza breaks are run-over.

In short, Larkin has created a form in which there is tension. On the one hand, we have stanzaic and rhyming regularity. On the other hand, the short second line of each stanza, and syntax and sense that cut across the pattern, break up the poem's form. This may be one of the reasons why 'The Whitsun Weddings' is a heightened, dramatic experience to read, despite its discursive, anecdotal voice and subject matter.

The story is straightforward. Interviewed for *The South Bank Show* in 1981, Larkin explained that the poem arose from a railway journey between Hull and London on Whit Saturday, 1955:

> ... train that stopped at every station and I hadn't realized that, of course, this was the train that all the wedding couples would get on and go to London for their honeymoon; it was an eye-opener to me. Every part was different but the same somehow. They all looked different but they were all doing the same things and sort of feeling the same things. I suppose the train stopped about four, five, six stations between Hull and London and there was a sense of gathering emotional momentum. Every time you stopped fresh emotion climbed aboard. And finally between Peterborough and London when you hurtle on, you felt the whole thing was being aimed like a bullet – at the heart of things, you know. All this fresh, open life. Incredible experience. I've never forgotten it.[1]

This is precisely the story told by the poem. As we can now expect from Larkin, it is the multitoned, shifting voice of the speaker that provides richness of implication and finds complexity in the subject.

The speaker begins casually, with '*That* Whitsun' and the inconsequential details of 'One-twenty' and a 'three-quarters-empty' train. He is telling the story of the journey, so he does not bother to tell us what caused him to catch a later than usual train. This conversational voice is present all through the poem from time to time: the same speaker remarks that 'At first, I didn't notice what a noise ...' (l. 21), or 'for / Some fifty minutes' (ll. 59–60), or that marriages 'got under way'(l. 63). Along the way, however, the voice has modulated into a number of other tones. These follow the speaker's changes of attitude and mood as he comes out of his isolation to observe other people, then meditates the significance of what he sees. The process is one of slow recognition, a gradual absorption of signals from outside followed by increasingly intense speculation, and is comparable to the speaker's delayed recognition of shock in 'Dockery and Son'. We will try to follow the main developments of the speaker's mood, before looking at his dissection of the subject, the Whitsun weddings, more closely.

First, he comes out of his life and settles into the train. He is evidently a creature of long-established habits. Not only may he wake at the same time every *day*: this character catches the same train out of Hull, at Whitsun, every *year*. This year, however, he is late. Furthermore, the phrase 'getting away' and detail 'One-twenty' imply eagerness to leave, and irritation at whatever forced a change in his usual habits. Once in the train, then, his mood changes: 'all sense / Of being in a hurry gone', he can relax. This passive ease sets up the mood of the first stage of the journey, and during the first stage, the speaker becomes guardedly lyrical. He allows himself some powerful metaphoric combinations, such as 'tall heat that slept'; an effective, rhythmic rhetorical triad with symbolic overtones ('Where sky and Lincolnshire and water meet'); and sudden touches of intensity related to the sun, such as 'blinding' windscreens, the hothouse that 'flashed uniquely', and 'short-shadowed' cattle. We are carried into his viewpoint and the train's movement as 'hedges dipped / And rose'. All of these elements might create a rhapsodic response to the landscape; but they are intermixed with prosaic observations of uglier things, set in plain language: they 'smelt the fish-dock', passed canals with 'floatings of industrial froth'. There was a 'reek of buttoned carriage-cloth' and towns are 'nondescript', surrounded by 'acres of dismantled cars'. It is as if the speaker responds to natural rural beauty with a powerful upsurge of vague emotion, but holds himself in check with prosaic reminders. Each time he descends to the less beautiful, so his tone changes back to the merely literal, the matter-of-fact.

From the third stanza, he begins to notice the weddings and there is a second transition of mood. There has been vivid reference to the sunlight three times, and he now comments that its brightness prevents him from seeing what is in the shade. For a moment, the speaker becomes a caricature: he thought the merry sounds he heard came from 'porters larking with the mails', and so 'went on reading'. The phrase 'porters larking with the mails' comes from a gentleman's description of ordinary chaps having fun: it belongs in a film comedy of the period, perhaps an Ealing comedy. The sense of a gentleman passenger's detachment and superiority is consolidated as he 'went on reading'. When his compartment passes the actual wedding-party on the platform, the speaker begins in the same mood: girls are 'grinning and pomaded' in 'parodies of fashion, heels and veils', and we can catch the contemptuous tone: they are provincial, stupid, and look ridiculous. There is a change at 'irresolutely', which suddenly carries us from objective scorn (how ridiculous they are!) to the subjective (what are they feeling?). It is a sudden swing into the girls' perspective, from the speaker's, and takes us by surprise. The simile that follows brings a sudden identification of time and space (the end of an 'event' as the end of a platform) combined with vagueness ('something'). The conflation of time and space suggests the speaker being, as he says, 'struck', while a vague 'something' conveys his wish better to understand what he has witnessed.

The first wedding he notices, then, is both absurd and vaguely challenging. What is the challenge? The simile of lines 31–3 tells us: something 'survived' an 'event'. The speaker, then, has sensed that something more significant may be occurring, and there is a hint that it may constitute a victory over time. 'Something' may last, even after its time – its 'event' – has gone. The speaker is left in an ambivalent mood: amusedly scornful and deeply interested.

Intrigued, he leans out to watch at the next station, and a wedding happens for a second time. This section builds on the first, scornful side of the speaker's mood. Fathers, mothers, uncles, the girls' coiffures, clothes and colour sense are all observed for ridicule. There is no empathy in 'loud and fat' or 'shouting smut'. The speaker goes out of his way to paint the vulgarity of the scene, and seems to become carried away by defining the social milieu of these wedding-parties. Not only does he see them on the platform, he also imagines the receptions they have just come from and where these have taken place, in 'cafés', 'banquet-halls up yards' or 'coach-party annexes'. The speaker's satiric tone comes across from the oxymoronic effect of 'banquet-halls' (associated with palaces and high society) 'up yards' (conjuring up a community hall, or an outbuilding of a small country-town hotel); and of 'bunting-dressed' (celebration) 'coach-party annexes' (seedy commercialism).

However, as the weddings are described for a third time, the speaker's mood swings again. Now, his second response begins to dominate, and he searches in the guests' faces for an answer to his question: what is the 'something' that has survived the event? Again, the poem provides us with a transition as he notices that children find the weddings 'dull', before juxtaposing his two reactions in balance again: fathers feel success so 'huge and wholly farcical'. 'Huge' suggests the weddings' significance, but they are simultaneously ridiculous. However, it does not make sense that the fathers find their success 'farcical', at least not consciously: the speaker's perspective is still combined with the party's. Next, he uses a simile ('like a happy funeral') to convey how the women feel; and finally an assertive metaphor that dispenses with any distinction between his view and theirs: 'girls … stared / At a religious wounding'.

This third attempt to define the weddings is loaded with paradox: 'happy funeral', 'religious wounding', 'huge … farcical' are all poised on the edge of making fun, but are too paradoxical to provoke an easy laugh. These lines are also full of surprises: instead of something like 'wonderful', we read 'farcical'; instead of 'event', we read 'funeral'; and instead of 'ceremony' or 'ritual', we read 'wounding'. Each surprise is heavy with connotation. For example, 'funeral' brings images of death and mourning, coffins and graves and the colour black into our minds; while 'Religious wounding' may make us think of the spear in Christ's side, and the holes in his hands and feet; or (in a literary vein) the mysterious wound that may be healed only by achieving the quest of the Holy Grail.

There is a satiric effect on a more prosaic level, also. It is traditional for women to cry at weddings; and naïve girls will imagine loss of virginity on the wedding-night as both a mystery (religious) and bloody (wounding). Perhaps the tradition of hanging out the bloodied bedsheet the morning after, to show the world that the marriage has been consummated, also comes to mind. All of these elements, then, are part of the mystique and superstition surrounding weddings; and the speaker's third attempt to define the experience is exceptionally rich in implication, ambivalent and shifting tones and moods, and burgeoning connotations.

The weddings are not further defined in the final three stanzas. The train continues 'loaded with the sum of all they saw' – in other words, all the perspectives just mentioned, added together; the couples' 'lives would all contain this hour'. Otherwise, the effect of the weddings remains vaguely 'what it held', and is metaphorically a volley of arrows. The speaker, however, returns to the tone of the first part of the journey, which we have called 'guardedly lyrical'.

The lyrical elements bring images of fertility ('squares of wheat', 'shower' and 'somewhere becoming rain') and of weapons ('we were aimed', 'loosed', 'arrow-shower'). At the same time, the speaker holds his more romantic speculations in check by means of matter-of-fact observations, such as that the shadows are now long, the locomotive's 'gouts of steam', and the passing of 'an Odeon' and 'a cooling tower'. His firm grip on an anti-lyrical reality is supported by parts of his meditation. For example, he sees marriage as narrowing the options in life, because of 'the others they would never meet', and as a limiting event because 'their lives would all contain this hour'. This is reminiscent of the theory voiced in 'Dockery and Son', that what we do and choose in life will 'harden into all we've got'.

There are subtle hints, however, that the event has had an effect on the speaker as well as on the newly-weds. Habituated to thinking of London spread out in 'postal districts', he now has the astonishing idea of 'squares of wheat'; and, ambiguously, he implicitly includes himself in the power 'that being changed can give'. The final two lines are a study in ambivalence: 'swelled' implies growth; but a 'sense of falling' is ominous both for the speaker's mood and for the marriages. This arc-shaped movement is echoed by the 'arrow-shower' rising and falling, positive only in the final fertile word 'rain'. 'Rain' is, however, undercut by uncertainty: it is 'sent out of sight' to 'somewhere', not where the speaker is.

So ends our commentary of the speaker's experiences on a train from Hull. What is the effect of the whole? We have found sudden swings from cynicism to mysticism; from the matter-of-fact to a vague and metaphorical lyricism with images of fertility, of a potential, or at least partial, victory over time and death. The finale is, to coin a paradox, absolutely irresolute. The speaker's relationship to the weddings has also veered wildly, from superior scorn to empathy, and back to satire.

We have followed the character of the speaker through the poem, then. At this stage, it is useful to reread our commentary, looking for a broader overview of the poem's structure. Two points seem to stand out. First, that the journey described in the first two stanzas can be taken as an analogy for the weddings themselves. The sun-flashes on windscreens and hothouse prefigure the speaker's sudden reaction to a 'something' that 'survived' when he is 'struck', and begins to notice the weddings. Perhaps 'acres of dismantled cars' and 'floatings of industrial froth' correspond to the vulgar farce of these social rituals.

Secondly, the speaker's mood is symmetrically structured. He begins the journey in a state of tension between his lyrical and prosaic responses to the landscape. In the middle of the poem, he first combines and then swings between two opposed responses to the weddings: on the one hand detached, sneering, superior, and on the other hand earnest, sensitive, imaginative. For most of the final three stanzas, the speaker returns to the tension between guarded objectivity, and flights of metaphor, that characterised the start of his journey. These two forces are left in exact and unresolved tension at the end. It is as if the poem is a circle ending where it began. An inversion of dictions illustrates this structural point well. In the first section, the speaker describes 'acres' (a rural word) of 'dismantled cars' (industrial and urban objects); at the end of the poem this antithesis of diction occurs inverted: London's postal districts are compared to 'squares' (an urban word) of 'wheat' (from rural agriculture).

We have approached 'The Whitsun Weddings' by focusing on the speaker, in the same way as we approached the poems studied in Chapter 2. We will return to consider the poem's depiction of society, which is the subject of this chapter, after looking at 'Toads'.

'Toads' (*CP*, 89–90)

'Toads' is a straightforward monologue on a similar theme to 'Poetry of Departures' which we studied in Chapter 1, but this poem's voice is different. The speaker of 'Toads' is driven by the energy of anger directed against 'the toad *work*' and against himself for submitting to it. Prosodists can argue about whether the dominant metre is anapaestic or dactyllic, but it has the characteristic bounce and speed of these metres and is skilfully varied to present an argumentative and convincing tone of voice. So, the regular and irregular alternate in the sixth stanza:

Ah, **were** I cour**age**ous en**ough**
To **shout** *Stuff* your *pension!*

See how the opening line builds up speed in regular anapaests, and how the speaker's impatient fury bursts out of the rhythm. These are words he wishes he could say but knows he never will, and breaking the metre helps us to hear both his fury, and how tightly it is bottled up. Similarly, the opening line ('**Why** should I **let** the toad *work*') sets up the bounce and pace of the poem so that the stressed word '**Squat**' lands with a revolting, wet sound effect and with enormous rhythmic weight at the start of line 2. Again, this perfectly conveys the speaker's anger, hatred and revulsion at the situation in which he allows himself to be trapped.

A poem of quatrains in short lines and anapaests would be in danger of becoming monotonously bouncy, were it not for these natural variations of rhythm. Also working against the pattern of the form are both the occasional use of enjambement that helps to disguise short lines, and the fact that the majority of the rhymes are half-rhyme, so the alternating rhyme scheme is half-muted.

We have already begun to comment on the speaker's character: his is an irascible voice, filled with pent-up anger against his need to work for a living, and against himself for putting up with it. The speaker of 'Toads' is not a simple man, however, and his voice has three other tones into which he modulates from his most noticeable emphatic anger.

First, our speaker is whimsically literary. This side of his character takes over the third stanza. It is announced in the word 'folk' (archaic, rather than the expected 'people'), which leads into the alliterated list 'Lecturers, lispers, / Losels, loblolly-men, louts'. This is a satirical list: two contemporary types join three archaic terms. 'Lecturers' include many of Larkin's friends and colleagues, and his lover Monica Jones. The poem says they do no '*work*'. 'Louts' are just idle, no-good bullies. It is an ironic, and amusing, comment on society that the people who get away without having to '*work*' are all lecturers and louts!

In between these two terms are three archaisms. 'Lispers' are not merely people with a speech impediment. The speaker is referring to people who affect a lisp in order to seem fashionable or to attract women. There are references to lisping courtiers in Shakespeare, but it is possible that this allusion originates from Chaucer's Friar Huberd, who 'lisped for his wantownnesse', a character who lived in luxury as a parasitic hypocrite stealing from the church and society.[2] A 'losel' is a Middle English word for 'a worthless person; a profligate, rake, scoundrel'.[3] 'Loblolly-men' is an early modern word for 'a bumpkin, a rustic, a boor'.[4] Clearly, this speaker has a literary education, and becomes whimsically carried away by thinking up archaic words beginning with the letter 'l'. The poem does not explore why he does this. We may theorise that this enjoying words for their own sake is a way of diverting himself from his frustration and fury; but the poem provides no evidence to back up such a theory: instead, the transition from fury to old-word-play is left as a characteristic silence, in the structure of 'Toads'.

The speaker does this again in the sixth stanza. His furious shout '*Stuff your pension!*' neatly suggests the repetition of 'stuff' in the next line, and this brings on another literary quotation – this time 'the stuff / That dreams are made on' from Prospero in Shakespeare's *The Tempest*. Yet again, the speaker takes refuge in literary history to dampen his fury with the present. It is a form of avoidance: an oblique, allusive way of admitting that he does not have the courage to give up his job. In terms of the tone of voice, what we hear suggests one of those scholarly bores who cannot resist using a quotation, or making allusions to his knowledge, to show off.

A second new tone of voice dominates the fourth and fifth stanzas, which describe gypsies. They 'live up lanes' and warm themselves at braziers. From their position in the poem's clear argument, these would seem to be idealised stereotypes: people who live blessedly free from the need to make a living. However, as he describes them, the speaker increasingly separates his own taste from theirs. He clearly cannot imagine eating a diet of 'windfalls and tinned sardines', and eventually damns their wives as 'unspeakable'. So, while exploring an alternative to his own life, the speaker is actually closing it off. The tone builds up into a horrified reaction against gypsy life.

Finally, the speaker's voice passes through the emotions that launched his monologue, before settling into a calmer tone. There is bitterness in the return to 'Squats' at the start of line 26, and a combination of complaint and dislike as he describes his inner toad: notice the effect of distaste expressed by 'h' alliteration in line 27. Envy and contempt appear in 'blarney', and as at the start of the poem, these feelings are directed against both others and himself for their common vulgar desires: 'The fame and the girl and the money'. The speaker settles in the final stanza, carefully and analytically denying that either toad bears a causal relationship to the other.

The character presented in 'Toads', then, is furious and frustrated. He is caught between hatred of work, and fear. He twists and turns in this dilemma, and reveals several unattractive traits of character: he is a compulsive literary bore, reacts against gipsies with prurient revulsion, finds himself distasteful, envies the successful for whom he feels contempt, and derides all human goals. These twists and turns demonstrate the truth of the final statement: 'it's hard to lose either, / When you have both'. Remembering how the 'toad *work*' 'soils' with 'sickening poison', we can see that the speaker reveals a character soiled and poisoned by hating his own submission to society's demands.

We have looked at the characters who speak 'The Whitsun Weddings' and 'Toads'. We now turn to this chapter's question: what kind of a social and historical commentary do Larkin's poems provide? Thinking about the poems we have already met, four points suggest themselves as we begin putting together an answer to this question.

First, the 'speakers' of several of the poems share certain characteristics. Together, these are beginning to build up a commentary on the effect of modern life on the individual. Many of Larkin's speakers are unable to escape from dilemmas that naggingly persist. Many of their feelings are negative, and the circumstances make them feel helpless, weak. They often despise both themselves and others, and their outlook on life is soured and twisted. They do not trust others, life or themselves: instead, they are suspicious and uncertain. These characters cannot undertake action, as every time something is presented as a truth it is simultaneously undermined and therefore suspect.

Secondly, the poems contain a considerable amount of satire. This has been directed against several targets, from the pretentious double-barrelled 'Warlock-Williams' from 'Vers de Société' to the 'grinning and pomaded' girls of 'The Whitsun Weddings'. Vulgarity, tastelessness and shallowness are ridiculed when they appear either in the lower classes or among the 'chattering classes'. One idea that seems to recur is satire of lives dominated by material possessions: in 'Self's the Man', Arnold earns so that his wife can buy material things – the 'drier / And the electric fire', and their marriage contract, like a labour contract, is seen in terms of 'perks'. In 'Vers de Société', even reading has been reduced to the level of consumerism by a 'bitch' who has only ever read '*Which*'.

Thirdly, and related to the growth of material consumerism, the dominion of money has appeared, particularly in relation to the sale of one's labour and the imprisoning effect of this on the individual's life. In particular, Arnold's work in 'Self's the Man', and that of the speaker in 'Toads', brings them no happiness and is wasted. For Arnold, the only purpose of work is to pay for his wife and children. The speaker in 'Toads' sells six days of his life each week 'Just for paying a few bills!' Implicitly also in 'Poetry of Departures', regular wage-earning appears as a form of slavery and waste; and wage-slaves harbour romantic fantasies of escape, from '*He chucked up everything*' to become 'stubbly with goodness' ('Poetry of Departures'), to the carefree lives of gipsies, pictured in 'Toads'. The poems depict a world where, increasingly, people know the price of everything and the value of nothing.

The fourth recurrent idea is that of change for the worse. The speaker of 'Vers de Société', for example, must be widely read and better educated than the *Which*-reading 'bitch', and in the same poem there is some qualified regret about the passing of a more certain age, when the church provided a sense of community. In 'The Whitsun Weddings', rural beauty is marred by more recent commercial and industrial detritus: canals are polluted by 'floatings of industrial froth', and towns surrounded by 'acres of dismantled cars'. The speaker of 'Dockery and Son' conjures up an idyllic past of mischief, stable authority (the Dean) and 'dazzling' lawns. Only in 'Wild Oats' does social change appear in a positive guise, when the poet refers to newer and more liberal attitudes towards sex.

'Going, Going' (*CP*, 189–90)

By now we are used to the counterpoint of a casual conversational voice working against a strict form. The numerous run-on lines in 'Going, Going' typically undercut a fairly regular line length and metre, and an unchanging ABCABC rhyme scheme of all perfect rhymes. The first and final lines of the poem address us directly, and tell us that the speaker has moved from 'I thought it would last my time' to 'I just think it will happen, soon'. The change from initial to final attitude begins at the end of stanza three: '– But what do I feel now? Doubt?', and continues when he confides that 'For the first time I feel somehow … That before I snuff it'. The speaker is slightly apologetic as he offers his opinion of the state of the country, saying that he feels 'somehow' or 'just' thinks that it is going to the dogs. He also questions the cause of his change of mind: has he adopted such a jaundiced view of things simply because he is middle-aged (ll. 19–20)? In between presenting the speaker's state of mind, the poem gives a gloomy series of comments on the country's decay into an urban wasteland.

In each of the first three stanzas the speaker makes an attempt to shore up his faith that ugliness will not be totally victorious in his lifetime. Each attempt is flawed, however. First, he believes that the country ('fields and farms') will always be there, but the picture is spoiled by calling villagers 'louts', who climb 'Such trees as were not cut down'. Next, he suggests that some old architecture will be preserved; but this picture is also ruined. If no old streets are left, he says, 'We can always escape in the car'. We may ask: Where to? To treeless villages inhabited by 'louts'? Finally, the speaker admits to a vague, mystical faith in nature: that it will survive mankind's attacks upon it. There is less conviction, however, in his elaboration of this idea: 'Chuck filth …' expresses anger and disgust, and is more powerful than the next line. These three stanzas demonstrate failing faith.

The speaker then turns his attention to complaints, which continue almost uninterrupted to the end of the poem. People are seen as crowds of mindless consumers who scream for 'more'; capitalism is caricatured as 'a score of spectacled grins' on the business page, destroying the ecology for profit. These two groups, those who sell themselves for money, and those who exploit others for profit, are summarised as 'a cast of crooks and tarts'. The phrase has an aphoristic, final effect: it is a damning judgement on everybody. Its dual totality is echoed in 'concrete and tyres', and the final stanza's 'greeds / And garbage'.

In between these complaints, in the penultimate stanza, the poem attempts to define what is being lost. The speaker calls this 'England', and mentions 'The shadows, the meadows, the lanes, / The guildhalls, the carved choirs'. The style of these two lines is more lyrical, with the internal rhyme of 'shadows ... meadows', the triad of line 44 slowing into two phrases in line 45, which ends lingeringly on the alliterated spondee 'carved choirs'. The nostalgic interlude is brief, however: by the end of the stanza we are back with harsh 'k' and 't' sounds, angry about 'concrete and tyres'.

How does this poem develop the four points we discussed? First, the speaker belongs to the passive, helpless group we have identified. He has some uncertainty (he feels 'somehow', and is unsure of his reasons for his opinion – perhaps it is just 'age'); and he does not see that action could solve the problem facing him: 'greeds / And garbage' are too voluminous, and cannot now be 'swept up'. Like the others, this speaker is characterised with a hint of irony, suggesting that he may be no more than a grumpy old man. He seems to use 'young' as synonymous with thoughtless, in stanza 4, and wonders whether 'age' has soured his outlook. We also notice his selfishness: he cares about 'my time' and 'before I snuff it', not the environment that is being destroyed, and certainly not future generations: those domineering children 'screaming for more'.

Secondly, 'Going, Going' takes social satire to a more negative level. Where the 'grinning and pomaded' girls, 'loud and fat' mothers, and fathers with 'seamy foreheads' of 'The Whitsun Weddings' have their own emotional visions to set against the speaker's ridicule, there is no such saving grace for this poem's 'screaming kids' or 'spectacled grins'. They are consumers and exploiters, and presented as repellent groups, not human individuals.

'Going, Going' develops the theme of money further. The title is an auctioneer's phrase, suggesting that 'England' is being sold off; and the fourth and fifth stanzas assert that profit and materialism, later summarised as 'crooks and tarts' and 'greeds / And garbage', are to blame. Clearly, Larkin identifies capitalism as the arch-enemy of nature, history and beauty. On one side are exploiters who only care for money ('Five per cent profit'), and do not care about the environment; on the other side are consumers who only care for material goods ('more ... more ... more ... more ... more ...'), and do not notice the environment. The final stanza adds a further comment to this analysis: the exploiters 'invent / Excuses' for destroying the environment, saying that their work fulfils 'needs'. So, capitalists are hypocrites who disguise their profit-motive under the pretence of satisfying demand. We may be tempted to see this as a socialist analysis of the economy, but the emotional emphasis does not bear this out. First because of the contempt and anger the speaker expresses equally towards the exploiters and the lower classes (who are effectively called 'a cast of crooks and tarts' with the added secondary meaning of 'garbage'); and secondly, because the poem is framed by the speaker's selfishness in caring about 'my time' and 'before I snuff it'.

The sense of change for the worse is strong in this poem. Its vitriol is directed against a stupid, degraded population who are destroying everything the speaker values; and the idealised past appears in those two nostalgic, lyrical lines in the penultimate stanza, glorifying rural beauty, old architecture and traditional culture in 'books' and 'galleries'. In this poem, then, the sense of deterioration includes both of the strands we have encountered before: nature being destroyed by industry and commerce, and beauty and culture being destroyed by tasteless consumerism.

'Going, Going' adds to our appreciation of social and economic themes in Larkin's poetry. The other poems we have studied are ironic, but in the case of 'Going, Going' we may sense too slight a division between Larkin himself, and his speaker; and we may miss the human sympathy with which he treats the wedding-parties in 'The Whitsun Weddings', for example, or even Arnold in 'Self's the Man'. There seems to be no sense that the 'young' people with their 'screaming kids' in the M1 café have their own lives to lead and their own problems to face. Larkin's ability to see through – and undermine – his speaker, is one of his finest and most characteristic qualities. He is aware, for example, of the contradiction between the speaker's 'We can always escape in the car', and his ridicule of those who clamour for 'more parking allowed'. But we may decide that we miss, in this poem, the ambivalence we find so highly developed in others.

'The Building' (*CP*, 191–3)

'The Building' describes a hospital. On first reading, we realise that there is no continuous narrative like those in, for example, 'Vers de Société' or 'Dockery and Son'; although there are elements of story, as patients are called from a waiting-room and taken to their appointments, or visiting-hour comes. With the absence of anecdotal form, this poem also does not draw attention to the speaker's character: rather, it is a poem in which the poet addresses us directly. We also realise straight away that this is not conversation. In place of chatty openings like 'Sometimes you hear …', 'About twenty years ago' or 'That Whitsun, I was late …', the opening line of 'The Building' is consciously alliterated, the adjective 'handsomest' perhaps chosen to accentuate the breathiness of the line. Then, within the first stanza we are bombarded with metaphors and similes, and conscious linguistic combinations. We read of the 'lucent comb', 'close-ribbed streets … Like a great sigh', and meet a rhetorical imprecation 'but see', and the zeugma in which both 'creepers' and 'a frightening smell' hang.

Larkin's tone does vary considerably during the poem, however. In the same first stanza, the two matter-of-fact phrases about porters and not-taxis stand out. It is as if the poem stops to make these remarks, then starts up again for the zeugma and mannered inversion of the final one and a half lines. In the remainder of the poem, Larkin includes a great deal of incidental detail such as paperbacks, cups of tea, red brick, lagged pipes and so forth, but then slips easily into ambitious metaphor and allusive symbolism. See, for example, how the naturalistic detail of 'girls with hair-dos' who 'fetch / Their separates from the cleaners' introduces the invocation 'O world' and the metaphor that loves and chances are 'beyond the stretch / Of any hand from here!'

'The Building' consists of nine seven-line stanzas of iambic pentameter, and a single extra line at the end. The opening stanza has a tight rhyme scheme (ABABCBB), but for the rest of the poem there is no consistency: there are rhymes within stanzas (for example ll. 10 and 12), and rhymes between stanzas (for example, ll. 13 and 16, or ll. 19 and 22); and some lines do not rhyme at all. Similarly, enjambement is frequent, and every stanza except the first runs on into the following stanza.

Larkin allows himself a great deal of flexibility, then, and this enables him to employ a wide variety of modes and tones, and to mix pace and rhythms with rapid changes between them. See, for example, how repetition and a near-regular metre help the poem to accelerate as patients imagine the labyrinthine complexity of the hospital:

> For past these doors are rooms, and rooms past those,
> And more rooms yet, each one further off
>
> And harder to return from; and who knows
> Which he will see, and when?

Then, suddenly, metre is inverted, the line has an added syllable, and the poem brakes as we come down to earth: '**For** the **mo**ment, **wait**'.

The patients are described with a novelist's eye for details, such as torn magazines and 'half-filled shopping bags'. The quiet of the waiting-room is conveyed by mentioning coughs, and the noise of cups and saucers. Larkin also assumes the novelist's ability to know how people are feeling, as they look at each other 'guessing', and he goes as far as internal monologue when patients tell themselves to be patient and rein in their anxious thoughts: 'For the moment, wait, / Look down at the yard'. Here, unlike in 'Going, Going' or 'The Whitsun Weddings', ordinary people are described with sympathy, rather than contempt or disgust.

Fittingly, it is 'The Building' in contrast to 'Outside', that attracts figurative and symbolic treatment. Several images are applied at different points of the poem, and it is useful to begin analysing imagery by listing them, before we begin to look at connotations, links between images, or to interpret them as symbols.

Images for the building:
1 'The lucent comb': the hospital is compared to a honeycomb.
2 The waiting-room 'Like an airport lounge'.
3 The waiting-room 'like a local bus'.
4 'Here to confess' suggests a comparison with a church.
5 '[U]nseen congregations [of in-patients]' suggests comparison with a church.

6 '[T]he only coin / This place accepts' compares the hospital to a shop which accepts payment in the form of human life.

7 'This clean-sliced cliff'.

8 'Outbuild cathedrals' compares the hospital and cathedrals.

Images for the world 'Outside':

1 '[C]lose-ribbed streets' suggests earth as a body.

2 The streets are 'Like a great sigh out of the last century', which develops the personification of streets and the land on which they are built.

3 'A touching dream to which we all are lulled / But wake from separately'.

4 Elaborate ideas ('conceits') and ignorance make a material that 'congeals' (becomes more solid as it cools) and carries 'life'.

Having listed the images, we now want to notice anything significant about the list: can we find groups of images of similar types? Or, are there any trends: do images develop during the poem? We do this by making notes, summarising what we can see in the lists. Images for the hospital are of two kinds: it is compared to a place where you start or go on a journey; and to a religious building (see images 2, 3, 4, 5 and 8 in the list). The only images not part of one of these groups are those of a honeycomb, of a shop accepting human lives as payment and of a cliff. Images for the world outside begin with personification (see images 1 and 2 in the list), but the eventual extended simile 'A touching dream ... etc.' (ll. 45–50) becomes increasingly abstract as it is elaborated mentioning 'conceits' and 'ignorance' (images 3 and 4 in the list). Both the hospital and the world begin with concrete figures (a honeycomb, and 'close-ribbed' respectively) and end with more abstract figures (religion, in the form of 'cathedrals', and a sigh and then a dream, respectively).

The connection between imagery and the subject of the poem is clear. Starting a journey and travelling is an apt metaphor for the patients' journeys away from their day-to-day lives into illness, and towards death, as they enter the hospital. The comparison between the hospital and a religious building is also central to Larkin's idea, which is explained in the last stanza: both are 'a struggle to transcend / The thought of dying'. The unconnected image of the hospital as 'This clean-sliced cliff' carries connotations of both surgery and death in 'sliced'. A cliff is the end of land, the familiar, life; and the beginning of the apparently infinite, mysterious sea. Cliffs have often been used as figures for death.[5] With regard to images for the world outside, it is appropriate that we move from concrete surroundings, and as we enter the hospital, our day-to-day lives recede until they seem like a dream.

Two separate images for the hospital remain. The first, the 'lucent comb', provides a vivid picture of many windows, and perhaps of rows of lighted rooms on the tall building glowing at night; and as a honeycomb has innumerable little chambers, all geometrically arranged, the 'comb' image begins to convey the labyrinth idea that is developed later in lines 34–7 ('For past these doors are rooms ...'). The other image, of a shop taking life as currency, strengthens our impression that the hospital is impersonal and indifferent. It is a cruel and bitter idea, that our lives are rung up on the hospital's till as profit.

In this poem, then, Larkin draws together ideas we have met before. The idea that life is a misleading dream, that all our day-to-day aims and the material objects with which we fill our minds are ultimately irrelevant, has surfaced in 'Next, Please' as the illusory 'sparkling armada of promises'; and in 'Vers de Société' where the party will distract the speaker from thinking about 'other things'. In 'The Building', life is said to include 'your loves, your chances' and then cynically summarised as 'conceits / And self-protecting ignorance' and as a dream 'collapsing' in the face of illness and death. The idea that the modern world seeks something to replace the security and comfort that was once found in religious rituals has appeared in 'Vers de Société', where the party is seen as replacing Sunday service; briefly in the 'known bell' of 'Dockery and Son'; in the 'happy funeral' and 'religious wounding' marriage rites of 'The Whitsun Weddings', and is a major theme of 'Church Going' which will be discussed in the next chapter. In 'The Building', these two ideas are integrated: in the modern world, we deceive ourselves compulsively, and we desperately erect medicine in the form of a symbolic monolithic hospital, in a hopeless attempt to 'contravene / The coming dark'. The ritual aspects of our desperation are a hopeless attempt to replace religion. Larkin's poem concludes that all our efforts are futile.

The self-deceptions of life collapse, and the poem repeatedly presents its people as helpless. They sit 'tamely' and are 'resigned' and 'caught'. They have no control, having reached 'the end of choice' and being sent to 'their appointed levels', 'not knowing' whether they will return home or be admitted, but 'All know they are going to die ... somewhere like this'. The finality of entering the hospital also repeatedly drums through the poem. 'Homes and names' are 'in abeyance'; as patients are taken further in, the deeper rooms are 'harder to return from', and the world is 'beyond the stretch of any hand from here'. We have found this moment of shock, when we confront illness and death, represented in the 'huge and birdless silence' of 'Next, Please'; in the moon like an 'air-sharpened blade' in 'Vers de Société'; and more fully expounded in people who 'sense the solving emptiness / That lies just under all we do' in 'Ambulances'. In this moment, life and all its concerns become futile, meaningless.

In 'The Building', Larkin elaborates the ritualistic elements he sees in society, adding details to the analogy between religion, and contemporary attempts to 'contravene' death. In particular, he compares being ill to being sinful: an illness is an 'error' that we must 'confess'. The faith that a hospital can 'correct' us and cleanse us of some fault is implicit in this analogy. Other connotations include a sense of shame, of being dirty or soiled, and isolation, privacy, secrecy. This idea also appears in 'Ambulances', where ambulances are described as 'closed like confessionals'. The metaphor of 'congregations' of in-patients adds a further but ambiguous suggestion: a congregation worships. It is equally possible that the in-patients are worshipping the hospital and medical science itself; or that they worship death. The latter is perhaps more likely, as the final analogy with religion is between the 'propitiatory flowers' brought by visitors to their hospitalised relatives, and the sacrifices offered at a shrine or altar, to gain a deity's favour.

'Propitiatory' gifts to a deity also broadens the analogy, suggesting pagan religions as well as Christianity. So, in the final line, Larkin implies that people's behaviour at the hospital is something human beings have done ritually, instinctively, from time immemorial. He sees this behaviour as a mass ritual, with 'crowds' participating each evening. His verdict, however, remains the same: these gifts are 'wasteful, weak'. Death will not show favour, and relent, in response to these offerings.

'The Building' is a dense and complex poem, and contains strands of Larkin's themes that we can recognise but do not have the space to explore here. For example, the middle-aged who are at 'the end of choice' reminds us of life that 'hardens into all we've got' from 'Dockery and Son', or the empty past and a future 'so final. And so near' from 'The View' (*CP*, 195): 'The Building' has more to tell us about ageing. For now, we can briefly notice how 'The Building' completes its analogy between medicine and religion. Although the poem focuses on rituals associated with death, it also paints a quick picture of modern society as a world from which religion has gone. As patients look out from the hospital, it is significant that the church they see is 'locked', and ignored by the playing children and 'girls with hair-dos'. This is an aspect of the theme that we will return to in our discussion of 'Church Going' in the next chapter.

Concluding Discussion

What sort of a commentary on society do Larkin's poems offer? So far, the four poems we have studied have provided us with some initial insights, but this discussion will draw upon wider reference to develop a fuller view. The four areas we have identified so far are the effect on the individual of living in the modern world; satire of social types, attitudes and behaviours; the dominion of money and material goods; and a sense of change for the worse. We can begin by looking at each of these areas with wider reference.

The Effect on the Individual of Living in the Modern World

We have noted characteristics many of Larkin's speakers have in common. Typically, the voices we hear in his poems are uncertain of the truth and unconfident of their opinions. They suspect that the world is deceptive and that they may be deceiving themselves. Consequently, decision and action is impossible for these characters: they cannot resolve the dilemmas facing them, they cannot choose between different courses of action, and they do not believe that any action could be effective against whatever causes their misery or anxiety.

These speakers therefore often take the path of least resistance. So, it is not so much a decision as an acceptance that the decision does not matter, when the speaker of 'Self's the Man' recognises that both Arnold and himself – despite their different life choices – are likely to go mad; or when the speaker of 'Vers de Société' writes either accepting or declining Warlock-Williams's invitation. In 'Mr Bleaney' (*CP*, 102–3), having described the miserable outlook and listed the disadvantages of the room ('no hook / Behind the door, no room for books or bags'), the speaker suddenly says 'I'll take it'. The reasons why choice, decision and action are beyond Larkin's characters will be further investigated and discussed in the next chapter. So far, we have found two possible causes for their chronic passivity. First, in 'Dockery and Son', comes the suggestion that we are ruled by 'innate assumptions' that will decide our lives whatever we do: our lives are predetermined from birth and we cannot escape from our natures, which will 'harden into all we've got'. Secondly, the forces ranged against our fulfilment are simply too great to oppose. There is too much 'garbage' to sweep up, therefore no point in attempting anything.

'As Bad as a Mile' (*CP*, 125) gives a succinct version of the first of these points, where the speaker imagines his failure 'spreading back up the arm / Earlier and earlier', until he believes that it was already there and inevitable even before anything started, when there was only 'The apple unbitten in the palm'. The poem hints that this may be a distorted view, however: missing the wastebasket with an apple core is just bad luck, perhaps; but this speaker is increasingly convinced that his failures are fated. So Larkin gives expression to a negative determinism, but at the same time suggests that it may be an embittered distortion of reality.

The second idea, that there are overwhelming forces ranged against us, affects Larkin's speakers in several of the poems. For example, in 'Toads', the speaker tells us that 'it's hard' to lose either work, or your need for security, 'when you have both'; while in 'The Building' the sheer size and cost of the hospital intimidates each patient, convincing them that they are guilty of 'error':

> It must be error of a serious sort,
> For see how many floors it needs, how tall
> It's grown by now, and how much money goes
> In trying to correct it.

As individuals, Larkin's speakers cannot challenge what the rest of society has created. Several poems convey a feeling of helplessness because adverse circumstances are a *fait accompli*. The speaker realises what is happening only when it has happened, and even then there is nobody to blame. 'Going, Going' tells us that 'Most things are never meant. / This won't be, most likely', but England will be destroyed all the same. 'Homage to a Government' (*CP*, 171) regrets the loss of the British empire, commenting:

> It's hard to say who wanted it to happen,
> But now it's been decided nobody minds.

Fatalism, uncertainty and overwhelming hostile circumstances seem to catch Larkin's speakers and grip them so firmly that they are unable to break free or even move out of the way. In the next chapter, we will consider some of the wider philosophical and cultural ramifications of such a world-view. For the present, we should ask how far material conditions conspire to promote this negativity.

Satire of Social Types, Attitudes and Behaviours

We have encountered satire of unfashionable provincials in 'The Whitsun Weddings' and 'Going, Going'; and of middle-class socialites in 'Vers de Société'; while the ordinary people in 'The Building' waiting-room are precisely observed. Thinking about Larkin's presentation of different social types, three points arise: the brevity with which he hits a satirical target, the wide range of both the targets he satirises, and the attitudes his speakers adopt.

The first of these qualities is found in almost all the poems. See, for example, in 'The Building' how the word 'hair-dos' (not 'coiffures' or 'hairstyles') defines the girls' working-class culture as they 'fetch ... separates' (not 'collect ... clothes') from the cleaners. The satirical implication is that their 'hair-dos' are the most important thing about these girls, in their own vacuous minds as well as in the poet's eyes. This occurs suddenly, in a poem which does not otherwise subject its population to ridicule. Similarly, in 'Toads', gypsy women are described. The simile 'skinny as whippets' is straightforward: it gives a visual image, and implies speed of movement. Notice, however, the word 'unspeakable'. This simultaneously defines both the gipsy wives' manners and coarse behaviour, and the speaker's horror of them. In Larkin's poems, sudden effects achieved with only one or two words abound. Other examples are 'spectacled grins' from 'Going, Going', the 'crowd of craps' from 'Vers de Société', and numerous others elsewhere such as the outrageous 'shoptalking shit who leads me off / To supper and his bearded wife', or the wittily combined 'weed from Plant Psychology', from 'The Dance' (*CP*, 154–8).

Larkin's satirical targets are widely varied. We have noticed two social types (provincial working class, and pretentious middle class) to which he frequently returns; but there are many other satirical portraits, and thumbnail sketches. We will identify three of the more prominent.

Many of the personae Larkin adopts take the form of lonely men in temporary settings. These speakers contribute to the composite self the poems gradually build and project, 'the poet', and as such, we will revisit them when we discuss how Larkin depicts the poet's role in Chapter 5. However, there are also other characters who inhabit hotels, rooming-houses or nursing-homes. 'Friday Night at the Royal Station Hotel' (*CP*, 163) exemplifies the sense that there are innumerable, faceless travelling people in society and explores the accommodation provided for this army of salesmen; 'Livings I' (*CP*, 186) adopts the voice of a representative in farm supplies; and 'Livings III' (*CP*, 188) carries this strand of investigation into an exercise in absurdity, in the voice of an Oxford don.

'Friday Night at the Royal Station Hotel' proposes a gentle series of paradoxes. The poem's motif is declared in the opening three words: 'Light spreads darkly'. Paradox then suggests abundance and vacuum as crowded 'Clusters of lights' shine on 'empty' chairs; turns to community and isolation as the chairs 'face each other' yet are 'coloured differently'; and reaches its apogee in the dining-room's 'larger loneliness', an almost-oxymoron that conveys the grandiose size of the hotel-shell within which transient people exist, an effect echoed by the counterpoint of an empty booming sound in 'gone' and 'room' (ll. 8 and 9), in contrast to the lush 'full ashtrays' the salesmen have left behind. This poem is rich in surprising, disturbing combinations: see, for example, the 'shoeless corridors' or the 'loneliness of knives and glass'. In the final line, 'waves' are envisaged behind 'villages', perhaps hinting at an analogy between, on the one hand, the immensity of nature ('waves') in contrast to tiny human settlements ('villages'); and on the other hand, the vast, grandiose hotel in contrast to its futile and isolated transient population. In addition, the poem's 'full ashtrays', unused 'knives and glass' and 'unsold evening paper' paint a picture of waste and leftovers.

'Livings I' is a less melancholy poem. The speaker adopts some of the cant language of the hotel-dweller: 'the boots' carries his bag, and he sleeps in 'a single'. This vein of mimicry continues into the hotel-bar gossip of the middle stanza. We hear the conversation as a kind of referential shorthand, lacking articles and linking constructions: it is 'Whisky' (not 'a whisky'), and 'price of stock', while discussion uses euphemistic phrases ('taking the knock') or the understated boast ('makes ends meet'). There is a staccato rhythm of incomplete syntax and frequent full-stops that began with the small ads in the local paper: 'For sale. Police court. Motor spares.'

The travelling salesman's reflections, in the final four lines, are limited. All he can conceive is to 'wonder why' he lives in this way, and to say 'it's time for change' without any suggestion that he can envisage a different life. The central effect of this poem is of a meagre existence. Notice how the rep's case is 'lean' and he takes a 'single'; how the place names are coyly given with blanks ('the —*shire Times*' for example) creating half-words, just as later we have half-sentences in the Smoke Room conversation, before 'Later, the square is empty'. Mixed in with this effect of thinness is parody of a provincial Englishness like that in an Agatha Christie novel. The coy blanks in place names set the scene somewhere in the home counties, but it does not matter where; and the list of 'Clough, / Margetts, the Captain, Dr Watterson' also brings such stereotypes to mind. The poem's one metaphor contextualises the meanness of the speaker's life, and his utter lack of individuality, by providing a dazzling contrast to his dulness: 'a big sky / Drains down the estuary like the bed / Of a gold river'. As we may expect from Larkin in this almost-sympathetic, almost-contemptuous mood, the bright image of a 'gold river' is ambivalent: does it suggest a wonderful elsewhere, a free and glorious life the salesmen may embrace at the end? Or is it just his business delusion, a greedy vision of wealth? The final line has an ironic effect almost as marked as sarcasm, dating the salesman's mitherings on the eve of the great stock-market crash of 'nineteen twenty-nine'. The poet seems to laugh: 'Ha ha! The poor blighter wants change, does he? He'll get more than he bargains for'.

'Livings III' exhibits a similar vein of paradox between leanness and plenty to that we found in 'Friday Night at the Royal Station Hotel'. The butler's name 'Starveling' contrasts with the abundant 'piles the logs' as candle flames both 'grow thin, then broaden'. The final stanza expands on this idea: six lines emphasise emptiness, cold and silence, in contrast to the fullness of the final two:

> Above, Chaldean constellations
> Sparkle over crowded roofs.

However, the greatest satirical fun in this poem is the level of absurdity to which Larkin takes the dons' conversation. Their talk has no consistency and no practical point, and we are tossed from academic to trivial and back again in a ridiculous series of irrelevancies chained together by insistent alliteration:

> On rheumy fevers, resurrection,
> Regicide and rabbit pie.

These three poems share certain features. In particular, they all suggest personal and spiritual poverty, as an emptiness within grand or sumptuous surroundings; they mimic a paucity or absurdity of dialogue;

and they all propose – with varying degrees of confidence – a potential magnificence in nature, which gleams unnoticed outside the shells of hotel or college, as '*waves … behind villages*', a 'gold river' and 'Chaldean constellations'. The implication is that the sales reps and dons who inhabit such half-worlds are caught within them. They, like their surroundings, become emptied and meaningless; and they fail to notice life's potential. We will return to the question of how far Larkin's poetic 'persona' shares their experience, in Chapter 5.

Advertising is another recurrent target of Larkin's satire. 'Sunny Prestatyn' (*CP*, 149) describes one obscenely defaced advertising hoarding, while 'Essential Beauty' (*CP*, 144–5) explores the relationship between advertising's impossible dreams of life and the tawdry reality of experience.

The advertisement in 'Sunny Prestatyn' shows a girl who was 'too good for this life'. However, even before she is defaced, the poster's cynical sexual appeal is emphasised. She kneels in 'tautened white satin' and her arms are spread 'breast-lifting'. The advertiser's intention is clearly defined: it is from her 'thighs' and 'spread breast-lifting arms' that sexuality expands over the beach, palms and hotel of Prestatyn. The second and third stanzas report how the poster is defaced. The gross obscenity of the vandals' work is more honest than the original poster's innuendo, but the poem's irony lies in the fact that both are unmistakably sexual. This suggests a number of comments on the relationship between advertising and its public, which are the fruits of Larkin's satire. So, for example, we can comment that the advertisement was a success: it aroused exactly the response at which it aimed. Or, that advertising aims to titillate our coarsest instincts, and people respond at a coarse level. Or, that the original image was impossibly idealised and sanitised: the advertisement peddles a dream, not coarse reality. Keeping these many implied comments in mind, we can reread the poem and recognise that many of the phrases are dense with irony. How many possible ironic meanings, for example, lurk in the simple statement 'She was too good for this life'?

'Essential Beauty' deals with advertising hoardings in general rather than the one poster of 'Sunny Prestatyn'. Various examples are listed, such as 'giant loaves' and 'motor-oil and cuts of salmon', all subsumed under the category 'sharply-pictured groves / Of how life should be'. The contrast between advertised ideal and seamy reality is explained: these images 'Reflect none of the rained-on streets and squares / They dominate'. However, a more serious point dominates the final phase of the poem, which focuses on all of us: people, consumers. First, Larkin reminds us of a fundamental tenet we have met several times in his poetry: that it is human nature to fill our minds with impossible dreams, in order to ignore or suppress thoughts of death. From the 'sparkling armada of promises' in 'Next, Please' to the 'touching dream to which we all are lulled' in 'The Building', Larkin has insisted on the human need to dream. So, in this poem, he describes us looking at the dream-world of advertising with 'live imperfect eyes / That stare beyond this world'. The next section, however, points out that the advertisers lie to us and abuse our trust. Alcohol is presented as 'white-clothed ones from tennis-clubs' when the reality is 'the boy puking his heart out in the Gents'; and finally, 'dying smokers' are beguiled by an alluring female image 'walking towards them'. The ironic sting is in the final line, when the smokers actually die still deluded by erotic dreams: 'smiling, recognising, and going dark'. The whole expresses anger at a mendacious industry that peddles lethal drugs with false idealised images; but ironically, Larkin also suggests a certain twisted kindness in the dream. At the end, the smokers die with their dream standing 'newly clear', perhaps happier than they would be facing the truth. The title reinforces this idea: even such false 'beauty' as we find in the dream-world of advertising, is 'Essential' as a diversion from an imperfect reality. One additional element from this poem is worth noting. The girl in the cigarette advertisement walks 'As if on water': so, advertising is yet another unsatisfactory attempt to compensate for the loss of religion.

We have referred to the composite persona of a poetic 'speaker' that emerges from the different characterisations in Larkin's poetry. However, this 'persona' is a shifting, unstable entity. In particular, the personality has moods and therefore takes radically different attitudes towards other people.

We have met this variation in mood most strikingly between 'The Whitsun Weddings' and 'Going, Going'. In 'The Whitsun Weddings', the characters are stereotypes, and their outward accoutrements appear ridiculous: Larkin notices how unnaturally the fathers wear their formal dress, for example, with 'seamy foreheads' showing their discomfort at the 'broad belts under their suits'; and the mothers are summarily dismissed as 'loud and fat'. On the other hand, the speaker of this poem is not hostile. He is ready to imagine the mothers' complex experience as at 'a happy funeral', and the fathers aware of a contradiction, feeling 'success so huge and wholly farcical'. The train then becomes 'loaded with the sum of all they saw'. In 'Going, Going', the speaker is in a different mood: he has no patience with the people in the poem. The crowd in the M1 café is simply, and damningly, 'young'; and their 'screaming kids' are just that – an unsatisfied, imbecile demand. Other poems display further varieties of the speaker's mood. There are almost as many as there are poems, but one example will suffice. In 'Vers de Société', the speaker is filled with anger and disgust at the 'crowd of craps' and the drivelling 'bitch' at the party; and Warlock-Williams's name is a contemptuous satiric invention. From this evidence the poem might seem a satire without sympathy. On the other hand, the speaker includes himself, the reader and all other people in the 'us' and 'we' who continue to attend boring social 'routines' for a shadowy reason, attempting to compensate for the absence of religion in the modern world. This is not the imaginative insight the speaker of 'The Whitsun Weddings' displays, and it is coupled with caricature as cruel and a tone more abusive than in 'Going, Going'. Nonetheless, this speaker evinces an interest in understanding what lies behind human behaviour that distinguishes his mood from that of 'Going, Going'.

The Dominion of Money and Material Goods

Larkin's poems portray a world in which virtually anything can occur for financial reasons. In 'Toads', the speaker sells himself for six days a week 'Just for paying a few bills', the speaker of 'Poetry of Departures' remains 'sober and industrious', Arnold slaves for material possessions, while in 'Going, Going' the 'spectacled grins' on the business pages justify their greed with 'excuses that make them all needs'. Larkin portrays the mass of consumers less sympathetically.

'The Large Cool Store' (*CP*, 135) describes the artificial appeal of the lingerie department; in 'Going, Going' the children scream for 'more' of everything and their weak parents, by implication, succumb to these infantile demands; and 'Sunny Prestatyn' demonstrates just how coarse commerce and consumption are: both the offers and the responses in modern economic life are on a sordid level. These are several examples, and there are many others, of the dominion of materialism.

The insight underlying all the various references to money in the poems is that modern commerce attacks values for which Larkin's speakers feel affection. We have noted the despoiling of the country-side, a complaint in both 'The Whitsun Weddings' and 'Going, Going'. Similarly, the pressure of money distorts people's lives, chain-ing the speaker of 'Toads', and Arnold from 'Self's the Man', to a working round from which they cannot escape. Many of the refer-ences to this fact are subtle, such as the feed salesman's 'gold river' of 'Livings I'; but whether more gently expressed, thundered in tones of outrage or mentioned with contempt, wherever money appears in Larkin's poems, it acts as an attack on nature and individuality, and it is a lie that breeds vulgarity and stupidity.

One further characteristic of commerce and money in these poems will lead us on to the question of change for the worse. In several of the poems, Larkin suggests that modern society is in a desperate state, frantically attempting to fill the vacuum left by discarded values, and particularly by religious belief. He sees that commerce profits from these needs, and offers to fulfil the dreams people need to live by. For example, in 'Essential Beauty' advertisers ensnare their public by pan-dering to dreams of 'live imperfect eyes / That stare beyond this world', and their promise is of one walking 'as if on water'. In 'The Large Cool Store', lingerie manufacturers pander to 'our young unreal wishes' with products that are artificial, but have the dreamlike appeal of an unnatural, other-worldly perfection: 'synthetic, new, / And natureless in ecstasies'. The people who buy these dreams seek an escape from this world, where 'nothing's made / As new or washed quite clean'. They are buying dreams of perfection, and Larkin likens this to believing in miracles. Clearly, this theme is also present in 'The Whitsun Weddings', where vulgar taste in fashion is part of the 'pure crust, pure foam' modern consumerism has added to an ancient ritual, a 'religious wounding'.

'The Building' presents another comment on financial power. In this poem, society is seen as desperately throwing money into medicine, attempting to erect an institution so huge and complex that it may 'outbuild cathedrals' and help to 'contravene / The coming dark'. Indirectly, the poem depicts money as a sort of pagan divinity: people feel awed and guilty when they see 'how much money' is poured into this vast effort.

Larkin is clear that human beings need to dream, and do so compulsively, in order to suppress the intolerable fact of death. Money, commerce, consumerism are shown playing a large part in modern society's hopeless and tacky dreams. The economic system has a coarsening and tyrannical effect as it profits from human weakness, our desperation to clutch at any diversion from 'the solving emptiness / That lies just under all we do'.[6] This need to preserve a dream of 'armadas of promises', and to participate in rituals such as social occasions, dancing, weddings or offering 'propitiatory flowers', has always existed. The dominion of money in the modern world, however, has brought these activities down to a coarse, degraded level: the economic system is inseparably involved in Larkin's perception of change for the worse.

Change for the Worse

Examples of deterioration in taste and to the environment litter Larkin's poems. Probably the most comprehensive statements of England's decline come in 'Going, Going' and 'Homage to a Government', where the speakers envisage the total victory of commerce with England becoming 'first slum of Europe', and decry the Wilson government's 1969 decision to withdraw all troops from East of Suez, as a betrayal of imperial responsibilities. Many critics have found these to be Larkin's least acceptable forays into public affairs;[7] but it is still important to recognise them as consistent with a number of more subtle perceptions about time and change we find among the poems. We may also accept them as no more than the more extreme characterisations, or 'voices', by means of which Larkin dramatises a personality. These are, perhaps, the composite speaker in his bitterest and most angry mood.

More seriously, we have noted how the poems chart a decline in several aspects of twentieth-century life. There has been a decline in education and culture, so that the speaker of 'Vers de Société' has to endure the 'drivel of some bitch / Who's read nothing but *Which*'. Scholarship has become a business, forcing Jake Balokowsky to study a poet he hates in order to get 'tenure'.[8] The countryside has been spoiled, for there are 'acres of dismantled cars' around every town, and 'that will be England gone' until we are left with only 'concrete and tyres'. Finally, there has been a decline in public taste and behaviour. In 'The Large Cool Store', people buy uniform, mass-produced garments for work, and even their erotic dreams are cheapened to 'machine-embroidered' lingerie, 'Bri-Nylon, Baby-Dolls and Shorties'; and in 'Going, Going', the parents and their screaming children are equally infantile and demanding. We already noted that 'Wild Oats' and 'Annus Mirabilis' suggest change for the better: they highlight more liberal sexual mores in society, and express envy for those growing up in a less restrictive society. However, both of these are comic poems, ironically undermining the very changes they chart. 'High Windows' returns to this theme, balancing the speaker's jealousy of the young with a previous generation's jealousy of him, because he grew up free from the bonds of religion.

The crucial question remains: how far should we read the poems as dramatic characterisation, each one a monologue from a slightly different speaker, although speakers with much in common? Do the poems build a series of related responses to postwar England, responses that vary in mood and focus; some of them broad satires on their speaker's own inadequacies, resentments and repressed desires, while others lash out at vulgarity or ugliness? Is Larkin laughing at his nostalgic personae and their myth of a pastoral idyll that was England in the 'good old days':

> The shadows, the meadows, the lanes,
> The guildhalls, the carved choirs.

Or is Larkin deluded, and therefore limited, because he believes in this myth?

We can argue that Larkin mocks the pastoral myth of Old England, gently overdoing the lyricism of its expression; and that his poetry, taken together, represents a series of largely comic dramatisations. The humour is often subtle, and is wry enough to leave a bitter – even sometimes a despairing – taste. But the central effort is to adopt various personalities, thus exploring individuals' responses to the postwar period. Some of these personalities are grumpy and vituperative old men.

This view is supported by three observations. First, there are the subtle lyrical parodies, and undercutting self-doubts, found in Larkin's voices. Secondly, we have noticed that there is no consistency in his attitude towards nostalgic memories. For example, in 'I Remember, I Remember' (*CP*, 81–2), the speaker derides Lawrentian and Dylan Thomas-ish myths of childhood, mentioning the garden 'where I did not invent / Blinding theologies of flowers and fruits' and 'the bracken where I never trembling sat' for a first sexual experience. Even in 'To the Sea' (*CP*, 173–4), which celebrates childhood holidays, the speaker is objective enough to recognise 'the cheap cigars, / The chocolate-papers, tea-leaves, and, between / The rocks, the rusting soup-tins'. Such evidence suggests that there was no blindness in Larkin's portrayal of the past, and that his hints at a mythical 'old England' are parodic. The third reason for taking this view lies in the more serious and consistent interest the poems display. Many of Larkin's poems explore human behaviours that are not limited to one period, and in particular the rituals we engage in as social animals.

These rituals are age-old. From time immemorial, mankind has invested in rituals which give meaning to the main events of a human life. Larkin's poems refer to this subject matter in guarded tones: it is the 'marriage, and birth, / And death, and thoughts of these' men-tioned in 'Church Going' and ascribed to a 'hunger ... to be more serious' people will feel 'forever'.

'The Whitsun Weddings' is clearly a poem upon such a theme: unit-ing a couple is a social event, and a rite in the sense that it touches on life and death (remember that the mothers feel as at a 'happy funeral'), prim-itive male instincts to procreate (notice the fathers' irrational feelings of 'success') and sacrifice ('a religious wounding'). We have repeatedly found that Larkin's descriptions of his contemporaries refer back to a continuity in human behaviour. So, the summer holiday in 'To the Sea' will continue to occur as 'half an annual pleasure, half a rite', and the poem stretches in time, referring to early childhood and just before death. In 'The Building', visitors lay sacrificial offerings of 'propitiatory' flowers on the altar of death, as people have always tried to mollify the violent forces of nature; in 'Essential Beauty', advertising panders to a much older human need to dream; and in 'Vers de Société' the social occasion is perhaps a substitute for the community of a place of worship.

Larkin makes hesitant, undercut, but recurrent affirmative suggestions about these human rituals. The 'crowd of craps' attending Warlock-Williams's party are 'playing at goodness', and the speaker wonders whether there is some positive value in such rituals 'because, however crudely, / It shows us what should be'. At the end of 'The Whitsun Weddings', however ambiguously, the imagery connotes fertility in London as 'squares of wheat', and the message of the weddings, that falls as an arrow-shower, 'somewhere becoming rain'. Most of all, Larkin's speaker seems uncharacteristically humble as he watches parents 'clumsily undressed', teaching children by 'a sort of / Clowning' and helping the old, in 'To the Sea'. He celebrates the positive power of long-continued rites, saying that 'It may be that through habit these do best', even though his own isolation implies that he will never be able to join in.

We have commented that many modern activities are portrayed, in the poems, as desperate substitutes for religion; as fulfilling the same function as faith and observances used to fulfil. Larkin's interest in rituals of behaviour underlies these insights about his social context. Religion, and both older and newer rituals, all speak of the same effort: the struggle to make life tolerable and to maintain an affirmative illusion, to contravene 'The coming dark'.

Girls, Women, Misogyny

The publication of Larkin's letters in 1992 unleashed a furious reaction against his misogyny.[9] This in turn has fuelled critical debate concerning how women and sexual relations figure in the poems. Certainly, the *Letters* display some unpleasant characteristics in Larkin the man. Resentment of women, sadistic urges, accusations against women and suspicion of them join together with crude obscenities, accounts of masturbation and a predilection for pornography, to give us a thoroughly unattractive picture. The casual comment 'as far as I can see, all women are stupid beings' (*Letters*, 63) is one of the least offensive remarks.

Reading 'Wild Oats', 'Deceptions', 'Lines on a Young Lady's Photograph Album' (*CP*, 71–2), 'High Windows', 'The Dance', 'Self's the Man' and many poems will quickly impress us with the seriousness of this charge against Larkin. There is abundant evidence of a peculiar, often hostile and sometimes abusive attitude towards women in all of these poems. Does this mean that Larkin's *oeuvre* is sexist?

Asking this question opens up an insoluble range of options, all of which ultimately hinge on the same question we have reached in relation to Larkin's commentary on society. How far should we read the poems as a dramatic characterisation: each one a monologue from a slightly different speaker, although speakers with much in common? Or, does Larkin share the deplorable attitudes some of his speakers adopt? The *Letters* suggest that many of the elements we find in his speakers were present in Larkin's private thoughts and in his own character. On the other hand, how tongue-in-cheek are his wry comments to male friends in the letters? Are these facts relevant to our estimation of the poetry?

It is, of course, impossible to find a single answer to these questions. It is unrealistic to think we can forget the sordid side of Larkin's character, and approach the poems as 'pure art', hermetically sealed away from their origin and context. Even if this were a worthwhile critical exercise, we simply cannot do it now that the letters have been published. On the other hand, the poems are not merely the man who produced them: it would be ridiculous to reject Larkin's poetry for purely biographical reasons. Ultimately, the answers to these questions are likely to be individual answers; and they will depend on your response to irony and tone, as well as on your individual sensibility.

The only way to explore our responses is to reread the relevant poems and attempt to make our minds up. We can begin this process now, facing one of the more controversial poems. You should then develop your own opinions by studying further poems. Here, we discuss 'A Study of Reading Habits'.

'A Study of Reading Habits' (*CP*, 131)

This poem is simple in its surface meaning and form. The lines are short, rhymes are strong and regular, and the language is colloquial, with several phrases drawn from a particular kind of adventure-story writing (for example, 'dirty dog' and 'ripping times'). The speaker dreamed of being a hero when at school, and of being a vampire-villain and brutalising women when he grew up. Now he recognises that he is a failure in both these roles, so he has stopped reading the books that fuelled his dreams.

In relation to the misogyny controversy, our questions focus on the second stanza. In this stanza, books have led the speaker to fantasise about being a vampire, leading him to fantasies of brutal sex and violent attacks on women. The word 'ripping' has its slang meaning of 'exciting' but also implies violent attack and violation; while 'clubbed with sex' is a particularly vicious phrase. In this stanza, sex is something men do to women with physical force. The woman's experience is not considered. Finally, the image he uses for women is a sweet object to be consumed: they are 'meringues'. The eruption of violence and sadism into the fantasy in lines 11 and 12 tends to overshadow 'me and my cloak and fangs', but this idea should also be noticed. The speaker imagines being a vampire, which is revealing for three reasons. First and most obviously, because a vampire drinks his female victim, so this is another consumption image like the meringue idea. Secondly, because a vampire can operate only in the dark, clearly a comment on the speaker himself who is a weedy myopic boy. He would never punch someone 'twice my size' in daylight. These fantasies are absolutely restricted: they must be hidden away, fostered in secret, never acted upon. Finally, a vampire has hypnotic power over his female victim. Magically, he puts her into a trance before having his wicked way with her. As we have already observed about 'meringues', this turns the woman into a mere object deprived of character or humanity.

In the final stanza the speaker admits what has been clear all along: he is too weak, frightened and myopic to succeed in either of the two macho enterprises of which he dreams. He cannot dominate women but 'lets the girl down before / The hero arrives'; and he is 'yellow' and 'keeps the store' while more courageous males go out to battle. However, it is the balance of ironies in the final two lines that reverberates through the whole poem. The speaker has failed both in his real life and in his sordid fantasy life. The only solution is the ambiguous 'Get stewed', meaning both 'go away' and 'get drunk'. The final line has an angry tone, complaining that books have deceived him: 'Books are a load of crap'.

What can we make of the poem as a whole? It has the quality of self-knowledge and self-confession we are familiar with by now, so that the final twist blaming books is akin to 'Or lied' at the end of 'Reasons for Attendance', for example, or the ambivalent 'useful to get that learnt' from 'Wild Oats'. The subject of the poem is equally convincing. The speaker shows how his upbringing as a weedy, myopic boy in a masculine culture which glorifies fighting and sexual violence, has turned him into a secret fantasist dreaming of rape and sadism. There is even an ironic acknowledgement, when the speaker blames books at the end, that he is still a disabled personality: he turns to alcohol instead of his fantasies, to dull the pain of failure.

Finally, Larkin's language throughout the poem has hinted at another judgement. The speaker should have known these books were 'crap', because they are cheap rubbish anyway. We can deduce this from the cant phrases 'the old right hook', 'dirty dog', 'lark', 'ripping times' and 'the dude', all of which belong with schoolboy slang of the Billy Bunter and *Boys' Own Comic* era. In short, the speaker has been a fool, and a very obvious fool.

Recognising this does not in any way diminish the insoluble fact of his failure, however; and the poem gives no hint of any more successful course of development. All he can do, in the end, is 'Get stewed'. So, 'A Study of Reading Habits' is typical of Larkin. The speaker is a character who cannot escape from his dilemma. He is partly aware of his own errors and self-deceptions; while the ironic poet behind him also portrays his tendency to take a vicious revenge on those he thinks have victimised him (such as women). Nothing in the poem provides any answer to such questions as: What else could a weedy, short-sighted boy have done? Or, what can he do now? The poem is reductionist, nihilist, negative. It is also complete, a typically thorough Larkin structure of utterance and silent ironies.

What about women? We have noticed the image of 'meringues', and this is appropriate to the egocentric boyish speaker. Women make no appearance in this poem, except as objects men will attack or possess. The poem is strictly limited to its interest in the male malfunction and neurosis, and this absence of interest in the problems of sexuality and relationships from a woman's point of view may strike us as a limitation. The most telling moment comes in line 9, where the speaker fantasises about being a vampire, with the power to hypnotise and so both dehumanise and immobilise his female victim. If we then go on to read 'Wild Oats' and 'Lines on a Young Lady's Photograph Album', say, we will begin to see that images of women framed or transformed into static photographs and pictures are common in Larkin's poetry. These images are both disturbing and exciting to Larkin's speakers: they can be owned in a sense because they are objects, no longer living beings (in the way that he keeps snaps of 'bosomy' in his wallet, in 'Wild Oats'); yet they also present him with an insuperable problem because they are unattainable. See, for example, the imagery of eating 'too much confectionery, too rich' and the excitement of 'My swivel eye hungers from pose to pose' as a speaker pores over photographs of his female friend (*CP*, 71). Psychoanalytical criticism quickly connects these confused, contradictory emotions with an urge towards sadistic attack that is present in both 'A Study of Reading Habits' and, for example, 'Sunny Prestatyn'.

It is arguable that women are treated in an objectifying, dehumanising manner even in poems that are gentler in their language. So, for example, the speaker of 'Broadcast' (*CP*, 140) knows that his mistress is in the audience at a concert he listens to on the radio. Tender though the poem may be, the speaker remains separated, out of contact, and the woman is described within the frame of a concert and framed by the auditorium: she is at the other end of a wire and a loudspeaker, just as the woman in a snapshot is at the other end of a lens. Equally, in the unfinished poem 'The Dance', the woman is 'acting more / Than ever you would put in words' and the speaker's neurotic responses are tied to conventional signs in her body-language: we can argue that the poem is no more than a closer account of 'The wonderful feel of girls' than is given in 'Reasons for Attendance'. The woman again fails to become more than an object representative of her sex.

We have already suggested that this controversy is ultimately a matter for each reader. My own feeling is that women as human beings are absent from Larkin's poems. Women figure as objects to be viewed, contemplated, resented, defiled or attacked in the various ways that his speakers' inadequacies and culturally ordained neuroses demand. This is a limitation, but it is one of which Larkin is acutely aware. In the arena of sexual relations, the subject matter of Larkin's poems is, strictly, male neuroses; and these he does in fascinated and deeply perceptive detail. He weaves a web so perfectly self-defeating, underlaid with balanced ironies, that his poems on this subject are dazzling. He does not write women as human beings because it would have been beyond his speakers' range. We can argue that expecting Larkin to 'do' women would be as absurd as expecting Jane Austen to 'do' a factory labourer, rather than the '3 or 4 Families in a Country Village' that was her chosen subject matter.[10] Larkin's subject matter is the neurotic postwar male, and nobody does him better.

The evidence of the *Letters* is of doubtful use. Whatever kind of a man Larkin may have been, his letters have the potential to be just as misleading as other evidence. The poems remain valuable, because of the distance of ironic self-criticism that exists between the poet and his 'speakers'. This distance is built into the fundamental structure of thought in nearly all of the poems. If Larkin himself was the twisted inadequate many of his speakers portray, then the poems show life successfully transformed into art.

This defence of Larkin is not entirely watertight. There are no factory labourers at all in Jane Austen's novels, but it remains a disturbing fact that there are numerous women treated as objects in Larkin's poems. In pursuing these issues and making up your own mind, it will be particularly useful for you to read and consider 'The Dance', 'Deceptions' and 'Love Again'.[11]

Methods of Analysis

In this chapter, we have continued to use the approaches and techniques developed in previous chapters. As we are increasingly familiar with Larkin's poems, however, we have been able to be less exhaustive. In particular, we have been more selective in our description of the poem's form, and in analysing metrical and rhyming features. This amounts to an increasing ability to pick out what is significant, and increasing confidence to spend less time on merely formal matters. You will find that you take a more direct line to your particular interests, in this way, as you gain experience and confidence.

We have made use of two additional approaches in this chapter.

(A) Pursuing a theme by formulating specific leading questions

1   In the last chapter, we kept the solitaire/solidaire theme in mind. So, we paused at each stage of analysis to consider what was revealed about the Solitaire/Solidaire dilemma. This method keeps you on the track of the theme you are interested in and ensures that your conclusions are relevant to that theme. It boils down to asking the same question again and again, after every stage of analysis. In the last chapter, we repeatedly asked: *what does this tell us about the Solitaire/Solidaire dilemma?*

2   Answering such a question is already quite complicated. You may, if you wish, break your question down into its constituent parts:
    (*a*)   What does this tell us about withdrawing, being isolated, being alone?
    (*b*)   What does this tell us about joining in, relationships, socialising?
    (*c*)   How does this affect the balance of the speaker's feelings about isolation and joining in?

3   In this chapter, we have taken on a theme made up of a more complex mix of elements. The method is the same: we repeatedly ask, *What does this tell us about society and work?* However, this is a very big question, which embraces:
    (*a*)   What does this tell us about human behaviour?

(*b*) What does this tell us about social rituals?

(*c*) What does this tell us about social class?

(*d*) What does this tell us about the power of money?

(*e*) What does this tell us about the labour contract, or the slavery of work?

(*f*) What does this tell us about commerce and mass consumerism?

(*g*) What does this tell us about the attitude towards women?

(*h*) What does this tell us about male neuroses?

4   Of course, we could go on adding to this list of questions. Thinking about the current chapter, we realise that we have asked another group of questions as well, which duplicate this list but focus on the speaker's attitudes in particular:

(*a*) What attitude does this express towards the slavery of work?

(*b*) What attitude does this express towards mass consumerism?

(*c*) What attitude does this express towards women?

and so on. Furthermore, Larkin's attitudes are usually complex; that is, he entertains mixed feelings about these topics. So, the answer to one of these questions may consist of two or more parts. For example, we noticed that in 'The Whitsun Weddings' Larkin's description of the 'grinning and pomaded' girls suggests contempt for their vulgar taste; yet his insight into their feeling that the wedding is a kind of 'religious wounding' suggests a more sympathetic attitude. It suggests that the speaker imagines their personal experiences.

5   So, when you are pursuing a particular theme through a study of the poems, the method to use is repeatedly to formulate, ask and answer leading questions. This will ensure that your conclusions remain relevant to the topic you are studying. However, you will often find that you need to break your questions down into their common-sense constituent parts. Breaking larger questions down into more specific ones helps because the answers to specific questions will be clearer. The more precise the question you ask, the more precise will be the insight you reach.

6   Remember the caution we discussed in Chapter 2: asking leading questions about a particular theme may lead you to pass over other important aspects of a poem. For this reason, it is vital to

reread poems repeatedly, considering different themes and features each time. This helps to keep your overall appreciation of the poems in balance.

(B) Analysing imagery by listing image-ideas and considering the resulting list

1 In this chapter we carried out an analysis of the imagery (metaphors and similes) in 'The Building'. We did this because there are many figurative ideas in that poem. The method is made up of three stages:

(*a*) Make a list of the images in the poem.

(*b*) Consider the list of images, looking for groups of similar image-ideas, or any progression of image-ideas.

(*c*) Consider how the analysis of images contributes to your understanding of the poem as a whole.

2 We followed this method with 'The Building' because the poem is particularly rich in imagery and the list of images is easier to think about than the whole poem with its figurative ideas in context. However, many Larkin poems contain a surprisingly small amount of imagery. It is often not necessary to go through the above three stages, when considering imagery in a Larkin poem.

3 On the other hand, a single image in Larkin can reflect the insoluble structure of the poem as a whole. We found this with the simile of London's 'postal districts packed like squares of wheat' in 'The Whitsun Weddings': the hint of natural fertility in 'wheat' is counteracted by the restrictive 'packed' and 'squares'. This reflects how the poem as a whole frames the weddings' potential with cynical doubt.

Suggested Work

In this chapter, we studied four poems in detail. We then followed up our interest in various themes by reading more widely among Larkin's poems, and by referring back to poems studied in previous chapters, in the concluding discussion. This provided a wider range of reference and more detailed understanding of themes from the initial four poems.

It will be worthwhile to practise this process.

1 Look again at 'Sunny Prestatyn'. Then browse the *Collected Poems* to find other poems that focus on the artificial and superficial. You may begin this process by reading such poems as 'Posterity', 'The Large Cool Store', 'Faith Healing', 'Essential Beauty'; and by returning to reconsider 'Self's the Man' or 'Next, Please' from this particular point of view.

2 Look again at 'The Building'. Then browse the *Collected Poems* to find other poems in which social and materialist preoccupations are a form of denial. You could begin by looking through a group of hospital poems, such as 'How', 'Hospital Visits', 'The Old Fools' and 'Ambulances'. You may then come across such poems as 'Skin' and 'Continuing to Live' which will further inform your appreciation of these themes in Larkin's verse.

3 Look again at 'A Study of Reading Habits'. Then browse the *Collected Poems* to find other examples of speakers' attitudes towards women. You may begin by reading 'Deceptions', 'Lines on a Young Lady's Photograph Album', 'Talking in Bed', 'The Dance' and 'Love Again'; and by returning to reconsider 'Wedding-Wind' and 'Wild Oats'.

As you pursue these enquiries, you can ensure that you continue to build your appreciation of the topic by formulating and asking relevant leading questions, as described in Methods of Analysis above.

4

'Tilting a blind face to the sky'

Poems analysed: 'Church Going' (*CP*, 97–8); 'An Arundel Tomb' (*CP*, 110–11); 'Sad Steps' (*CP*, 169); 'Aubade' (*CP*, 208–9); 'High Windows' (*CP*, 165)

Larkin repeatedly hints that his speakers are concerned with questions about the purpose and value of life, and the powers (if any) that control our existence: who or what runs the universe? He does not believe in any of the answers canvassed – the most abiding impressions the poems leave are of a repetitive but futile natural cycle, and a void or blankness behind.

This chapter discusses how Larkin tackles the subject of existence in poems that are overtly concerned with either religious faith or death. The first poem we will look at is 'Church Going'.

'Church Going' (*CP*, 97–8)

The voice we hear in 'Church Going' is that of a natural, conversational speaker. He begins as if in the middle of telling us about his holiday: 'Once I am sure there's nothing going on ...'. Most of the lines are iambic pentameter, but the metre is far from rigid. See, for example, line 21 where we have to treat one 'wondering' as two syllables and the other as three before the line will scan; or the irregularity of line 12 ('**Cleaned**, or res**tored**? **Some**one would **know**: I **don't**'). Natural phrasing cuts across line endings giving numerous enjambements, and four of the stanza breaks continue the same sentence. The nine-line stanzas have an elaborate rhyme scheme (ABABCADCD), but the enjambements and some off-rhymes (for example, *this/use*, and *do/too/show* in the third stanza) dampen down any formal impression. There is one exception: the comic doubled rhyme of *surprising/grow wise in* in the final stanza. This is just one level more sing-song than the surrounding language, possibly to poke fun at the delusion of growing 'wise in' a church.

Colloquial phrases help to characterise the speaker, providing humour and irony. There is comedy in his ignorance of church architecture ('some brass and stuff / Up at the holy end'), and we laugh when he looks for a gesture of respect, realises he isn't wearing a hat so he cannot take one off, and plumps for removing his cycle-clips instead. This ignorant and mischievous church visitor runs his hand around the font, mounts 'the lectern' (climbs to the pulpit?), and jokingly tries out his voice with 'Here endeth'. The echoes 'snigger briefly'. In short, he behaves very like a naughty schoolboy.

On the other hand, he did feel a need to show respect, removing his cycle-clips 'in awkward reverence'; he lays a serious charge against religion, which promotes 'a few / Hectoring large-scale verses'; and he is embarrassed and self-conscious that his 'Here endeth' makes much more noise than he expected. With unconscious irony, the speaker comments that the church has been silent for 'God knows how long', yet finds the silence 'unignorable' and 'tense'; and he asserts his ignorance of the building in a defensively abrupt tone: 'I don't'. So, we have a neat character-portrait of the speaker. It is clear that the speaker is not indifferent to the church, and is affected by its solemnity. He acts against his own response to the place, however: he defensively covers up his 'hunger ... to be more serious' with flippant humour and schoolboy mischief.

The rest of the poem plays out these character traits in a discursive meditation presented as the casual 'wondering' of the holiday-maker as he leaves a church that was 'not worth stopping for'. It is tempting to follow the loose thread of his thoughts, and mistake this holiday whimsy for the subject matter of the poem: indeed, this has often been done. If, on the other hand, we keep the speaker's character in mind, we should recognise that this voice is tricky, defensive and self-deceptive. The first two stanzas have revealed him as peculiarly unable to cope with visiting a church. He cannot behave properly, and mixes compulsive impudence with embarrassment and the comic solemnity of the bicycle-clips. He is annoyed by his own ignorance (remember the curtness of 'I don't') and 'Hectoring' church authority. It is at this point that he appears to introduce a meditation:

> Yet stop I did: in fact I often do,
> And always end much at a loss like this,
> Wondering what to look for; wondering, too,
> When churches fall completely out of use
> What we shall turn them into ...

We should follow these shifts of thought with the speaker's character in mind, and therefore with suspicion. Let us summarise:

1 He realises that he repeatedly stops to visit churches. This puzzles him: 'Yet' tells us that he knows his behaviour is illogical.
2 He always wonders 'what to look for'.
3 Then he wonders what will happen to churches when society ceases to use them altogether.

Listing his thoughts in succession like this helps us to see the glaring omission, the question he does not ask which resonates through the subtext of the remainder of the poem. It is another example of a powerful gap or 'silence' lying behind the 'utterance' of the poem. He does not ask the obvious question: Why do I keep on visiting churches? Instead, the speaker turns the question away from himself to an external something ('what to look for') and then further afield to the generalised 'we', the whole of society. Notice also that by the end of these few lines, the church has ceased to be a puzzling place that arouses his compulsions: it has become a mere building, ready for ruin or tourism but no longer deeply personal to the speaker. We can conclude, then, that the speaker's so-called meditation is an exercise in avoiding the puzzle within himself. Now we are ready to follow this speaker's twists and turns through the remainder of the poem.

Sure enough, the 'meditation' proves to be wittily amusing but banal, full of stereotyped characters and with a touch of commonplace, sentimental emotion. He begins with the tourist industry, including some satirical digs at its profit-motive. Cathedrals will be kept 'chronically' on show; the neatly alliterated 'parchment, plate and pyx' creates a silly sound, and there is ambiguity because 'plate' could be silver and gold, or the collection 'plate', and the 'pyx' is a container for both the communion host and newly minted coins; then, nature and commerce are comically juxtaposed in 'let the rest rent-free to rain and sheep'.

Just before the third stanza ends, the speaker's mind turns to superstitions. This is a new bout of meditation, and the way it takes over a line sooner than expected suggests the speaker's eagerness to think about something. Again, we should suspect him of avoiding the real puzzle, drowning it out with commonplace laughter about witches and ghosts. Notice the word 'dubious' (l. 28), reminiscent of the gypsies' 'unspeakable' wives in 'Toads': this is the class voice of respectability, declaring that one does not mix with such women. Nonetheless, the speaker is surprised during this phase of his bogus meditation, and we should be careful to follow his characteristic modes of thought as the surprise occurs.

Having caricatured superstitious thrill-seekers, he is led back towards his true problem, which he mentions in vague terms: 'Power of some sort or another'. He manages to pass off this thought with the belittling 'games ... riddles' and dismiss it as 'seemingly at random'. He is keen to return to his caricatures, and the artificial 'topics' of his meditation. So, he produces a grand aphorism under the title of his current topic: superstition. 'But superstition,' he intones, 'like belief, must die'. This line sounds wonderful. The grand abstract nouns are sweeping, and the zeugma perfectly constructed with the hard-hitting, monosyllabic verb 'die' kept to the end. How good the speaker must have felt as such a fine aphorism came to him. He continues in the same vein with a fine rhetorical question: 'And what remains when disbelief has gone?' But wait! The sense, the entire context of 'Church Going', cries out for 'what remains when *belief* has gone?' This seems to me one of the most extraordinary moments in Larkin: his speaker adds the prefix 'dis-', reverses the meaning to 'disbelief' and utters what appears to be an unintended mistake. This is a subtle piece of characterisation by Larkin, and we will return to consider how it complicates the effect of the famous final stanza.

It has all the characteristics of an unconscious slip, because the speaker does not notice it. He answers his own rhetorical question just as if he had asked about the end of 'belief', not '*dis*belief': the church, he says, will decay, and nature will take over: 'Grass, weedy pavement, brambles, buttress, sky'. The picture of a buttress holding nothing up, outlined against an empty sky, suits the speaker's apparent thinking about the death of religion. It is a gothic picture of ruins and the following two lines add a suggestion of sentimental nostalgia for the church's 'shape' and 'purpose'. In this mood, the speaker recovers, and diverts himself with another whimsical question ('who / Will be the last, the very last') which leads him into another bout of satirical caricature. This time his target is antiquarians, comically presented as church-junkies: he imagines a 'ruin-bibber' who is 'randy', and a 'Christmas-addict' who, like a drug-addict, seeks a 'whiff' of old church rituals. This diversion is amusing, and the caricatures have a touch of acid. In terms of the speaker's character, he is taking out his earlier annoyance at his own ignorance on those who 'know what rood-lofts were': another hint of his inner disturbance.

In the final two stanzas, the speaker makes another attempt to define what the church once provided. His idea is that religion held the three major events of life, 'marriage, and birth, / And death', together 'unspilt'. Furthermore, religion gave these events significance because they were 'robed as destinies'. Now that 'belief' has gone, these rituals and the 'compulsions' that make us seek them are found 'Only in separation'. Presumably this means that the main events of life have lost any sense of a unified purpose: religious belief used to be a framework linking them all together within the one great ritual of life on earth. Now, they are isolated and pointless moments, the result of mere 'compulsions'.

Finally, the speaker becomes more personal, acknowledging that 'It pleases me to stand in silence here', and allowing that the church, and the land on which it stands, are both 'serious'. We have now followed our spiky, tricky speaker through several twists and turns. Following his acid caricature of church-junkies, he gradually approaches the subject he has tried to avoid so far. This is a movement towards a more affirmative outlook, recognising the value, the 'power of some sort or other', as he called it, of religious faith. It would be wrong to suppose that this movement is without qualification, however. The speaker's cynical nature still struggles: he knows that religion has died, and calls it the 'ghostly silt' in a pun on the archaic meaning of 'ghostly' (spiritual) and the common (gothic/superstitious). The church is an 'accoutred frowsty barn', and he questions what it is 'worth' in a tone which leaves us unsure whether he means its spiritual value, or the price of property. So, although the speaker recognises his own pleasure, he still explicitly denies belief, and denigrates religion as 'ghostly silt'.

We approach the final six lines of the poem in this context: the speaker struggles against confessing his impulse towards the church. Many critics have found a positive message in the final stanza of 'Church Going'. Andrew Motion, for example, claims that 'the fear of death and the loss of religious belief are counteracted by an ineradicable faith in human and individual potential';[1] and David Lodge finds that the finale 'comes as a thrilling surprise after the downbeat, slightly ironic tone of the preceding stanzas'.[2] Having followed the movement of the speaker's thoughts and emotions through the poem, our analysis cannot agree.

What happens to the speaker's voice in these final lines? First, he moves away from the 'me' of line 54 to the distant 'someone' who ends the poem. That is, his idea about the value of religion becomes less personal, more theoretical. Secondly, the grander rhetoric of the triad 'all our compulsions meet, / Are recognised, and robed as destinies' is not sustained to the end. Instead, there is the almost silly rhyme of 'surprising' and 'grow wise in', which makes growing wise sound funny. Thirdly, the urge which makes someone 'gravitate' towards church ground is called 'hunger': surely not some transcendental 'ineradicable faith', but rather a primitive need. Finally, the speaker leaves us with a wry comment that undercuts the whole finale. Perhaps churches make him feel 'serious' only because there are so many corpses buried all around them. The poem's finale, then, cannot be construed as a 'thrilling surprise' or indicating 'ineradicable faith in human ... potential'. It is an equivocal, ambivalent ending to the poem. In 'Church Going', personal emotion is disguised as impersonal theory, while wry irony and cynicism allow no softening of the speaker's habitually secular, anti-metaphysical outlook.

We should now bring the speaker's astonishing slip into consideration. This slip transforms the poem. 'Church Going' declares that the problem is the loss of religious faith, and this problem dominates all the poem's 'utterance': the speaker's narrative, his meditation and his final theory explaining the attraction of religious sites. The prefix '*dis*belief' exposes a completely different perspective. The problem is how to lose rational cynicism, not the loss of religion at all. The revealing 'slip', together with the obvious unasked question (*Why do I keep on visiting churches?*), alter the poem's focus radically. It is no longer the story of a man searching for lost faith. Rather, it is the story of a man struggling to divest himself of his twentieth-century secular rationalism. He struggles to set himself free from his *dis*belief, but he is frightened and has no idea what can take its place.

This is a crucial dilemma. When he imagines what might come after *dis*belief, our speaker is frightened and nonplussed. Life may have meaning, and his cynical self recognises that committing himself to 'marriage, and birth, / And death' might satisfy a primitive 'hunger' and fulfil his natural 'compulsions'; but he cannot bring himself to do so as it is a leap into emptiness. Instead, his final thought is a cautious question about the origin of his feeling for churches: perhaps it is nothing more than a morbid attraction to graveyards.

This perspective on the poem opens out another odd combination we might not have noticed otherwise. It is convention to think of birth, marriage and death as the three defining events of a life; but the speaker goes further than this. All three reappear, in line 56, as 'our compulsions'. This implies that death is a compulsion, and even, indirectly, that we 'hunger' for death.

'Church Going', then, is an unresolved tangle. The different attitudes towards both belief and disbelief that Larkin has built into the poem in layers of self-deception, equivocation, ambivalence and irony cancel each other out. If we consider our study of other poems, such as 'Self's the Man' or 'Vers de Société', we should recognise that this unresolved quality is intentional. The poem is a representation of the speaker's dilemma, and we 'unravel' it at our peril. So, what can 'Church Going' tell us about 'the purpose and value of life, and the powers (if any) that control our existence', the topic we chose for this chapter?

First, religion itself does not appear to come into the question. Just as in 'Vers de Société', so in this poem again, the problem is its absence. There is no question that the poet or speaker might find religion: he will not. His attitude towards religion is anthropological, rather. He recognises the social and emotional benefits religion used to bring to individuals and the community, and expresses some nostalgia for these effects. But there is no doubt in his mind that the 'ghostly silt' has 'dispersed' now, and will never be recovered. Further, the 'propitiatory flowers' which conclude 'The Building', and the comments on wedding rituals from 'The Whitsun Weddings', are consistent with the desires that 'Church Going' explores. It is not that we want a God, a supernatural – that is impossible in the modern age – it is rather that we want to find some cohesive meaning in life, in the natural. This speaker would not approve of returning to religion, anyway, as his comment on 'Hectoring large-scale verses' makes plain.

In the literal sense, the poem cannot tell us anything. On the other hand, it presents the speaker as a twentieth-century man wrestling with these questions, and it recreates the sheer complexity and depth of the disturbance they cause him. At the very least, the poem tells us that questions concerning the purpose of existence are central to the experience of a twentieth-century atheist. 'Church Going' may also suggest that we are in thrall to an unexpected form of fear. As modern rationalists, we no longer fear a loss of faith. On the contrary, what we fear is any form of positive belief, and the loss of our safe, cynical rationalism which defends us against the risk of being wrong.

'An Arundel Tomb' (*CP*, 110–11)

This poem takes on the form with which we are now familiar: a situation or anecdote sparks off a wider meditation. In this case, the speaker sees the tomb, which is a medieval effigy of a noble couple, and notices that the couple are holding hands. The event that gave rise to 'An Arundel Tomb' was a visit Larkin and Monica Jones paid to Chichester Cathedral in the winter of 1955–6. The poem acknowledges that the couple's hand-holding pose is probably 'A sculptor's sweet commissioned grace' and a 'stone fidelity / They hardly meant'. After the poem's publication, Larkin discovered that the linked hands were added when the monument was restored in Victorian times. He did not feel that this knowledge invalidates the poem.

The technique is masterly and the poem beautiful. The integrated ABBCAC rhyme scheme, with its understated use of minor rhyme words (such as 'until', 'and', 'in' and 'they'), and the natural linking of the final three stanzas, are typical features. See also how the gentle 'tender' is framed within the alliterative 'sharp … shock'; how 'Persisted' is withheld to the start of the next stanza, somehow increasing its obstinate, enduring sense; how breaking the line between 'light' and 'Each summer' seems to imitate the repetitive renewal of the years, and breaking the line between 'bright' and 'Litter of birdcalls' has an almost onomatapoeic effect; how the alliterated phrase 'smoke in slow suspended skeins' lingers like the smoke itself.

Beautiful and often lyrical, with its resonant affirmative final line, 'An Arundel Tomb' has given rise to widely varied critical interpretations. Many of these focus on arguments about Larkin's pessimism or optimism: how much weight can we attach to that final line, in the light of the constant interplay between the stone love-story that has 'Persisted, linked' through 'altered people' to an 'unarmorial age' when time has changed the air to 'soundless damage', on the one hand; and, on the other hand, the suggestions that lasting love is a delusion, an 'Untruth' they 'hardly meant' and no more than 'a sculptor's sweet commissioned grace / Thrown off'? If we return to our method and consider the character of the speaker, it is clear that 'An Arundel Tomb' is, in this respect, a typically Larkinesque complex: a structure in which different and contradictory impulses make a tense dynamic whole, never likely to be resolved. This speaker is sensitive to the 'sharp tender shock', and his desire to believe in the ideal of enduring love can be heard in the effort he puts into 'almost-instinct almost true'. However, he is also cynical enough to place the defining word 'Untruth' at the start of a line, and the ironic use of the heraldic 'blazon' in the same final stanza. There is no resolution of the dilemma here, only tension right to the end.

In this chapter, we are interested in a different aspect of the poem: its concern with the ways in which people, their lives and their stories are made. We should begin by remembering 'Dockery and Son', which proposes the theory that our birth (and perhaps our childhood) brings with it 'innate assumptions'. These 'assumptions' determine our 'habit' and eventually 'harden into all we've got'. Similar suggestions that life deprives us of freedom and steadily 'hardens' can be found in 'Home is So Sad' (*CP*, 119), where marriage, 'A joyous shot at how things ought to be', leaves behind a static detritus of memorial objects: 'the pictures and the cutlery. / The music in the piano stool. That vase'. Several poems referring to photographs or albums[3] also attest to this concern, as do the imaginings of gradual ruin, and even the final line, in 'Church Going'. These images of life undergoing a metamorphosis into something lifeless and fixed, are determinist. Larkin's frequent return to these ideas is a testament to his concern with existential questions about what, if anything can, constitutes freedom; and where, if anywhere, lies an individual's human essence.

With 'An Arundel Tomb', then, we will attempt to follow the metamorphosis of the stone couple through time, remembering that the undercutting irony of this essay in enduring love is the fact that the entire story takes place after death. At the start of the poem, death has already deprived the earl and countess of individuality. Their faces are 'blurred' and clothing 'vaguely shown'. So far, change is simple hardening: his 'jointed armour' and the cloth she wears 'stiffened'. Memorial convention has provided them with little dogs under their feet, which render them 'absurd'. As far as the speaker is concerned, this transformation into effigy is unremarkable. The reason for the poem is the 'sharp tender shock' of their joined hands. We have already commented that these three words are hard–soft–hard both in sound and connotation.

In the third stanza, the speaker introduces the question of mind in a negative: 'They would not think …'. The earl's and countess's minds are local in both space and time: the joined hands are for 'friends' and not for 'long'. Instead, their thoughts are continued by the sculptor they commissioned, and focus on prolonging their names rather than their relationship. The couple's expectations are utterly wrong. Very early in their 'stationary voyage' through time, their dependent community (the 'tenantry') disappears, and people can no longer read Latin. So, the 'names around the base' they thought to preserve are quickly meaningless, and attention focuses on the accident they 'hardly meant' instead.

Because of this context the phrase 'Rigidly they / persisted' becomes ambiguous. On the surface it would seem to present the couple as determined, their effigy surviving the centuries. In the context of their short-sighted hopes, however, it comes to have a different implication. The ambiguity of this phrase suggests that the couple are now prisoners of their stone existence. Nothing they intended has come to pass, and something they did not intend is happening. Trapped in their hardened stone casing, they are impotent to protest, and must endure and suffer this 'Untruth'. The speaker contrasts their helpless rigidity with the fluid continuity of nature, its seasonal round, and time which brings 'endless altered people'.

The metaphor 'Washing at their identity' makes this point clear. Their rigidity in stone is likened to a rock in the fluid sea of nature and change. Their 'identity' has changed from what they intended, and the 'endless people' have, like water eroding over centuries, washed them into a new shape. In other words, time has projected a new identity and meaning onto them, gradually, inevitably. In the final four stanzas, then, a conflict between the couple's intention, and the inevitable and contrary action of time and nature upon them, is described. They have no chance of victory. The power of 'time' (including its snows, sunlight and birdsong) to 'transfigure' them is unchallenged.

'An Arundel Tomb' explores the existential question, but with a wry and humorous obliqueness. In the early part of the twentieth century, existentialism examined the new post-religion consciousness. Put simply, the modern individual does not believe in an eternal 'soul' or essence that comes from God. When we are born, we exist, but our self or individual 'essence' is a blank. Starting from this premise, philosophers proceeded to two insights. First, that self-consciousness in a being subject to death is inherently absurd because death and consciousness are contradictions. To say 'I am not' is a contradiction, an absurdity, because the pronoun 'I' asserts consciousness and therefore existence. The 'absurdity' of life is also apparent in the mismatch between a tiny consciousness and a vast universe. Secondly, that we can pursue and achieve true freedom through our actions: the way we live, if we live free from constraints, will create our individual self, our 'essence'. This is necessarily a very broad summary; but it clearly shows how Larkin has comically moved the goalposts in the version he provides.

'An Arundel Tomb' asks: how do we attempt to 'make' meaningful lives for ourselves? Can we do so? In answer, the poem shows that the earl and countess attempted this and failed. They now suggest a meaning that is in conflict with their intentions. Their attempt to make a meaningful monument lost its intended meaning quickly after their death; and worse, it grew another quite different meaning over succeeding centuries. These individuals had no choice or freedom. Their helpless efforts had no chance against the power of nature and time. The metaphor of water 'washing at' stone, and the contrast shown between their 'rigidity' and the fluid continuity of nature, adds a further comment on metamorphoses. It seems that human efforts are artificial, and tend to harden, to petrify; whereas a long, patient and completely unpredictable process of time and nature renders these hardened human memorials impotent, or distorts them into falsehood.

The comic element in 'An Arundel Tomb' comes from its original perspective on the problem. Far from considering life from a starting-point of birth, this poem uses the starting-point of death. Larkin always insisted that much of his verse was intended to be amusing, and we can imagine him laughing as he wrote about a couple struggling, posthumously, with existential doubt!

At this point, and before we move on to look at 'Sad Steps', it is worth remembering that we have met this comment on existence before. In 'Dockery and Son', the speaker has a vision of 'innate assumptions' that control the individual's actions and destiny. He points out that these have nothing to do with 'what / We think truest, or most want to do', which 'warp tight-shut, like doors'. This is another picture of the individual's impotence, our inability to control our destiny or 'make' our lives.

'Sad Steps' (*CP*, 169)

This poem begins in the idiom of one of Larkin's irreverent, common-tongued speakers, like the man in 'Vers de Société' and his 'crowd of craps'. However, from the shock of seeing the sky when he parts the curtains in the second line, the idiom changes. He is 'startled' and, later, 'shivers slightly'. In between these reactions, we read a wildly powerful description of the sky.

What does he see and why does it affect him so strongly? Two qualities of the sky are emphasised: first, it is enormous and endless, an impression reinforced throughout by 'cavernous', 'high ... separate', 'Immensements', and the 'Far-reaching singleness of that wide stare'. Secondly, there is a high wind and the sky is full of rapid movement: there are 'rapid clouds', it is 'wind-picked' and the moon 'dashes' through clouds like 'cannon-smoke'. The view from his window, then, impresses him with wild movement and immensity. The speaker connects this with something 'laughable' and 'preposterous': clearly the sudden contact between himself and the immensity of the sky gives him a feeling of absurdity, because individual consciousness is out of proportion to the endless universe. This, in turn, reminds him of his own insignificance and mortality.

The speaker focuses on one particular aspect of his mortality: the 'wolves of memory' and the ideals he once believed in: love and art. He concludes that the immensity of the sky reminds him of 'the strength and pain / Of being young; that it can't come again'. The final line puts forward the cyclical continuity of natural life, setting this against his own comparative impotence. Although his youth is gone, he reflects, it is 'undiminished somewhere' for others. In other words, he sets the objective, 'being young', against the subjective, that for him it 'can't come again'. It is an argument that cannot be resolved.

Our speaker has been shocked by the immensity of the sky, in contrast to his own insignificance in the universe. The comfort he tries to find, in the final line, refers to the fact that nature, and therefore such positives as 'being young' continually renews itself. This suggestion, like the images of fertility at the end of 'The Whitsun Weddings', can hardly balance the pain of knowing his own nothingness. Indeed, it could be argued that his own annihilation is even more painful: it seems even more senseless and unfair, in the knowledge that others are still young. The next poem we look at, 'Aubade', explores death, the annihilation of self, more fully.

'Aubade' (*CP*, 208–9)

'Aubade' was composed in 1977. There is a 'speaker' who introduces himself in the first line: 'I work all day, and get half-drunk at night', and like 'Sad Steps', the poem is set in the small hours waiting for dawn. The title is ironic, since an 'Aubade' is traditionally a poem in praise of dawn, generally involving lovers who must part, or urging a lover to wake. Larkin's 'Aubade' provides a bitter slant on the tradition, focusing on bleak thoughts of death as dawn approaches. If daylight brings relief to this pessimistic speaker, it brings it only because 'Work has to be done'. As in 'Toads Revisited' (*CP*, 148), work is welcomed because it will 'Help me down Cemetery Road'.

The rest of this poem, however, is in Larkin's late manner: there is none of the amused self-mockery or self-doubt of the earlier speakers, none of their ambivalence. Such character ironies are absent, giving us no reason to suppose that there is a distinction between the speaker and Larkin himself. Also typical of the later manner is the tendency to definitive or aphoristic lines. So, in a line that has become famous, religion is 'That vast moth-eaten musical brocade', and death 'The anaesthetic from which none come round' or 'no different whined at than withstood'. Lacking irony and seeking definition, the poet has no need to create tension between shifting conversational dictions, and a complex form, as he did in poems such as 'Dockery and Son' or 'The Whitsun Weddings'. Instead, the rhyme scheme (ABABC-CDEED) is regular and firmly used, there are fewer enjambements, and each stanza terminates in a full-stop.

The subject of 'Aubade' is declared in the first stanza: 'Unresting death'. The poem is one of the few major works to appear after *High Windows*, Larkin's final collection, and makes one of a group of sombre orations (another might be 'The Building' which we studied in the last chapter) which cemented Larkin's reputation for pessimism and morbid subject matter. 'Aubade' certainly is about continual thoughts of death; but there is a danger in stereotyping Larkin as this gloomy middle-aged speaker, even if this character is not satirically undercut. If we approach 'Aubade' with the same care as we approach other poems, we will realise more exactly what it is about death that occupies the poet.

The opening stanza tells us more than that the theme is 'Unresting death'. The speaker is conventionally frightened: death is 'a whole day nearer now', and he has a 'dread / Of dying'. Death is 'always there' and 'Unresting'. However, two other characteristics of thinking about death also appear. First, it makes 'all thought impossible'; and secondly, he not only fears 'dying', he also fears 'being dead'. The conventional fears are of something that is active, something that moves or is an event: 'nearer now', 'Unresting' and 'dying'. These suggest that death is an action, something death does or something you do when you die. The other two elements, 'Making all thought impossible' and 'being dead', introduce the effort to express absence and emptiness, death as a blank negative, which gains dominance and urgency as the poem continues. 'Impossible' is given prominence by the changes in pace between the inverted first foot and the spondee that lead up to it: '**Mak**ing **all thought**'. In the context of death as an 'impossible' concept, the two words 'being dead' are virtually an oxymoron. If you are dead, you are not 'being', and vice versa. Death is impossible to experience because it is the absence of sensation and thought; and this is the problem to which the poem returns again and again. We should now follow the development of the speaker's ideas.

'Flashes' gains power from its position at the start of line 10, and conveys both the suddenness and the blinding and therefore unthinkable concept of death, and this effect of paralysing the brain is underscored in 'The mind blanks at the glare'. The poem then attempts to express this 'impossible' or inexpressible realisation of death. First, the poet dismisses 'remorse' and the lack of achievement in life. We may recognise the ideas here, from earlier poems. For example, 'failure and remorse' make up the intolerable misery the speaker can escape by socialising, in 'Vers de Société'; and the idea of life unable to 'climb / Clear of its wrong beginnings' is reminiscent of the 'innate assumptions' theory in 'Dockery and Son', where birth limits our freedom and eventually 'harden[s] into all we've got'. In 'Aubade', however, these concerns are introduced by 'Not' and 'nor'. The second half of stanza 2 struggles to express what the recognition of death is. The poet attempts this four times: 'total emptiness for ever', 'sure extinction', 'Not to be here' and 'Not to be anywhere'. These are two positive descriptions and two negatives. Such repeated attempts to convey death actually convey the speaker's desperation, and his inability to put the realisation into words. The problem with which this poem struggles is, in fact, linguistic and logical. As we commented on 'being dead', death is not 'being' but its opposite, for which there are no words. This stanza, by stripping away other ideas, and repeatedly attempting to describe a vacuum, shows the speaker's intellectual and verbal helplessness.

In a further negative, 'No trick dispels' the speaker's fear. Two 'tricks' are then mentioned and dismissed, just as two causes of misery were dismissed in stanza 2: religion, and 'specious stuff' or philosophers' syllogisms. The proposition about '*No rational being*' is, of course, irrelevant. Larkin is unable to overcome the contradiction between consciousness and death. All thought assumes the pronoun 'I': *I think, therefore I am*. Logic, and language, are incapable of framing the absence of 'I'. How can 'you' think about the absence of 'you'? The speaker's horror is precisely because 'all thought' on death is 'impossible', and because language is not capable: death goes beyond the power of words. His dread 'Flashes' and his 'mind blanks at the glare'. The point is that he is not a '*rational being*' at all, he is a terrified being. Yet again, he enters into a desperate struggle to find words. He makes another four (at least) attempts to explain to us what he means:

> no sight, no sound,
> No touch or taste or smell, nothing to think with,
> Nothing to love or link with,
> The anaesthetic from which none come round.

There are further descriptions of the undescribable in the final two stanzas, but there is also a gradual return to more familiar living activity. Fear of death is now placed in context 'just on the edge of vision'; and the terrible time before dawn is also placed: 'when we are caught without / People or drink'. Attempts to convey the speaker's horror continue as well. He describes how 'it rages out / In furnace-fear' in a violent, painful image reminiscent of 'dread ... / Flashes afresh'; and death as a non-human absolute is present again in its indifference: 'no different whined at than withstood'.

In the final stanza the long-awaited dawn arrives. The poem's ending is a counterpoint: death occupies three lines, and the awakening world a further six. This time death is said to be 'plain as a wardrobe', and it seems that this is because the speaker's dilemma is crystal clear. He knows that he 'can't escape' death, but he 'can't accept' this. His final comment on this dilemma is even amusing: 'One side will have to go'. It is possible to hear this as a flippant irony, since the speaker knows perfectly well that he can lose neither his knowledge nor his refusal to accept it.

The final six lines, devoted to a world waking up to its daytime activities, simply reinforce a point that has already appeared: that our fears are rampant when we are 'caught without' other things on which to focus. Andrew Motion finds the final stanza 'stoic where the previous three had been terrified'.[4] We may see something other than stoicism, and feel that the terror of the previous stanzas hovers over this one as well. The speaker is grateful to everyday things (telephone calls, letters) *because* thinking of death is 'impossible'. Meanwhile, everyday things are not presented in positive terms: telephones 'crouch' like animals waiting to pounce; the world is 'uncaring / intricate rented', a reminder of the vulgar dominions of money and work; and postmen are 'like doctors', bringing letters that will occupy our minds and therefore act as painkillers to dull the thought of death. The separated single-sentence line 'Work has to be done' expresses exactly the same insight as the final two lines of 'Toads Revisited': work has no intrinsic value; it is merely a distraction from horror.

We have mentioned 'gaps' or 'silences' in the structure of Larkin's poems before, and identified several examples. 'Aubade' creates an enormous silence, by struggling so desperately and repeatedly to express death. It is a silence beyond the reach of language and beyond the ability of thought, as the poem makes plain. There is another silence after the poem ends: terror will return before dawn on the next morning, and the one after that; and it will stay 'just on the edge of vision, / A small unfocused blur' throughout the day, as well. Furthermore, terror will push the speaker to drink, in his desperation to numb his feelings. All of these facts are clear from the poem, but not put into words at the end. They echo like an insoluble future after the poem has finished.

In the above commentary on 'Aubade', we have focused our attention on the poem's demonstrative failure to express death, and the philosophic and linguistic limits that are revealed by the speaker's struggle. One further point also arises. We are conscious individuals born to death, and there is an inevitable mismatch between our consciousness, our individual sense of existence, and the entire universe that ignores us. This mismatch, or lack of proportion, was one of the characteristics of human life described as 'absurd' by philosophers in the early part of the twentieth century. This term denotes elements that are true but, in logical terms, so irreconcilable as to be ridiculous. In its struggles with the contradiction between personal consciousness and death, 'Aubade' is a poem that confronts the absurd: that which does not make sense about being born.

Before we move on to look at 'High Windows', it is worth noting the pedigree of some of Larkin's insights in 'Aubade', which develop themes reminiscent of a poet he admired. The insoluble dilemma of 'can't escape' and 'can't accept' may remind us of Thomas Hardy's 'I Look into My Glass'.[5] In this poem, Hardy imagines losing passion at the same time as losing youth, because he could then face death with 'equanimity'. The poem regrets, however, that this is impossible, for passion 'shakes this fragile frame at eve / With throbbings of noontide'. Such a combination of desire to live and hope, and consciousness of the approach of death, is present here and also echoed in 'the strength and pain of being young', in 'Sad Steps'. Similarly, Larkin's inability to lose either fear or the longing for something else, reminds us of the dualism between factual bereavement and irrational hope, expressed in the final two lines of Hardy's 'The Voice':

> Wind oozing thin through the thorn from norward,
> And the woman calling.[6]

Hardy's 'The Voice' was written soon after his wife's death: she is 'the woman calling' in the quotation above, while the factual cause of the noise that has woken him is the wind. Larkin wrote the first three stanzas of 'Aubade' during the time of his move from the University flat in Pearson Park, to his own house in Newlands Park in Hull. This was not a voluntary move: it was forced because the University had sold the Pearson Park house, and Larkin felt resentful, ill at ease in his new surroundings, and depressed. He finished the poem, adding the final stanza, three years later and eight days after his mother's death. It is noticeable that the occasion of 'Aubade' makes no appearance, however. Larkin's treatment of the theme is more negative than Hardy's, simply because he omits any connection with personal desires and passions. In 'Aubade', death is the 'impossible' or absurd fact that is neither escapable nor acceptable. Larkin's poem is, perhaps, more bleak because he has removed personal grief from the landscape.

'High Windows' (*CP*, 165)

We will not dwell on the first four stanzas. The speaker is a familiarly colloquial and conversational voice, the poem taking on the aura of somebody's 'thought' that might be part of a conversation in the pub. The tone is along the lines of 'Do you know what suddenly occurred to me today?' Intensive use of off-rhymes (such as *she's/paradise, back/dark*) and of enjambement (twelve of the twenty lines) works against the rhyming quatrains in Larkin's typical manner. This allows the natural voice in 'couple of kids', or 'I wonder if' and 'forty years back' to modulate into momentarily angry coarseness ('he's fucking her') and more reflective language ('Bonds and gestures pushed to one side / Like an outdated combine harvester'). There is no difficulty over the idea: the speaker resents and envies the sexual freedom of the young because there was no such latitude in his youth. He then realises that his parents' generation may have envied him his freedom from religious guilts and fears of damnation. It is at this point, expectation perfectly massaged by beginning the new thought 'And immediately ...' at the end of stanza 4, that the poem's subject appears to change.

It is no accident, however, that meditating the changes the twentieth century has brought, and particularly the deaths of religion and sexual taboos, should bring the speaker face to face with another infinite, empty sky. The final stanza is perfectly poised to provoke several competing interpretations. One possible ironic meaning undercuts the older generation's envy: yes, the young can live more freely, but they must live in an empty universe, having lost the reassuring structures of religion. Similarly, sexual relationships have lost their importance, a reductive view of love already hinted at by the coarse verb 'fucking'. Another thought is that the 'high windows' represent the speaker's sudden perspective across generations; yet there is nothing for him to observe through the glass. A third suggestion is that none of these petty details matter, anyway, because we all face death, and an indifferent sky.

The silence in 'High Windows' concerns the relationship between the final stanza and the rest of the poem. The link, 'And immediately / Rather than words comes the thought', tells us nothing. Yet the determinedly colloquial tone of the first four stanzas, and the extreme contrast between this and the final stanza's metaphorical rhetoric, is so surprising that it provokes the question: Why? How can a poem move from the awkward earthiness of 'And guess he's fucking her and she's / Taking pills', to the beautiful extended stresses of 'deep blue air', or the perfect tripled cadence of 'Nothing, and is nowhere, and is endless'? The surprise is so great, we could say that it is absurd for a poem to do this. Perhaps this is the point: the poem itself enacts the mismatch between human life and the universe it inhabits. It does so by exploiting the dislocation between the fourth and fifth stanzas, and by the 'gap' the poet leaves where any relationship between the two might appear.

Concluding Discussion

We have found that Larkin confronts the particular philosophical dilemmas of a twentieth-century thinker in all of the poems we have studied in this chapter. In each case, the fact that he looks at the universe through the eyes of an atheist is a significant element.

Larkin's feelings about religion vary. In 'Church Going', his behaviour displays irreverence and mischief, before he moves on to a meditation which contains nostalgic elements. In 'Aubade', on the other hand, there is a dismissive and contemptuous definition: 'That vast moth-eaten musical brocade / Created to pretend we never die'. Clearly, in the later poem the speaker has less time for the exposed lies that have left him facing death so directly that his 'mind blanks at the glare'.

We have discussed some other references to the religious past in Chapter 3. These take the form of mild regret that some social rituals, and social cohesion, no longer exist; and the poems focus on people's efforts to replace the beliefs that have been lost – whether by attending pointless social gatherings, as in 'Vers de Société', or by erecting a vast ritual temple against the onset of death, as in 'The Building'. The poems also explore the idea that religion was a 'shell' for timeless human behaviours, for rituals that existed before Christianity, and will continue to exist in altered forms now that God has 'gone'. Such rituals particularly focus on courtship events (for example, dancing) and weddings, but also include ineffectual propitiatory offerings laid on the altar of death. This theme suggests a continuity of primitive behaviour and mystical experiences, universal to human beings irrespective of their particular cultural circumstances.

All these related themes seem to be viewed from one point of view, however. Larkin's speakers observe themselves and others taking part in a persistent and ultimately fruitless attempt to avoid, ignore, deny or suppress the thought of death. The fullest confrontation with the 'black-sailed / Unfamiliar' occurs in 'Aubade'.

The twentieth century began in the shadow of hugely influential determinist thought from the second half of the nineteenth: Marx, Darwin and Freud were perhaps the giants of this intellectual change. Larkin's relation to determinism was uneasy. He wrote down and collected his dreams when he was an undergraduate; yet he expressed himself uninterested or unwilling to investigate, when anybody suggested that he might find an explanation for his problems in his own childhood. For most of his life, Larkin expressed no interest in politics or social theory, and when he did, his views were erratic but predominantly right-wing. On the other hand, the poems often leave an uncompromisingly determinist effect behind them. There are the 'innate assumptions' that 'harden into all we've got', in 'Dockery and Son'; but there are also many less direct examples, where it appears that freedom and choice cannot exist. In 'Wild Oats', for example, the entire disaster of a seven-year affair appears to have been dictated by a shy young man being brought up to mistrust and fear his sexuality. In this chapter, we have studied 'An Arundel Tomb', which presents an entirely original angle on the questions of freedom and choice. It is an elaborate and beautiful joke because it examines the issues *post mortem*, but we found that the balance of its effect is weighted against the possibility of freedom. In 'An Arundel Tomb', however, the determining force is more or less chaotic, not the restricting accident of birth proposed in 'Dockery and Son': people are endlessly 'altered' and the future is entirely unpredictable. All we are sure of is that our perceptions will, in the end, be 'Untruth'.

'Church Going' ironically suggests another form of entrapment within the cultural environment. The speaker's apparent slip, asking what follows when '*dis*belief' has gone, introduces the idea that cynicism itself can become a safe haven from doubt. Just as previous generations did not have the courage to abandon the reassurance of religion, so in the twentieth century, a freethinking atheist may be scared of relinquishing the rational scepticism that keeps him safe from disappointment.

Larkin, then, seems to include the problem of confronting death in one or another guise, in nearly all of his poems; and death seems to be recurrently associated with images of the sky and of emptiness. We have the sky's combination of violence and vastness, seen in 'Sad Steps'; a sky 'white as clay, with no sun' from 'Aubade'; the 'deep blue air, that shows / Nothing, and is nowhere, and is endless', from 'High Windows'. In 'Church Going', we may see a symbol of the church's lost function in the modern world: overgrown ruins ('weedy pavement, brambles') lead to 'buttress, sky'. In this image, religion may figure as a ruined support, holding up nothing, set against an empty sky.

In 'Aubade', suggestions about an experience of the absurd, from earlier poems, become greatly expanded. The speaker's description of the shock of death emphasises its disproportion, illogic, the mismatch between humanity and an indifferent universe: it makes 'all thought impossible', 'the mind blanks', and the speaker finds he 'can't escape' and 'can't accept'. The poem struggles to express and re-express the absence that is death, and shows that language is not capable of it despite the repeated negatives 'no sight, no sound,' and so on. In 'Sad Steps', he finds 'something laughable' and 'preposterous' in the sky; and the suddenness of the final stanza of 'High Windows' enacts the disproportion, the inexplicable relationship, between humanity with its temporal and parochial concerns, and the empty sky.[7]

Opinions about religion and death do not vary very much between Larkin's poems, then. What do vary, however, are the moods of the poems. These can range from the self-deprecating comedy of 'Wild Oats', to the emotional confusion of 'Church Going'; and from the ironic amusement of 'An Arundel Tomb' to the seriousness of 'Aubade'.

Methods of Analysis

In this chapter, we have employed the same repertoire of analytical approaches as in previous chapters, and we have again focused on a particular interest. We have not added new techniques to the analytical armoury. However, we have made two important efforts that deserve to be emphasised here, if only as a reminder that all approaches to poetry should remain careful and open-minded.

1 *Be flexible.* In previous chapters we found that many of Larkin's poems are like 'characterisations' of the speaker: his personality is woven into the poem in layers that are ironically related one to another, and the character of the speaker adds an important dimension to the subject matter. This 'character' feature of Larkin's poems, we found, often undercut the meditative and thematic content, finally rendering the whole poem either uncertain, or impossible to resolve. 'Vers de Société', 'Reasons for Attendance' and 'Wild Oats' are typical examples of this kind of poem. In 'Reasons for Attendance', for example, the final line is a revelation of the speaker's character which causes a re-evaluation of the entire poem.

    In this chapter and the last, however, we have come across poems that do not respond to our 'characterisation' approach in the same way. These poems, mostly from Larkin's later work, do not develop the speaker's character as ironic, so that his utterances are undercut or devalued. They do not display the layers of contradiction and self-deception that encircle an insoluble issue like fortifications, in many of Larkin's poems. Instead, we seem to read the poet's single character, and this is expressed directly, not undercut by irony. The voices we hear in these poems, then, are more reliable and authoritative. They may modulate between different dictions, and employ conversational techniques to create an impression of friendly intimacy, or common speech; but they are not constructed over an ironic weave of self-contradicting uncertainties. When writing in this later manner, the poet's overriding concern seems to be to express his ideas in verse. Poems we have studied, that are written in this different manner, include 'The Building' and 'Aubade'. These were composed in 1972 and 1977 respectively, so we have called this more direct style Larkin's 'later manner', despite the fact that there are examples of 'characterisation' poems from the 1970s, as well.[8]

Having realised the comparative absence of self-negating irony in these poems, we have adapted our approach and treated them differently. Put simply, we have devoted less effort to analysing the speaker's character. We have concentrated on following the train of emotion and thought in the poem instead, and applied our minds to more conventional interpretation. The important point is to be flexible: look at your response to each poem, and use your observation and sense to choose which analytical approaches will be most fruitful. It is frustrating to study a poem with pre-conceptions, hoping to unearth something that is not there. Recognise this quickly, move on and try a different approach.

2   *Careful reading and careful thought can be crucial.* This is true of any study, of course. However, in this chapter, we have found instances where it is particularly true of studying Larkin. In many of the poems we have studied, Larkin practises mis-direction. In other words, he encourages us and points us towards a particular conclusion, only to pull the rug from under us and show that we had adopted a superficial, over-confident view. There are many

poems that do this: 'Vers de Société', 'Self's the Man', 'Toads', 'Reasons for Attendance', 'Annus Mirabilis' and 'Wild Oats', to name only a few. In this chapter, we have found that very careful thought indeed is necessary to a reading of the whole. Two examples are worth remembering now.

When we studied 'An Arundel Tomb', we faced the power of that sonorous final line, 'What will survive of us is love'. Critics have argued for decades about the balance between optimism and pessimism in this famous poem. However, we noticed the phrase 'Rigidly they / Persisted', and the accent placed on 'Persisted' by its position at the start of a stanza. The word is highlighted, our attention drawn to it, and we commented that this weighting provokes ambiguity. Do we admire their persistence, or do we see it as obstinacy? Noticing this led us, in turn, to think of the phrase in its context. The preceding two stanzas explain that the couple's intentions have been thwarted, and their new significance is an unintended accident. So, as a result of careful reading and thought, we recognised 'Persisted' in a different, more complex way. Such rigidity is a sign of their helplessness, and we respond by pitying them, trapped in their stone representations while the world changes unpredictably around them.

The simpler example of careful reading comes from 'Church Going'. Most commentaries focus on the overt theme of religion's decline, and the social function it no longer fulfils. However, we read the line 'And what remains when disbelief has gone?' with care, noticing that '*dis*belief' reverses the expected meaning. This, which appears to be the speaker's unconscious slip of the tongue, certainly adds a further dimension to the whole of the rest of the poem. It adds depth, for example, to our understanding of the speaker's part-mischievous, part-compulsive behaviour, described in the first two stanzas. Arguably, the apparently accidental prefix 'dis-' shifts the emphasis of the poem and leads to a reappraisal of the final stanza's significance.

So, it is self-evident that careful reading and careful thought can be crucial when you study poetry. With Larkin, however, the point is worth reiterating again and again. He will mis-direct us with all the power of his consummate poetic skills, persuading us with the sonorous finality at the end of 'An Arundel Tomb', and with the fine musicality and rhythm of lines 55–7 from 'Church Going'. It is up to us to read carefully, and think carefully, so that we pick up the half-buried details that may shift the subject matter, or the balance, of a poem.

Suggested Work

In this chapter, we have considered Larkin's responses to the twentieth-century atheism and rationalism in which he was brought up. In each of the poems we have looked at, we have found that he explores these issues more or less in relation to the problem of death. Religion once provided a belief to 'contravene / The coming dark'; but Larkin, and others in a world of declining faith, have to face the intolerable prospect of complete annihilation, and the absurdity of 'nothing to think with', in other ways. At the same time, we have found that the poems vary greatly in mood, from comedy, through ironic amusement, and resignation, to bleak terror. We have also found a degree of affirmation in some poems, albeit limited, such as the lines describing light and birdsong from 'An Arundel Tomb', or the 'sun-comprehending glass' from 'High Windows'. It is worth pursuing the varieties of Larkin's treatments of themes of death and absurdity through a wider reading of his poems.

Look at the theme of death in 'The Old Fools' (*CP*, 196–7); then look at the early poem 'Under a Splendid Chestnut Tree' (*CP*, 43–4), 'Continuing to Live' (*CP*, 94), 'Age' (*CP*, 95), 'The View' (*CP*, 195) and 'Faith Healing' (*CP*, 126). Identify the role of religion in these poems where it is present; and consider the responses to death or an atheist outlook that are presented. For each of these poems, try to judge the balance between cynical and affirmative elements. Then compare them, identifying shifts in mood.

5

Travel, Skies and Observation

This chapter is not divided into detailed analyses of particular poems. However, the following poems receive considerable attention: 'The Whitsun Weddings' (*CP*, 114–16); 'Dockery and Son' (*CP*, 152–3); 'Arrival' (*CP*, 51); 'I Remember, I Remember' (*CP*, 81–2); 'Arrivals, Departures' (*CP*, 65); 'Here' (*CP*, 136–7); 'Lines on a Young Lady's Photograph Album' (*CP*, 71–2); 'Deceptions' (*CP*, 32). Several other poems are also referred to in passing.

In this chapter we look at the poet's role, and his relation to the world around him. It is noticeable that many of Larkin's poems place the speaker, or observer, on a journey either by road or rail, so that travel may be considered as a metaphor for the poet's relation to his surroundings and subjects. It is equally noticeable that many of Larkin's speakers observe through one or another form of frame, such as a window ('Sad Steps', 'High Windows', and parts of 'Vers de Société' are examples we have met) or a photograph ('Lines on a Young Lady's Photograph Album' and 'Wild Oats' come to mind). Rather than choosing a few poems for detailed analysis, we will refer to many, because this topic is best suited to a wide-ranging survey. However, we should begin by reconsidering the travel poem Larkin chose for the title of his second mature collection: 'The Whitsun Weddings'.

Journeys

Let us look at the speaker's situation in 'The Whitsun Weddings'. First, he enters the poem from the rush of ordinary life. He was 'late getting away' and is concerned about the time. This suggests that the journey itself is an exceptional interlude: as he remarks, he feels 'all sense of being in a hurry gone' once in the train. One feature of travelling, then, is that it is a gap in time. Also, responsibility is transferred from the individual to the vehicle, and this is conveyed in the poem as the pronoun 'I' changes to 'we' in line 6. As the journey begins, then, the speaker is taken out of his life, as it were, and placed in a timeless, passive interlude. At the same time, he loses individual responsibility and becomes a part of 'we', the train.

During the poem the speaker's role is that of an observer. He begins by observing the countryside, then settles to read, until the weddings obtrude on his consciousness and he becomes increasingly absorbed by them. His only action, however, is to penetrate the frame that divides him from these events, when he 'leant / More promptly out next time, more curiously'. For most of the poem the communal pronoun 'we' persists. Then, in the penultimate stanza, he draws a distinction between 'They' – the newly married couples – and 'I': their marriages 'got under way', while 'I' thinks of London. Afterwards, the communal 'we' reasserts itself strongly: 'we' were aimed, 'we' raced and 'we' slowed.

As the newly-weds, couple after couple, board the train, the speaker appears to identify with them in something akin to the liberation from 'hurry' he felt in stanza 1. 'We', that is the train and all aboard including the speaker and the couples, are 'Free at last'. However, they have also absorbed, and are 'loaded with the sum' of everything the wedding-parties on the platform 'saw'. This seems to describe a curious interaction: the speaker identifies with the couples and the train, yet 'we' have also been watched, so there are two classes of observer. The speaker observes, and the wedding-parties observe. The wedding-parties take in 'a secret', 'a religious wounding', even 'success so huge and wholly farcical', while all of these also load the speaker and his trainful of fellow-passengers.

All of this interaction between observer and observed, between vehicle and the non-travelling world, is called 'this frail / Travelling coincidence'. The final lines suggest that such a 'coincidence' has 'changed' them. It is natural for the couples to be 'changed' by their wedding-days, but the speaker appears to have been changed as well, because the whole final stanza is firmly couched in the collective 'we'. The consequence of this 'frail / Travelling coincidence', then, is that the speaker as well as the newly married couples are invested with 'all the power / That being changed can give'.

The observer's status in 'The Whitsun Weddings', then, is more complex than that of a mere onlooker. The poem suggests an interaction between the train-ensconced, passive poet, removed from his life and from time, and the life he observes. He leans through the window into the world of the weddings, and is part of the 'Travelling coincidence', loaded with the power of wedding-ritual. The other relevant point from this poem is that the farewell parties stand on the ends of platforms 'As if out on the end of an event'. The platform end where a journey starts is symbolic of a particularly intense moment people experience 'on the end of' a mysterious social ritual such as a wedding.

We should notice, in passing, that Larkin chooses to mention a triad of elements – sky, water and land – as slipping away at the start of a railway journey, in both 'The Whitsun Weddings' ('Where sky and Lincolnshire and water meet') and in 'Dockery and Son' ('Canal and clouds and colleges subside'). In 'Dockery and Son' the speaker is 'ignored' as he catches his train, and has found 'the door of where I used to live: / Locked'. This may remind us of 'The Whitsun Weddings', as in both cases the speaker seems to be excluded from contact with day-to-day life as the journey starts. In 'Dockery and Son', meditation begins on the train, and leads to sleep.

The stop at Sheffield, in stanza 3, frames the remainder of the poem. The speaker places himself precisely within a symbolic system: he stands on the end of the platform and looks at 'the ranged / Joining and parting lines' which 'reflect a strong unhindered moon'. Interpreting this speaker's situation is quite simple. The 'joining and parting' lines clearly represent the paths of different people's journeys through life: his own and Dockery's 'lines' parted years before but the Dean's remark means that they have momentarily 'joined' again. The train journey is therefore a journey through life, all tracks leading where the poem itself leads, towards 'the only end of age'. In this poem it seems appropriate that our lives run on 'lines' that will take us in different directions irrespective of our wishes. This symbol suits the determinist tone of stanza 5, with its theory of 'innate assumptions' that 'harden into all we've got'.

There are other poems in which travel and vehicles figure. 'Arrival' (*CP*, 51) records the speaker moving to a new town. The focus is on his freedom from both the past, and any ties to the life of his new home-town, that begins so energetically as a morning 'flashes', windows 'flock open' and 'curtains fly out like doves'. In contrast to this activity, expressed in images of teeming life, the newly arrived speaker finds his 'past dries in a wind'. He wishes to lie down under the town's 'indifference'. The moment of his arrival is celebrated, then, as a special time when he can be solitary:

> For this ignorance of me
> Seems a kind of innocence.

He is aware that this state is temporary, for he will 'wound' it by meeting people and settling in to the life of the town; but he wishes the moment of exclusion from time and life to be prolonged: 'Let me breathe till then / Its milk-aired Eden'. The final line suggests that such moments outside ordinary life – like the railway journey of 'The Whitsun Weddings', and this short period after arriving in a new place – are special, because they are an exception to all other times; and all other times are 'A style of dying only'.

'I Remember, I Remember' (*CP*, 81–2) presents the detached experience of a train passenger from a different angle. The speaker finds himself, to his surprise, in the town of his birth and childhood. As in 'The Whitsun Weddings', he breaches the window-barrier that separates observer from the world outside: 'I leant far out, and squinnied', looking for familiarity with the town he once knew well. However, a barrier remains: Coventry has changed, and he does not recognise anything. Instead of contact, the speaker finds himself separated, excluded and ignored, and relapses back into his journey: 'A whistle went: / Things moved. I sat back'. This event is comparable to the few lines preceding his train journey in 'Dockery and Son', when he found the 'door of where I used to live: / Locked'. There, we have the impression that his failed attempt to find his past in Oxford pushes him out of life and onto the train. Here, he is unable to re-enter a past he believes is through the carriage-window, and he is whisked away by the continuing journey.

We have been developing the idea that a journey is, in some sense, a metaphor for the poet's relation to the world. He is in a temporary situation and in a position withdrawn from everyday life. While the train carries him past others, there is a barrier between him and the real life in which they are immersed. In 'The Whitsun Weddings', the poet's observation of others also entails a form of interaction: he is able to become part of a collective experience that leaves him 'changed'. In other poems, however, we find him alternately longing to preserve his isolation, and hopelessly searching for some form of contact with the past, but pushed back into his travelling isolation by failure. Clearly, the interface between journeying, observing poet, and the ordinary life of towns and communities, is a complex division, charged with the poet's changing emotions. The barrier itself attracts ambivalent urges: sometimes the poet longs to break it down, and at other times he wishes to defend his isolation behind it.

In passing, we should notice that the travelling poet shares experiences with patients in hospital, or in an ambulance. The patient in 'Ambulances' finds that 'the unique random blend / Of families and fashions' that has been his life, 'At last begin to loosen'; and in 'The Building' those in the waiting-room are on 'ground curiously neutral, homes and names / Suddenly in abeyance'. These evocations are reminiscent of the speaker in 'The Whitsun Weddings' who finds a timeless state, separated from his day-to-day life, as he catches the train. We can suggest that being taken out, or ejected, from the muddle and crowds of everyday living is an important part of the poet's circumstances whether presented as a railway journey or a terminal illness. It is, of course, a double-edged benefit. In both cases, whether train or hospital, it clears the mind and provides perspective; on the other hand, being 'caught without / People or drink', or contemplating the 'joining and parting lines', can lead to a confrontation with 'unresting death' that is always there: 'age, and then the only end of age'.

'Arrivals, Departures' (*CP*, 65) is an inversion of 'Arrival'. This speaker could be an inhabitant of the town that was new and strange in the earlier poem. Travellers arriving and leaving disturb the town as people are 'nudged from comfort' because the strangers are 'Horny dilemmas at the gate once more'. This is, however, another poem about the potential for contact, and therefore for relationships, between travellers and a settled community. The refrains chanted on arrival and departure are both pessimistic. Possible relationships are a mistake, an invitation saying '*Come and choose wrong*'. So, should the traveller depart? '*O not for long*' is the refrain. Only the speaker believes that contact might have resulted in 'happiness'. The poem as a whole leaves us with its 'Horny dilemma'. The town's resident wonders whether he can 'safely' avoid making contact; while travellers are caught in a hopeless bind between wrong choices on the one hand, and temporary journeying isolation on the other. The dilemma of travelling, a metaphor for the fraught, unsettled relationship between the poet and his community, is never resolved.

'Here' (*CP*, 136–7), the poem Larkin wrote after six years in Hull, celebrates that town's

> ... domes and statues, spires and cranes cluster
> Beside grain-scattered streets, barge-crowded water ...

and its 'cut-price crowd' of 'residents from raw estates'. On the other hand he describes it as a traveller's backwater, a 'terminate' place where 'only salesmen and relations come'; and the poem is in the form of a journey. We approach Hull 'Swerving east' then 'swerving through fields' and 'swerving to solitude' (all in the opening stanza), and the town itself is a 'surprise' before the journey takes us right through and out at the other side, over the desolate plain of Holderness to the seashore where 'Ends the land suddenly'. The triple repetition of 'swerving' suggests that the journey itself is rather like a roller-coaster and lends a hair-raising quality to the swift passage through the crowded town centre. The poem finally celebrates isolation, not Hull at all: 'Here is unfenced existence: / Facing the sun, untalkative, out of reach'. Those who regard 'Here' as evidence of Larkin's affection for Hull may not have followed the journey to its conclusion. On his journeys, then, the poet is tortured by anxieties about potential contact between his exiled, observant persona, and the communities from which he is sealed away; but his isolation is a recurrent motif, ending 'Facing the sun, untalkative, out of reach'. In some poems, the poet's isolated exclusion is an accident of circumstances; but in 'Here', it is the journey's aim.

'Facing the sun', at the end of 'Here', suitably reconnects the motif of travelling with the image of a poet contemplating the sky, another figure that makes frequent appearances among Larkin's poems. We met this idea in 'Sad Steps', in the evening view from solitude in 'Vers de Société', and in the sudden opening out to 'deep blue air' at the end of 'High Windows'. This image, like that of the traveller, remains problematic. The journeying poet is out of control, relaxed, passive, curious, fearful, exiled, by turns. Similarly, the poet facing the sky is sometimes relieved, sometimes haunted by remorse, sometimes attracted and fascinated, and often terrified.

Framing Devices

In our discussion of journeys, we have realised that the carriage-window is simultaneously a frame and a barrier, and we picked out two occasions – in 'The Whitsun Weddings' and 'I Remember, I Remember' – when the poet pushes through this frame, broaches the window-barrier, in his curiosity and eagerness. This motif links with a number of poems in which the poet's relation to what he observes is defined by a framing device.

The most obvious of these is 'Lines on a Young Lady's Photograph Album', in which the speaker looks at photographs from the past of an attractive girl.[1] This poem further underlines the volatility of relations between the poet and what he observes, as the speaker passes through intense emotions while contemplating the desired girl's past. He begins in a voyeuristic state, and is clearly sexually excited by the challenge of gaining access to the album. The opening words, 'At last you yielded up the album', tell us plainly that there has been a flirtatious chase; and the double entendre continues with the graphic 'which, / Once open, sent me distracted' and a rash of obvious eating imagery: 'confectionery, too rich'; 'I choke'; 'nutritious images'; and so on. Larkin spares no effort to characterise the speaker as rather disgusting, slavering over the album: 'My swivel eye hungers from pose to pose'.

The album presents a challenge, however: the speaker's insecurities appear as the pictures 'strike at my control', and his jealousy is aroused by 'disquieting' chaps, photographs of male friends from her past. These elements are the natural corollary to his initial sexual excitement, before he diverts himself into a meditation on photography and the past. Photography is objective, and the past hurts – 'lacerates' – because it is the past and will never be recovered. Photography, then, persuades him that she was 'a real girl in a real place'; and this in turn hurts him because it is the past, unreachable. The crucial development is between the speaker's original excitement, when the pictures were mere 'poses', objects to be looked at; and his new perception, that they represent real life. His response is to 'cry'.

He is deeply disturbed by the photograph album: how can he reach an emotional equilibrium? First, he recognises that his tears contain an element of luxury: there is misery in being excluded from the pictures, and so from her real past life. On the other hand, there is relief that he can indulge his emotion safely, because their love affair is also over: they are 'free to cry' and no future together will 'call on us to justify / Our grief'. This point is underlined for us. The speaker is comforted because he can mourn her 'without a chance of consequence'. His emotions become more and more comfortable until he reaches the point of seeing the album as a frame into which he can pack away, and preserve, what he wants from both her past, and their relationship:

> It holds you like a heaven, and you lie
> Unvariably lovely there,
> Smaller and clearer as the years go by.

At the same time as he reaches such a comfortable conclusion, luxuriating in his tears, the speaker completes and satisfies the sexual arousal with which the poem began. He deals with his jealousy by reflecting that her past is just as unreachably past for any other man as it is for him ('a past that no one now can share'); and he steals a picture, 'this one of you bathing', presumably to titillate his lust in the future.

'Lines on a Young Lady's Photograph Album' is a comic poem showing how a voyeur achieves his vicarious pleasure, but it is also more than this. When attempting to explain his poetry, Larkin wrote that creating a poem is 'the only possible reaction to a particular kind of experience, a feeling that you are the only one to have noticed something, something especially beautiful or sad or significant'.[2] This poem wryly acknowledges a more complex and emotional relationship between the poet and his subject. He desires the subject because it excites him; but (as in the trains) he is immobilised between desire and inevitable failure. He seeks to preserve what he sees, and he is jealously possessive. Finally, his success in owning a 'snapshot' means that the moment is held 'like a heaven' and 'unvariably lovely': in other words, the poet feels that he has gained a victory over time, change and death. The ironic undertow of sexual inadequacy, luxurious sorrow and illicit theft forms a comic, derogatory counterpoint to this metaphor-story of object and observer, and acknowledges that Freud's comments about artists are also accurate. Art is not only the preservation of beauty and a victory over time and death; it is also a rather seedy process by means of which the inadequate artist exploits the 'wishful constructions of his life of phantasy' to obtain 'honour, power and the love of women'.[3] We remember that this element is alluded to again when the speaker of 'Wild Oats' keeps photographs of 'bosomy rose with fur gloves on', in his wallet.

We have read 'Lines on a Young Lady's Photograph Album' as a metaphorical essay on the poet/observer's relationship with his subject, life. This is a justifiable approach to the poem because the motif of observation through a frame or window is a recurrent feature of Larkin's poems. In 'Reasons for Attendance' (*CP*, 80), for example, the poet's dual motives appear again. The speaker is drawn to 'the lighted glass / To watch the dancers', and his ambivalent motives in remaining outside include dedication to 'that lifted, rough-tongued bell / (Art, if you like)', as well as the possibility that he is merely inadequate and has 'lied' to himself. As in 'Lines on a Young Lady's Photograph Album', the poem's structure suggests a Freudian explanation of the artist's motives. 'Art' is placed as the alternative to the 'wonderful feel of girls': art is the alternative to sex. In 'Whatever Happened?' (*CP*, 74), the past is immediately 'gone, thank God!' By the next day it is 'kodak-distant' and we say that 'Perspective brings significance' as an excuse for ridding ourselves of the real experience by reducing it to a picture: 'What can't be printed can be thrown away'. This parallels the snapshot he steals in 'Lines on a Young Lady's Photograph Album', which leaves her 'smaller and clearer' as time passes. In these poems, Larkin seems to admit that he gratefully discards part of the real experience when he reduces and distils that experience into poetic form. Notice that all the problematic violence of jealousy and grief is disposed of, when the 'Young Lady' is reduced to a trophy snapshot and becomes 'smaller and clearer' as time passes.

If these poems do portray the poet's relation to his subject, Larkin clearly implies that creating a poem is a morally questionable activity. Specifically, he seeks to preserve something, but in an idealised and dehumanised form. The girl in the photograph is held by the picture 'like a heaven', thus satisfying the poet's urge to escape from the emotions of real life into an idealised world: the image connects with his wish to breathe his isolated 'milk-aired Eden' in 'Arrival'. Furthermore, his desire for this idealised state is often explicitly driven by guilt, shame or failure.

If we appear to be taking a cynical attitude to the act of poetic composition, this is because such cynicism is present in the poems. Thinking back to the first two chapters, remember that one of our initial observations was that Larkin's poems leave us with unresolved ambivalences. The structure of insights in such poems is carefully constructed so that different solutions are balanced against each other, and cancel each other out; and we have often been able to identify a gap, or 'silence', where we might expect a causal explanation. We have also remarked that alternative readings often set a higher, intellectual or artistic solution against a lower solution. This 'lower' solution may be vulgar or shameful (as in 'Lines on a Young Lady's Photograph Album' or 'Wild Oats'), or self-deceptive (as in 'Self's the Man' and 'Church Going'), and is often comic. There is no question that Larkin regarded the process of poetic composition as something complex, mysterious and wonderful. Equally, he consistently revealed the 'lower' motives that contribute to the making of poetry.

Before moving on, it is worth noticing that there are explorations of literary framing devices as well as the visual frames we have discussed. In 'I Remember, I Remember', for example, the speaker considers his childhood in Coventry and immediately enters into a parody of famous literary childhoods penned by D. H. Lawrence and Dylan Thomas. These word-pictures are surrounded by negatives: the garden 'where I did not invent / Blinding theologies', the family 'I never ran to', the bracken 'where I never trembling sat' and the doggerel that 'was not set up'. The language, heavy with parodic irony, mocks the other authors' tricks in turning their early experiences into passionate verse and prose. Such parody suggests that words have the power to turn an ordinary childhood into something significant, and mocks the process. Larkin's speaker goes further than this, however. The invention of 'theologies', stories of passion and early literary brilliance are all egocentric boasts; and Larkin's negatives deny the validity of these just as he exposes the authors' literary tricks. Finally, we should notice that the theologies were 'Blinding', and that experience 'became a burning mist'. Larkin's poem, then, not only attacks the overblown style of such childhood memories. It also suggests that they reveal no insight: they are merely vague, exploiting mystery to cover a lack of clear understanding. 'I Remember, I Remember' explores literary 'pictures' of childhood. Seeking a valid reality behind these constructs, the speaker comes to a nihilistic conclusion: 'Nothing, like something, happens anywhere'.

Another literary frame is considered in 'Deceptions', the poem that provided the title for *The Less Deceived*. The origin of this poem is an anecdote from Mayhew's *London Labour and the London Poor*. The story of a rape evokes sympathy for the victim, and the speaker responds appropriately:

> Even so distant, I can taste the grief,
> Bitter and sharp with stalks, he made you gulp.

From this point, however, the poem grows to question the literary frame through which a reader reaches this past event, and which determines the reader's response. 'Deceptions' then creates an alternative in which the victim is 'less deceived' than the rapist, whose violence leaves him in 'fulfilment's desolate attic'. This poem has been highly controversial.[4] Our point here is that Larkin's speaker distrusts the literary frame, and seeks to reinterpret the past event. As in 'I Remember, I Remember', this process of denying the frame leads him to reframe the supposed significance of the event.

In addition to specific framing devices and journeys, there is a more general sense in which Larkin places his speakers in itinerant or temporary circumstances. So, for example, the speaker of 'Church Going' removes his bicycle-clips, his church visit both casual and compulsive, but clearly in passing; and the speaker of 'Poetry of Departures', although ensconced in 'my life, in perfect order', is not settled, and dreams of walking out on *the whole crowd*. In 'Mr Bleaney' (*CP*, 102–3), the speaker rents a room that is sparse and negative: 'Bed, upright chair, sixty-watt bulb, no hook / Behind the door, no room for books or bags'. These details enhance our sense that the speaker arrives without encumbrances such as 'books or bags', and the lack of settled comfort is emphasised by the missing lampshade and armchair. The speaker breaks off at 'bags', and says 'I'll take it', his eagerness again suggesting that the room's very emptiness suits him. Even the thoughts aroused by renting the room are temporary: the speaker gives up wondering about both Mr Bleaney, the previous occupant and himself in the final three words: 'I don't know'.

We can suggest that such poems are merely examples of a wider, more generalised sense that Larkin's works exude: the underlying truth that all life's experiences are temporary. Even with speakers at their most settled, many of Larkin's poems turn on the fragility of our lives, our short existence and an ever-present awareness of death. We have seen this in 'Aubade' where, despite his repetitive routines ('I work all day, and get half-drunk at night'), the speaker finds that an overwhelming awareness of death is 'always there'. In 'Talking in Bed' (*CP*, 129), the intimacy that might erase such thoughts is ineffective: instead, the speaker is aware that 'Outside, the wind's incomplete unrest / Builds and disperses clouds about the sky'. Conversely, some speakers cling to their settled routines in order to drown out negative thoughts. We remember how the speaker in 'Aubade' waits for the telephone to ring, or letters to be delivered; and how work will 'help' the speaker 'down Cemetery Road' in 'Toads Revisited'.

Concluding Discussion

Much of the discussion in this chapter has filled out conclusions that have been apparent from our previous studies. For example, we were already aware of the prevalence of a death-theme in Larkin's poetry, and we knew that issues of isolation and exclusion bedevil many of his speakers. However, these discussions have raised further questions also, about how we receive and organise our perceptions of life; and about our relation to events either as they pass or in the past. The following are points we have noticed.

1   Larkin often uses journeys as metaphors. These journey-metaphors have a dual significance. First, they suggest a journey through life. It is in this sense that the wedding-guests on the end of a platform are 'out on the end of an event' in 'The Whitsun Weddings', and the speaker in 'Dockery and Son', also on the end of a platform, contemplates the 'joining and parting lines' of his own and Dockery's lives. This sense is also suggested in 'Here', where the helter-skelter journey through life terminates at the seashore, 'Facing the sun, untalkative, out of reach'. Secondly, journeys are a metaphor for the poet's relation to ordinary life: he is withdrawn, taken out of time and out of contact with hum-drum routine. Such journeys allow the poet to explore how he perceives reality, meditates upon what he sees and attempts to respond. On train journeys, the speaker is additionally trapped in the vehicle and his journey determined by the 'joining and parting lines'.

2   We compared the poet's state of separation from ordinary life in railway trains with the separation he describes in ambulances and hospitals. The suggestion is that, like the terminally ill, the poet/observer is separated from others by an unnaturally continuous awareness of death.

3   The end of the journey in 'Here' exemplifies another metaphorical figure found frequently in Larkin's poems: the poet facing the sky. We find this motif in 'Talking in Bed', 'Sad Steps', 'High Windows' and many other poems. The sky is often filled with the unceasing movement of clouds, and is also 'cavernous', showing

'nothing, and is nowhere, and is endless'. We have suggested that these skies represent coming face to face with futility, change and either death or infinity. The effect on the poet is usually to paralyse him. In 'Sad Steps' 'One shivers slightly, looking up there', and in 'Talking in Bed' the conviction that people are insignificant ('None of this cares for us') overwhelms the couple's intimacy and silences them. In short, it has the effect described in 'Aubade' of making 'all thought impossible' and leaves the poet 'untalkative, out of reach'.

4   Thinking back to Chapter 4, we can interpret these skies as representing the absurd because they remind the poet that his ego and consciousness are ridiculous in the context of infinite indifference. They give the poet/speaker a sudden shock of absurdity.

5   Many of Larkin's poems and speakers observe through a framing device. In this chapter, we noticed the framing carriage-windows in poems of railway journeys, and looked at 'Lines on a Young Lady's Photograph Album' in some detail. We noticed the turbulent emotions through which the speaker passes. This poem is suggestive about the process by which life is turned into art. There is a shameful and comic characterisation of the speaker, and at the same time the half-claim of a pyrrhic victory over time and change that keeps the woman 'Unvariably lovely'. Other poems such as 'Whatever Happened?' and 'Maiden Name' (*CP*, 101) further explore this theme.

6   As we might expect, Larkin's poems refuse to resolve the question of the artist's motives, methods and character. There is a higher strand in which we find noble ideals such as that 'rough-tongued bell / (Art, if you like)' and claims of a victory over time and change. At the same time, there is a lower strand: the seedy character of the voyeur and social inadequate, reducing life to a comfortable trophy, and modulating his real pain into a melancholy he can indulge and enjoy. Larkin does not reject either of these versions. Like many incompatibles in his poetry, they continue in uneasy coexistence.

7   We also mentioned some literary framing devices, the parodies of D. H. Lawrence and Dylan Thomas in 'I Remember, I Remember', and the Mayhew anecdote that gives rise to 'Deceptions'. In both

cases, the poem's speaker invalidates the literary artefact. In both cases it can be argued that his rejection of the literary frame leads him to nihilism: 'Nothing' in one poem, and a shocking inhumanity in the other.

8   There is a sense in which Larkin's whole *oeuvre* can be said to be about writing, since so much is devoted to exploring interactions between a lone, isolated speaker, and the world he observes; and to constructing a permanent uncertainty about what he feels, what he thinks, what he wants and why he wants it.

Suggested Work

This chapter has referred to a number of poems, but there are important contributions to the question of the observer's relation to his world, that we have not mentioned. It will be rewarding to study further poems, and reach your own conclusions about the complex of attractions and repulsions, and the pleasures and fears of both society and isolation, that they explore.

Look at 'To the Sea' (*CP*, 173–4). This can be considered as a journey poem as the speaker is an itinerant visitor to the beach; or as primarily concerned with memory; or as exploring a social ritual. Look at 'Livings II' (*CP*, 187–8). Here, the speaker appears to celebrate isolation within a savage natural world. Finally, study 'The Dance' (*CP*, 154–8), a detailed exploration of the speaker's ambivalence in the face of society and relationships. In this poem, it will be revealing to trace the speaker's moves from temporary situation to temporary situation, and his feelings about each of them.

6

'Double-yolked with meaning and meaning's rebuttal': Conclusions

This is a short chapter that suggests some tentative working conclusions based on the studies we have carried out in Chapters 1–5. The quotation that is the chapter's title comes from 'If, My Darling' (*CP*, 41), and expresses a complex, unresolved response to existence. In the poem, Larkin imagines his 'darling' jumping into his head and being driven to distraction by what she finds there, because everything is 'double-yolked with meaning and meaning's rebuttal'. Metaphorically, our approach to Larkin's poems has attempted to 'jump, like Alice' into his head – or more precisely, into the place from where all his poetic voices speak. At some moments during our study, we may have been tempted to 'be stopping [our] ears' like the poem's 'darling'. This is not the final effect of Larkin's poetry, however. Despite his assiduous self-characterisation as an indecisive, misanthropic, irritable and irritating man, the poems remain entertaining, pleasing and fascinating. Why?

1 Most of Larkin's poems are immediately accessible, intelligible as stories and characters. In the preceding chapters, we have argued that each poem is built as a carefully balanced structure of ideas. They are balanced because the ideas are constructed to cancel each other out, or to 'undercut' each other.

153

2   The missing ideas are often as significant as those that are fully expressed. In other words, Larkin constructs 'silences' in his poems that are often as important as the 'utterance'.

3   We have called the elements Larkin uses to structure his poems 'ideas'. This is a general term we have used for convenience. 'Ideas' includes attitudes, reactions, opinions, impulses and emotions as well as concepts.

4   Opinions, impulses, emotions and attitudes have energy: they push you towards choices, and actions; or they push you away from actions. Therefore, the structure of a Larkin poem is dynamic: 'ideas' are in a state of energetic tension, pushing against each other, undermining each other, overwhelming each other, turning each other around.

5   A 'dynamic' structure is made up of energy. Larkin creates dynamic structures that are balanced between opposing energies so that they remain, held in tension, in a sort of unresolved equilibrium. No one energy is allowed to dominate, so the poems remain caught in balance with no possibility of movement, change or resolution.

6   In several of Larkin's poems, the 'silence' is a place where we expect to find a causal relationship between two ideas explained, and the poem does not explain. If there were an explanation, the poem could be resolved either one way or the other. This would remove the structure's balance, enable the poet to decide, take action: the whole problem of the poem would be resolved. However, there is no explanation, only a silence. Therefore, the silence in a poem often holds the whole poem in shape. To put it another way, without the silence, there would be no poem. For an example of such a balancing silence, think back to our analysis of 'Wild Oats' (see Chapter 2 above). The story told in this poem, by implication, provokes two distinct reactions to the speaker: either we sympathise with him because his upbringing has left him too shy, awkward and embarrassed to find happiness; or we are repelled by his selfishness because he uses the 'friend in specs', wasting seven years of her youth, so that he can get pornographic excitement from snapshots of 'bosomy', and be set free from committing himself to any relationships for the rest of his life.

The poem does not tell us which young man is the 'real' speaker. The tone of the phrase 'Useful to get that learnt' remains ambivalent. The poem's silence on this vital question keeps the ambivalence alive and prevents us from responding with either sympathy or revulsion. We have to continue responding with both. Therefore, the 'silence' in the poem keeps the poem's structure in unsettled equilibrium.

7   Such balanced dynamic structures are pleasing. We have argued that these structures constitute the 'shape' of a Larkin poem: this is its aesthetic appeal, its 'beauty'. Each poem is a closed system, made up of contrary energies held in equilibrium.

8   The 'balance' of such shaped poems is the insoluble dilemma explored in that poem. The structure therefore re-enacts the impossibility of resolution, choice, decision, or movement.

9   We have looked at some of the dilemmas most commonly explored in Larkin's poems. These have included solitary or social living; staying single or committing to a relationship and marriage; the routine of work or adventurous escape; unsatisfactory reality, or art (and recovering the past); belief or disbelief; choice or determinism; affirmation or complaint. Many more insoluble dilemmas, and offshoots of these, have come up during our study of Larkin's poems.

10 Many of these issues seem to hinge on choices between solitary or lonely living on the one hand, and joining in with society or committing to a relationship, on the other hand. Those mentioned as solitary or social living, staying single or committing to a relationship and marriage, the routine of work or adventurous escape, unsatisfactory reality or art, can all be seen as belonging to a *Solitaire, Solidaire* dilemma.

11 However, the poems about these dilemmas are also about the impossibility of making a choice. Think back to our analysis of 'Self's the Man', for example. The choice between living single (the speaker) and marrying (Arnold) is the *Solitaire, Solidaire* dilemma on the surface of the poem. This so-called dilemma vanishes, however: both are selfish, and life may drive both of them mad. Therefore, the poem is not ultimately about the dilemma. Rather, it is about choice: is there such a thing as

choice? Is it futile? How can we choose when both courses are uncertain?

12 So, we can argue that the poems we have studied are almost all related to the underlying issues facing twentieth-century people. These issues are a consequence of being born into a world without a religious faith, dominated by rationalism and determinism. In such a world, it was difficult to find a satisfactory purpose in life, or a reason for living, because rationalist and determinist explanations of life tended to undermine belief in ideals and emphasise the insignificance of humanity in a vast mechanical universe. Furthermore, determinist explanations of human behaviour have tended to emphasise instinctive or biological drives that people find upsetting. Society thinks of such drives as shocking, low or vulgar. For example, Marx taught that history is about social groups or 'classes' pursuing their own interests and destroying each other violently; Darwin taught that biology and evolution is a vicious struggle between species, for survival; and Freud taught that love between the sexes is driven by infantile sexual lust, including patricidal and incestuous desires. Determinist explanations of life were disturbing, morally shocking and socially unacceptable.

13 Therefore, the search for a purpose in life that is pleasing, because it is morally higher than the vulgar mechanics of biology or economic power, was problematic for twentieth-century people.

14 We have found that many of Larkin's poems are balanced between higher and lower interpretations of life. In other words, the poems propose morally acceptable, affirmative or humane explanations of the speaker's circumstances; and cynical, pessimistic, selfish and disturbing, often coarse explanations. Larkin's art is to keep the two possible perceptions of life in play, not allowing either to be completely overruled. In this way, his poems re-enact twentieth-century dilemmas.

15 It is in this sense, that life either has a satisfying meaning or has no acceptable meaning, that the quotation in the title of this chapter is central to the experience Larkin's poems express and

recreate for the reader: life is 'double-yolked with meaning and meaning's rebuttal', and remains so without resolution.

These conclusions are, inevitably, broad generalisations: so-called 'conclusions' from a study of literature are never definitive, in any case. My aim in putting together the above ideas has simply been to draw upon ideas and insights that have come from our analyses of poems, in order to suggest a viable way in which Larkin's works can be read, appreciated and understood.

PART II

THE CONTEXT AND THE CRITICS

7

Larkin's Life and the Literary Context

The Life

Philip Arthur Larkin was born in August 1922, in Coventry, where his father Sydney was the Borough Treasurer. He died at the beginning of December 1985. His life therefore spans a childhood in the 1920s, the stock-market crash and the Great Depression, the rise of Nazism and international tension in the 1930s, the Second World War, postwar reconstruction and expansion, the 'swinging sixties', and extended into the first part of Mrs Thatcher's prime ministership in the 1980s. Historical background relevant to Larkin's literary output is the subject of the next chapter. Our present business is to sketch Philip Larkin's life. We will then enter into a brief discussion of the literary context in which he grew up and to which he contributed.

To make a coherent narrative of Larkin's life in such a small space as is available, we will take four threads in turn: education and work; personal and family life; writing and publication; friends.

Education and Work

Larkin was very short-sighted, tall and ungainly even as a child, and stammered. His father sent him to King Henry VIII School in Coventry, a good academic day school, where he stayed from the

161

age of 8 until he left to become an Oxford undergraduate at the age of 18, in the autumn of 1940. At school he was regarded as able but not having any remarkable ability, until he reached the sixth form, when he began to excel in English. He later pointed out that his stammer led him to pass lessons in constant fear of being asked to say something by the teacher; and many of his schoolfriends remember that he was an inventive planner of their mischief and pranks. By the time he left school he had already begun to write novels, stories and poetry.

In March 1940 Larkin took entrance examinations at St John's College, Oxford, and passed; in the summer he gained distinctions in English and History in the Higher Certificate examinations; and in the autumn he went up to St John's to read English. In December 1941 he was called to an army medical, which he failed due to weak eyesight, to his great relief. He was informed on New Year's Day 1942 that he would not be called up and could continue at university. Although Larkin himself was exempted, Oxford as a whole had to adapt in wartime. Numbers of his contemporaries were called up and had to interrupt their degrees, and numbers of the dons were also absent on active service, so that aged scholars were called out of retirement to teach. In the summer of 1943 Larkin took a First in his Schools, and became a BA.

A month after accepting his degree in full academic dress, with his admiring family looking on, and on his birthday as it happens, Larkin was interviewed for the Civil Service, and in September he was interviewed for the Foreign Office code-breaking outfit at Bletchley Park. He was rejected for both of these positions. Wondering what he could do in the way of a job, Larkin noticed an advertisement for a librarian in Wellington, Shropshire, and applied. He got the job, and started there on 1 December 1943. On his arrival, he found an antiquated and dilapidated library and he rented tiny, depressing digs. He feared loneliness and worried that he had made a terrible decision in taking the job. Although his letters consistently complained that Wellington was a dull place and the library a drudgery, and he affected contempt for this small backwater, Larkin was in fact an exceptionally successful librarian during the two and a half years he spent there. He transformed the library, lobbying the local Library

Committee for funds, and introducing a wider variety of books onto the shelves, including some modern authors who shocked some of the locals. He brightened the appearance of the library itself, reorganised the cataloguing and loans systems, built up interlibrary loans, and began a correspondence course to take Library Association examinations, the professional qualification for librarianship. Many Wellington people have put on record that Larkin had an invigorating and enlivening influence on cultural life, and that he brought a much larger and more varied clientele into the library, which had been almost moribund before his arrival.

In June 1946, feeling that he must escape from Wellington, Larkin applied for and was appointed to a sub-librarianship at the University College of Leicester. He started work there in September and stayed for four years. The college held about 200 students in 1946, and had quadrupled in size before Larkin left. The library kept pace, rapidly growing in size, budget, numbers of books and numbers of staff. Larkin finished his correspondence course and passed final Library Association exams in 1947. His colleagues remembered him as 'always fun to work with. He would lighten tasks with a keen sense of humour'.[1] The job at Leicester appears to have been quite congenial and, professionally, with the expansion of the library and catering to undergraduates and faculty, Larkin gained knowledge and experience he was able to use later in his career at Belfast and in Hull. The momentous event that occurred while he was working in Leicester was Sydney Larkin's death, in 1948.

In the summer of 1950, Larkin obtained a job as sub-librarian at the Queen's University, Belfast. He travelled to Ireland to take up his post in September. Again, he stayed in the job for four years. As a sub-librarian, Larkin was put in charge of Readers' Services. He was responsible for supervising the reading room, the stacks and the issue desk; and he also took charge of the book bindery and the photographic department. His job involved managing eighteen junior members of staff. This was a much bigger job than he had held at Leicester, and he was also asked to tour university libraries in England, and to contribute ideas for the remodelling and expansion of the library, which went ahead in 1952. After this, however, Larkin became familiar with his responsibilities, and the routine of the library became increasingly dull to him. Eventually, he applied for the job of Chief Librarian at the University of Hull, and was interviewed in November 1954. He was appointed, and took up his duties in Hull the following March.

The University College of Hull had been an extension of London University until it received its royal charter and became the University of Hull in 1954, the year Larkin was appointed. What he found, when he started work, was a library that was about to be rehoused in a new, much bigger building and anticipated enormous expansion. Plans had been drawn up, canvassed and passed, in a committee process that had taken many months, and everything was nearly ready. Larkin had to familiarise himself with the plans very quickly indeed, and decide where he wanted to propose modifications. He immediately immersed himself in the detail and entered into discussions with the University Buildings Officer, the Vice Chancellor and the architects, arguing for the changes he saw were necessary, attending meetings and drawing up revisions. His revised plans were accepted before the end of 1955, and building was scheduled to begin in January 1958. As the Chief Librarian, Larkin spent two more years simultaneously overseeing and managing all the preparations for the new building and for moving the stock and running the existing library efficiently. He mastered the detail of the plans, and proved a first-class administrator. The library staff moved 250 tons of books into the empty new building in September 1959, and those first four years in Hull appear to have been a successful period in Larkin's career. He was proud of the new library, had friends among the staff with whom he socialised and had achieved a professional reputation and success. The Queen Mother officially opened the Brynmor Jones Library (stage 1) in June 1960, although it had been stocked and in use since the preceding autumn. Larkin was pleased that his spacious new office boasted a desk bigger than the American President's.

Stage 2 of the Brynmor Jones Library began to occupy Larkin's working day almost immediately upon the completion of stage 1. The long process of committee meetings, planning meetings with the architects and lobbying to secure the funding for stage 2 began within a year. Larkin paid detailed attention to the plans and was adept at including practical measures to enhance the library's usefulness to its 'customers' and easy running for its staff. He also delegated a great deal of the work to a highly efficient sub-librarian he appointed in 1962, Brenda Moon, who later became his deputy. The go-ahead for stage 2 was given at the end of 1963, and building was scheduled to start in 1965 and be completed in 1968. In the event, the seven-storey tower was finally ready during 1969. Larkin was proud of his achievements in creating such an impressive and successful library, a task that had occupied much of his attention for the whole of his first fourteen years at Hull.

However, when stage 2 was finished in 1969, the rapid expansion of universities that took place in the fifties and sixties had already begun to go into reverse: budgets were not keeping pace with costs and inflation, and as Librarian, Larkin now entered a period of fighting rearguard actions to defend his library from cuts. His biographer tells us that 'by the late 1970s he felt that his work had become as disappointing as his home life'.[2]

Larkin returned to Oxford on a Visiting Fellowship for two terms in 1970–1, and Brenda Moon took over the library in his absence. In 1969, at Larkin's instigation, the first Compton poetry fellowship was awarded to C. Day-Lewis, and the practice of having a visiting poet attached to the university continued for four further years, with Larkin's close involvement. Despite these and other diversions, the end of fourteen years of building and expansion left a gap. Now, there was no future objective to aim for, no need to plan. All that was left was to oversee the day-to-day running of the library he had built, and fight a depressing battle to defend his budget. Larkin's secretary Betty Mackereth wrote that her boss slowed down 'a bit, you know, as if he couldn't see the point of anything. He'd always get his work done, the library would always be very efficiently run, but he'd often have a bit of a nap after lunch'.[3] However, the impression of a dull but undemanding routine as 'the toad work' helped Larkin through the days of his life would be misleading. As the seventies turned into the eighties, university funding cuts became even more swingeing, and the computerisation of the library, largely organised by Brenda Moon because Larkin disliked computers, took place. These years continued to be a depressing battle: the number of staff in the library was reduced by twenty-five, and there was a constant need to make decisions to stretch the budget as effectively as possible, as well as to fend off further shrinkage. In 1980, Larkin discussed taking early retirement with the Vice Chancellor. A combination of being assured that he was still regarded as valuable, and fear of the empty days retirement would bring, kept him working. Deteriorating health, and attending hospital for tests, began to interrupt his work during the spring of 1985. The operation to remove his oesophagus took place in June, and Larkin attempted to return to work for part-days when the new academic year began in the autumn, but was unable to keep it up. He died on 2 December 1985.

Personal and Family Life

Larkin consistently portrayed his childhood as boring, his family as unhappy and himself as isolated from an early age. In 'I Remember, I Remember', he mocks the joy and passion of Dylan Thomas's and D. H. Lawrence's memories, insisting on the emptiness of his own early years: 'Nothing, like something, happens anywhere'. He complained that his father was strict, distant and autocratic; and his mother was feeble, complaining and a household drudge. There was a sister, Kitty, ten years older than Philip, who married in 1944 when Larkin was in his first job at Wellington, and went to live in Loughborough. The siblings remained on good terms throughout their lives, but he showed little interest in her and confided, in letters to others, that he found her dull. Larkin highlighted a horror of his parents' marriage as the defining experience that left him isolated, terrified of marrying, and incapable of committing himself, throughout his life. We may add that his feeling of isolation was probably also a natural consequence of weak eyesight and a pronounced stammer.

Larkin's father Sydney was an efficient and strict Borough Treasurer, and a daunting personality. He was proud of his son's educational achievements, encouraged him in his reading, and helped him to frame his first job applications. On the other hand, Sydney Larkin was an admirer of Hitler and regularly visited Germany, reportedly attending several Nuremberg rallies during the 1930s. Apparently the Larkins had a statue of Hitler on the mantelpiece, and

Sydney was well known for extolling the virtues of German efficiency in public. Furthermore, he treated his wife more or less as a servant, criticising her for any small failings in the home, and he was contemptuous of women. We can only imagine the feelings of a boy growing up in a provincial town where his father cut such an arrogant and controversial figure; and in a home where his mother submitted, but uttered constant long-suffering complaints. It must have been even more confusing for the child Philip, because Sydney was a clever and intellectual personality, and an indulgent father.

When he returned to live at home after graduating, Larkin found the atmosphere unbearable. He was relieved to move away, and from then onwards he dreaded Christmas visits, which he found irritating. Sydney Larkin died in 1948, at the age of 63. This event brought about a change in Philip's life. It partly curtailed his freedom for the next twenty-nine years until the death of his mother, Eva Larkin, in 1977. He felt responsible for looking after his mother now that he was the 'man' of the family, and he became involved in emptying and selling the family house in Coten End, Coventry. The plan was for Eva to buy a house in Leicester so that Larkin could live there as her 'lodger'. He did not relish this idea, dreading the invasion of his privacy and the irritations that living with his mother again would entail; but he felt it his duty, and in due course they bought a house at Dixon Drive in Leicester, and Eva and Larkin moved in.

As he had feared, Larkin felt suffocated and irritated by living with his mother. They shared the house until he left for the job in Belfast, in 1950, and Eva went to live with Kitty in Loughborough. Towards the end of 1951 Eva took a house in the same street, and was settled there for the next twenty years until she began to become weak and confused, and moved into an old people's home in 1971. She felt unsettled after a few months, and insisted on returning to her own house, living there until she fell and broke her leg in 1972. Philip and Kitty then placed her in Berrystead Nursing Home, between Loughborough and Leicester, where she remained until her death.

Larkin stayed with his mother for weekends and at Christmas, and took her for a week's holiday each summer, up until the time when she became too frail. He visited the nursing home dutifully and frequently during the final five years of her life. So, his commitment of time and effort in caring for his widowed mother was a part of Larkin's life from the age of 26, until he was 55. In other words, it persisted through most of his adult life. Andrew Motion certainly thinks that Larkin used this commitment to his mother as a way of controlling and moderating his relationships with other women. Eva's needs would come first (even though her feeble dependent personality drove Larkin to distraction), and no relationship with another woman could become an equal commitment, or take a decisive turn, while this was the case. While he was in Belfast, Larkin became infatuated with a Winifred Arnott ('Lines on a Young Lady's Photograph Album'), and carried on an affair with Patsy Strang, the semi-detached wife of a colleague. Since Andrew Motion's biography was published, it has also come to light that Larkin had a love-affair with the novelist Patricia Avis in 1952–3. She became pregnant by him, and then suffered a miscarriage. Avis later incorporated a fictional portrait of Larkin as the character Rollo Jute in her novel *Playing the Harlot, or Mostly Coffee*, written between 1957 and 1959. Apart from these, it appears that four 'other women' took second place to his mother in Larkin's life.

Ruth Bowman was a 16-year-old schoolgirl when she came into Wellington Library at the end of 1943, and met Larkin. They struck up a friendship and gave rise to local gossip by being together a great deal. Ruth went to King's College, London, in 1945, but their relationship continued and they became lovers. When Larkin moved to Leicester, they continued to see each other at weekends until, two months after his father's death, they became engaged to be married – but at some unspecified date in the future, and only perhaps. When Larkin was about to go to Belfast, they planned to marry and go there together, but only for one heady evening. There followed a few days of wavering before Ruth wrote returning the ring and breaking off the engagement, finally recognising that Larkin would never be fully committed to her. This affair lasted through seven years. It blew hot and cold, and for five of those years the couple lived in different towns. In the end, Larkin seems to have been so hesitant and his interest so insultingly unpredictable that Ruth was forced to break off the engagement.

Monica Jones was a Lecturer teaching English Literature at the University College of Leicester when Larkin arrived there as sub-librarian. They had been at Oxford at the same time, although they never met there. Monica wore bright clothes, was strong-minded and appeared independent, and she and Larkin gradually formed a friendship. They became lovers in 1950, a few months before Larkin and Ruth Bowman finally broke off their engagement and he left for Belfast. Larkin's love-affair with Monica Jones continued for the rest of his life, never interrupted even by his other affairs. They holidayed together every year and sometimes more often, and saw each other in Belfast, in Hull and in Leicester at weekends, and when Larkin visited his mother in nearby Loughborough. Many holidays were spent at a cottage at Haydon Bridge, Northumberland, which Monica bought in 1961. However, Larkin and Monica did not live together until she became ill in 1983. On her discharge from hospital, she was too weak and confused to look after herself, and moved into Larkin's house at Newland Park, in Hull. From that time, they lived together until Larkin's death two years later.

Maeve Brennan was a senior assistant librarian when she met her new boss, Philip Larkin, in March 1955. He tutored her for Library Association exams, which she passed in 1960, and they went out together to celebrate her success. Maeve Brennan charts the course of their increasingly warm friendship through further meetings, and attending conferences together, up to Philip's sudden collapse in March 1961 and his several weeks of hospital tests in London.[4] During this period they wrote to each other regularly, and they carried on a romantic association after Larkin's return to work. Brennan acknowledges that there was a naïve and escapist element in their relationship: 'By locking ourselves into a complex dream world, we shut out the pressures of the real world, and apart from a sixteen-month separation in 1973–4 our friendship continued on this heady course until 1978'.[5]

The course of Larkin's relationship with Maeve Brennan broadly supports both Andrew Motion's and Brennan's own theories about the poet's love-affairs. Motion describes a Larkin terrified of marriage and children, and determined to avoid recreating the angry misery of his parents' marriage. Consequently, he explains, Larkin felt a need to protect himself from committing to one partner by simultaneously carrying on more than one relationship. For most of his adult life, this need took the form of protecting himself from his long-term commitment to Monica Jones, by maintaining a romance with

Maeve Brennan: 'For years she had been urging him to choose between herself and Monica, and for years he had refused – creating, instead, a painful but potent stasis.'[6]

Brennan's theory is that Larkin's personality was 'dichotomous': 'Larkin distinguishes between love and sex, classifying love as illusion and sex as reality. This is surely the key to his romanticism. At a personal level it explains his approach to our relationship; why he separated love from sex and why, when illusion became reality, the affair eventually came to grief.'[7] Brennan builds upon this insight the suggestion that there was 'the nobler side of his [Larkin's] temperament' which she identifies as 'joy' and which corresponds to 'love as illusion'; and simultaneously another side including 'cynicism, malice, and disparagement of what he held dear', that she calls 'personal sorrow' and which corresponds to 'sex as reality'.[8] Brennan was a Roman Catholic, obedient to her church's rules against extramarital sex; and Larkin respected her principles from the time their romance began in 1961, until their period of separation in 1973–4. When their intimacy was rekindled in 1975, however, Brennan 'yielded to temptation, but only on *very* rare and isolated occasions'.[9] Certainly, and Brennan acknowledges this, Larkin suppressed the more malicious and irreverent side of his personality when in her company; and she was deeply upset by the revelations of 'the darker side of his character'[10] that came out when his letters were published, as well as by the discovery that he started another affair in 1975 about which she knew nothing.

Betty Mackereth became Larkin's secretary in 1957, and she has been identified as the 'loaf-haired' secretary mentioned in 'Toads Revisited'. However, it was not until 1975, the same year when his romance with Maeve Brennan was physically consummated, that Larkin and Mackereth began an affair. They had known each other and worked together for seventeen years, and their affair appears to have been an uncomplicated liaison including familiarity, friendship and unembarrassed sex. Betty Mackereth had no wish to compete in the emotional tug-of-war between Monica Jones and Maeve Brennan, and did not frighten Larkin with talk of marriage. Even after Monica Jones's illness, when she came to live with Larkin in 1983, he and Betty continued the affair, although they adapted by meeting less frequently.

Whether Larkin was a 'dichotomous' personality, or used his widowed mother and simultaneous affairs to hold the terrifying prospect of commitment at bay, or both, we cannot ultimately know. It seems likely that there is truth in both of these theories. Larkin's own account, in memoirs and in his letters, gives support to both ideas. It is also worth remembering that he had been an awkward and ungainly-looking boy, with thick glasses and a stammer, tall and unathletic. Andrew Motion suggests that he was ambivalent about his sexuality during his teens and while he was at Oxford, and describes an ardent – but unconsummated – friendship with a fellow under-graduate, Philip Brown. Add to these elements a society which encouraged 'A wrangle for a ring, / A shame that started at sixteen / And spread to everything'[11] and an early habit of masturbation and enjoyment of pornography, and we have all of the ingredients for the worst consequences of what D. H. Lawrence termed 'the dirty little secret'.[12] Lawrence complains bitterly against the Victorians' division of life into 'the sentimental lie of purity' and 'the dirty little secret'. We could argue that these two correspond quite closely to the two 'sides' of Larkin's personality that Brennan describes as determining the course of his romantic affairs.

Before leaving Larkin's personal life, it is important to record the shock, revulsion and controversy caused by the publication of Anthony Thwaite's *Selected Letters of Philip Larkin, 1940–1985* (1992), and Andrew Motion's *Philip Larkin: A Writer's Life* (1993). These revealed that Larkin habitually used coarse language and obscenities, in letters and in person; that his political opinions were more intolerant and reactionary than had been revealed in his life-time; that he regularly expressed racist opinions, and was abusive and contemptuous of women, in his private correspondence; and that he collected and kept a collection of pornography all through his life. Larkin's reputation suffered: he was attacked by Germaine Greer, and even those who admired his poems, like Alan Bennett, 'could not see how they would emerge unscathed' after he read *A Writer's Life*.[13] Since that time, a steady stream of further biographical information and personal material has been made public, and Larkin's personality, opinions and character have become a legitimate part of controversial critical debate.

Writing and Publication

Larkin's reputation rests almost entirely on his poetry. However, his first ambition as a writer was to become a novelist. *Jill* (1946) had been written in 1943 and 1944, and was published soon after he moved to Leicester. The main character is an undergraduate named Kemp who is made to feel socially inferior by public-school boys, when he arrives at university. He compensates by inventing a sister, Jill, and as the fantasy grows and begins to interact with his own character, he changes her name to give her the potential to become more than a sister. Kemp then meets a real girl, Gillian, who closely corresponds to the fantasy Jill. Kemp's gauche attempts to pursue Gillian end in humiliating disaster, and he ends the novel in a hopeless speculation about whether fantasy life or real life are to be preferred, and about whether they can – or should – ever be reconciled. Reviews of *Jill* were, on the whole, positive and respectful, but they fell some way short of Larkin's hopes for a literary success.

Faber published *A Girl in Winter* in 1947. The heroine, Katherine, is a junior librarian, a war exile in England, originally from somewhere in middle Europe. At the beginning of the novel, she is expecting to meet again a young man she last saw when she spent a summer holiday in England before the war. The middle section of the novel is a flashback that tells us the story of that summer. Robin Fennel was Katherine's penfriend, and she stayed one summer with him and his family. The summer's potential for romance culminated in Robin kissing her. In this middle section the novel explores a similar theme to that in *Jill*, where a character is first invented or created by letters, and only later becomes real. However, the situation is more complex in *A Girl in Winter*, for Katherine and Robin, although they have only their letter-created fantasies of each other when they first meet, are nevertheless both real people; and are therefore both makers and made. The final part of the novel returns to the present. Robin is now in the army and waiting to be posted overseas, and when he visits her, drunk, he asks Katherine to sleep with him. The final pages of the novel are preoccupied with Katherine's isolation, distancing herself from Robin and drawing strength from self-sufficiency.

A Girl in Winter received positive reviews and sold well, and Larkin was temporarily buoyed by thinking that he had a successful career as a novelist ahead of him. He failed to produce a third novel, however, despite beginning two and continuing the struggle to make progress with them for several more years. Gradually, writing poetry began to be more rewarding.

Larkin's first collection of poems, *The North Ship*, was published in 1945 by the Fortune Press, which had previously included ten of his poems in an anthology, *Poetry from Oxford in Wartime*. *The North Ship* received only one rather lukewarm review. Since Faber reissued it with a new Introduction by Larkin, in 1965, it has been accepted as the juvenilia of an established poet, interesting because his talent later blossomed, and as showing the influences – particularly of Yeats – that preceded the emergence of Larkin's own distinctive voice. In 1945, however, *The North Ship* virtually disappeared without trace. Larkin's next attempt at publishing poems was a collection called *XX Poems*, privately printed in Belfast in 1950–1. Again, the collection was ignored by the literary figures to whom Larkin dispatched copies. In 1954, a further selection of five poems was published by the Fantasy Press as number 21 in the series Fantasy Poets, but attracted little attention.

In 1953, three of Larkin's poems appeared in the second issue of *Listen*, a magazine brought out by George and Jean Hartley, a young couple living at Hessle on the outskirts of Hull. They founded the Marvell Press, and their first book was the first collection of Larkin's mature poetry, *The Less Deceived*, which came out in 1955. By the time this collection made his name as a poet, Larkin was living and working in Hull and had met and befriended the Hartleys. *The Less Deceived* had an odd beginning, the collection receiving hardly any notice when it was published: then, just before Christmas 1955, *The Times* included it in a list of the year's best books. From then, and on into 1956, Larkin's fame grew steadily with enthusiastic endorsements from *The New Statesman* and other journals, as well as praise from academics including F. W. Bateson of Oxford University.

In 1963 Larkin severed his connection with the Marvell Press and became a Faber author, negotiating with Charles Monteith, who became his editor and a long-standing friend. The result was the second major collection of Larkin's mature period, *The Whitsun Weddings*, which was brought out in England in February 1964, and in America seven months later. This collection, containing many of the poems still regarded as his masterpieces, such as 'The Whitsun Weddings' itself, 'Dockery and Son', 'Mr Bleaney' and 'An Arundel Tomb', firmly established Larkin on the map. His reputation was further enhanced by the reissue of his novel *Jill*, in the same year. The Arts Council awarded the book a prize for 'the best book of original English verse by a living poet published from July 1962 to June 1965', and in 1965 he was awarded the Queen's Gold Medal for poetry.

Larkin's now established reputation led him to be commissioned to edit a new *Oxford Book of Twentieth Century English Verse*, to replace and update the volume edited by Yeats in 1936. Oxford University Press approached Larkin in 1966, and working on the anthology was his reason for taking a two-term Fellowship at Oxford in 1970–1. Larkin's selection was published in 1973. He had stamped his own taste on the volume, showing his preference for poets who wrote in the tradition rather than experimental or Modernist writers. This provoked considerable controversy: some reviewers approved while others were hostile and complained about the poets and poems Larkin had omitted. It is a measure of Larkin's security about his position in the literary firmament that he found the controversy invigorating. A few years before, he would have found any negative review depressing and dispiriting.

The next, and final, collection of poems came ten years after *The Whitsun Weddings*: *High Windows* was published in 1974. It was an immediate success, both in terms of the public recognition accorded Larkin by reviewers and other luminaries, and in terms of exceptional sales (19,500 copies were sold in little more than a year). Larkin received honorary degrees, a glut of fan-mail and a flood of invitations to attend this or talk about that. Andrew Motion remarks that '*The Less Deceived* made his name; *The Whitsun Weddings* made him famous; *High Windows* turned him into a national monument'.[14]

In the final decade of his life, Larkin finished few poems, and only eight appeared in public. These varied from 'Bridge for the Living', the words of a cantata commissioned to celebrate the opening of the Humber Bridge and performed in 1981, to a few finished personal poems such as 'Aubade', which appeared in *The Times Literary Supplement* in 1977.

Larkin was also a journalist. In 1956, he began reviewing poetry for *The Guardian*, and in 1961 he started to write reviews of jazz for

The Daily Telegraph. As his fame grew, a variety of other prose pieces, articles, essays and introductions were requested or commissioned. A collection of the *Telegraph* pieces was published under the title *All What Jazz*, in 1970; and in 1983 Faber brought out a selection of Larkin's prose pieces and interviews entitled *Required Writing: Miscellaneous Pieces, 1955–1982*, the idea for which had been proposed as early as 1974. This volume contains a selection of pieces on jazz written for *The Daily Telegraph*, transcripts of Larkin's interviews with *The Observer* (1979) and *The Paris Review* (1982) and a selection of essays, articles and reviews under the headings 'Writing in General' and 'Writing in Particular'. More of Larkin's writings have been collected and published since his death, in particular the volume of *Selected Letters of Philip Larkin* that caused such a stir on its publication in 1992.

Friends

We cannot leave Philip Larkin's life without mentioning the friendships he formed, some of which were influential and long-lasting. Larkin made and kept in touch with numerous friends, and it would be impossible to give an account of all of them here. The following paragraphs summarise a selection of the friendships that seem to have been particularly important at various stages of his life.

At school in Coventry, Larkin made friends with Jim Sutton, Colin Gunner and Noel Hughes. At Oxford, he met Kingsley Amis, Bruce Montgomery and John Wain. In Belfast, he met Colin and Patsy Strang, and Judy Egerton. In his literary life he established friendships with Charles Monteith, Robert Conquest, George and Jean Hartley and Barbara Pym.

Sutton was a close friend at school: he and Larkin had planned their subversive, adventurous future lives together, with Sutton as a painter complementing Larkin's literary ambitions. When Larkin went to Oxford they began a regular correspondence in which Larkin often expressed his opinions, his emotions and the events of his life without restraint, as he felt that he could tell Sutton anything. When Sutton returned to Coventry after the war, they looked forward to resuming their close association; but this proved awkward, partly because their letters had been so open, and partly as their ambitions faced compromise with Larkin's job and Sutton running out of the money he had inherited from his builder father. They continued to write to one another for a few more years, then the correspondence died out. Sutton spent most of his adult life working as a pharmacist.

Colin Gunner was another friend from Larkin's schooldays. He remained a friend during Larkin's Oxford years, but they then lost contact with each other. In 1971 Gunner wrote to Larkin asking his advice because he had written the story of his war experiences and thought of publication. Larkin offered to read the book and helped with an approach to Charles Monteith at Faber. Although Gunner's book was not accepted, the friendship between the two was re-established, and they kept up occasional meetings and a steady correspondence until Larkin's death.

Noel Hughes was at school and then at Oxford with Larkin and they met occasionally in later years. When Anthony Thwaite collected essays and tributes for his anthology *Larkin at Sixty* (1982), Noel Hughes was asked for a contribution. His essay alleged that Sydney Larkin had been a member of The Link, a fascist group in England before the war, and described the atmosphere in the Larkin house as 'joyless'. Larkin objected and Hughes offered to withdraw his essay altogether. He was calmed down, and a few cuts to the essay were agreed; but the friendship between him and Larkin did not recover.

These friends are mentioned because they were at school with Larkin, and yet in the cases of Gunner and Hughes they were still in contact with him some fifty years later when they had become middle-aged men. The same point applies to Larkin's university friends Amis, Montgomery and Wain. Barely out of adolescence when they met, Larkin and Montgomery were regular drinking friends, and discussed each other's writing projects, throughout their twenties. After a trip to Paris they took together in 1952, the friendship cooled, partly because Montgomery, successful early in his life, began to ask for money; but they remained in touch until Montgomery's death in 1978. John Wain continued as a friend and correspondent throughout Larkin's life. Larkin hosted a party for Wain when he visited Hull to give a lecture, in 1965, and was writing to him about his Oxford honorary doctorate as late as 1984.

Kingsley Amis was both the most and the least problematic of Larkin's Oxford friends. The most problematic because his sustained literary success, his marriages and children, excited Larkin's jealousy and at the same time threatened the male-only nature of the friendship. Least problematic because Amis and Larkin remained on good terms. Amis's contribution to *Larkin at Sixty* was complimentary, all of a piece with an understanding and steady support Larkin had been able to count on.[15] At Larkin's funeral, Amis revealed that Larkin had once thanked him for a whole adult, lifetime of 'undiminished affection and admiration',[16] and it appears that this steadiness, as much as the wit and brilliance of the undergraduate, enabled their friendship to endure through more than forty years. At the same time, Amis's friendship could have been a burden at times. He was free with his opinion of Larkin's partners: he expressed contempt for Ruth Bowman, and he did not like Monica Jones (neither did she like him), so that, for Larkin's girlfriends, meeting Kingsley Amis may have been rather like being taken to meet the parents. Additionally, Amis used Larkin as a model in his hugely successful comic novel *Lucky Jim*. Seeing himself, and Monica, caricatured in a successful novel and therefore read about by thousands, did give Larkin some uncomfortable feelings.

Patsy Strang, with whom Larkin had an affair while in Belfast, became an alcoholic, and died in 1977. Judy Egerton was another friend from the Belfast days, when Larkin was a frequent visitor to her and her husband Ansell, a Lecturer at Queen's University. Ansell Egerton later proposed Larkin for membership of the MCC; and with Judy he carried on an intimate and sincere correspondence, clearly founded on close friendship, to the end of his life. Just as Larkin's letters to Jim Sutton provide an unparalleled insight into his life during the Oxford years and the war, so his letters to Judy Egerton give us a similarly personal impression of the mature Larkin.

Larkin made friends of several literary contacts such as Charles Monteith, his editor at Faber, and Robert Conquest (who shared – and even exceeded in daring – Larkin's taste for pornography). He also met numerous literary 'names', such as John Betjeman, Ted Hughes, Louis MacNeice and many others. One name stands out, however: in 1961 Larkin wrote to the novelist Barbara Pym, whose books he admired, suggesting that he might write an essay about her work. She replied, and these letters began a correspondence that continued until her death in 1980. When Pym had difficulty publishing her latest novel, Larkin was unswerving and practical in his support. He wrote of her talent in glowing terms to Monteith at Faber, in 1965, and continued to help her and reassure her that her book deserved publication. Larkin and Pym did not meet until 1975; but when they did this only confirmed their friendship and mutual respect. Larkin attended her funeral in January 1980, and compiled her entry in the *Dictionary of National Biography* in 1981.

This has been a summary of four main strands in Larkin's life, and is the best we can do in the space available. Inevitably, many events, details and people have been left out. For example, we have remarked that Larkin became famous, and a member of the literary establishment, after the publication of *The Whitsun Weddings*, but we have not mentioned his diligent work on committees – with the Poetry Society, the Arts Council, and chairing the Booker Prize committee – or many of his honours (CH, CBE) or honorary degrees. As far as possible, this biographical sketch has concentrated on conveying some impression of Larkin's personality, and summarising his own writing: his novels and journalism, and above all his poems.

The Literary Context

Three of Larkin's close friends became successful novelists. When he met Larkin at Oxford in 1943, Bruce Montgomery was already writing detective novels under the pseudonym Edmund Crispin. He also wrote poetry and fiction under his own name and is particularly remembered for the novel *The Moving Toyshop* (1946). John Wain was a writer whose most celebrated title is *Hurry on Down* (1953). Kingsley Amis is best known for *Lucky Jim* (1954), his hugely successful first novel in which the main character is partly modelled on Larkin; and he enjoyed a long career as a novelist, poet, journalist and critic. In fact, this group of friends are thought of as the kernel of a loosely connected coincidence of young writers who exerted a common and purposeful influence on the course of literature at the time.

The group also included Robert Conquest, D. J. Enright, Donald Davie and Elizabeth Jennings; but it was a loose grouping, and there were others, as well as writers who shared the group's aims temporarily, like the younger poet Thom Gunn, and sympathisers from an earlier generation such as F. W. Bateson. The group received their name 'The Movement' in a leading article in *The Spectator*, by J. D. Scott, which appeared in 1954. They were said to have a shared agenda and were described as changing the direction of literature, discarding their predecessors, redefining the writer's relation to his audience and changing literary taste. In order to understand how and why Larkin and his contemporaries were 'new' and controversial writers, we have to survey the literary context in which they grew up, the establishment they inherited. This will necessitate a very brief and generalised dip into literary history.

In the first decades of the twentieth century there was a revolution in the arts. Responding to the influence of the great determinist thinkers of the nineteenth century, such as Darwin, Marx and Freud; and to the unprecedented physical devastation and psychological disillusion in the wake of the Great War, artists and philosophers felt that they were confronted by a new intellectual landscape, and needed to devise new, experimental forms to express their new consciousness. The visual arts embraced first impressionism, then surrealism, cubism and the abstract; poets abandoned traditional forms based on metre and rhyme, and wrote 'free verse'; and novelists developed stream of consciousness writing or adopted plots and material subversive of the traditional. In *The Waste Land* (1922), T. S. Eliot wrote a free verse poem so filled with obscure and learned allusions, and so demanding in its intellectual structure, that only a scholarly élite could guess at its meaning – and even the élite could not agree. Virginia Woolf produced the stream-of-consciousness novels *Mrs Dalloway* (1925) and *To the Lighthouse* (1927), and James Joyce published *Ulysses* (1922). Both Woolf and Joyce adopted plots in which there was virtually no incident in the conventional sense: *Mrs Dalloway* recounts one day, as does *Ulysses*; and these novels have no climactic events or conventional ending: the novel stops, but life continues. D. H. Lawrence's novels focus on turbulent, semi-conscious emotions, and several (for example, *Sons and Lovers,* 1913, and later

The Rainbow, 1915) also display anti-endings; while his poetry is often in a passionate, rhapsodic free verse form. Lawrence also wrote explicitly about sexual love, shocking the Edwardian establishment. Modernist writers made free use of metaphor, myths and symbolism, or developed the combination of description and metaphor called 'magic realism'.

Several of the writers and artists involved in this process knew each other and formed a recognisable 'group'. The 'Bloomsbury set' adopted a bohemian lifestyle, dressed strikingly, and their behaviour, including cohabitation, open marriages and lesbian affairs, was deeply shocking to English society. In her essay *Mr Bennett and Mrs Brown,* an imaginary conversation between an ordinary woman and the traditional Edwardian novelist Arnold Bennett, Virginia Woolf explains that this revolution in the arts was necessary: the old, outworn forms were no longer relevant to real life, and had to be broken: 'And so the smashing and the crashing began. Thus it is that we hear all round us, in poems and novels and biographies, even in newspaper articles and essays, the sound of breaking and falling, crashing and destruction'.[17]

The artists who carried out these experiments in form, and attacked the leftover conventions of Victorian and Edwardian literature, became known as Modernists. We already remarked that Eliot's *The Waste Land* demanded a learned audience; and it was a characteristic of many Modernist works that, being experimental in form, they were also 'difficult'. Having discarded the mass popularity of, say, Dickens's social realism and sentiment, and refusing to tell a plain story, the Modernist writer was often accessible only to highly educated people with a special interest in the arts. Furthermore, as the 1920s moved into the 1930s, Modernist experiments also moved on and further narrowed their audience. So, for example, in Virginia Woolf's *The Waves* (1931), symbolic metaphor takes over and there is virtually no recognisable narrative left; and Joyce's *Finnegans Wake* (1939) is a vast trove of words but very obscure indeed. Even today, most people do not attempt to distinguish a good abstract painting from a bad one, and suspect that any 'expert' who pretends to be able to is just pulling the wool over our eyes. So, the Modernists contributed to a popular mistrust of art, and began to encourage the negative view that the world of artists is a high-falutin' place inhabited only by artists, experts and their hangers-on, out of touch with ordinary people's lives. When describing the decadent behaviour of the postwar generation in Europe, Stefan Zweig wrote that 'The general impulse to radical and revolutionary excess manifested itself in art, too, of course ... the comprehensible element in everything was proscribed, melody in music, resemblance in portraits, intelligibility in language. How wild, anarchic and unreal were those years'.[18]

As the Modernist revolution gradually became an artistic mainstream, poetry developed further. In the late 1930s, when a teenaged Larkin was beginning to read and write, the experimental forms of Eliot, Pound and their followers were giving way to two different branches of poetic style: lush, metaphor-rich effusions filled with word-music and expressive romantic emotion; and a more controlled diction and use of traditional metrical and rhyming forms. A good example of the former is the work of Dylan Thomas; of the latter, examples are the poems of W. H. Auden and John Betjeman.

Dylan Thomas published collections of poetry between 1934 and 1946. His work abounds in imagery surprisingly transferred and metaphors dazzlingly mixed, often creating the impression that the meanings of words are secondary to their music or their sensual associations. Just three lines from his famous 'Fern Hill' is enough to show his love of manipulating language:

> And once below a time I lordly had the trees and leaves
> > Trail with daisies and barley
> Down the rivers of the windfall light.

Such verse-music is intoxicating, and Dylan Thomas's bohemian life and riotous poetry readings became something of a legend while Larkin was in the sixth form and during his Oxford years. Another poet whose exploitation of language and rhythms is hypnotically impressive is W. B. Yeats, who published poetry from the 1890s to the late 1930s and was interested in mysticism and the occult. The verbal and passionate excesses of these poets and others like them, and their elevation of metaphor and effect above clarity of meaning, became anathema to the young writers of 'The Movement', who determined to change the direction of poetry away from verbal excesses and Modernist experiment. Their aim was to bring back the ordinary language of ordinary conversation: to write poetry in which the meaning is clear, and accessible to a wider audience.

The Movement writers – Amis, Larkin, Wain, Enright, Davie and the rest – wished to return to a direct traditional line that had been maintained during the 1930s, partly in the poetry of W. H. Auden and particularly in the works of John Betjeman. They focused on developing a seamless technique, crafting poems with a skilfully unobtrusive yet strict use of metre and rhyme, to create an impression of natural speech. They wanted the reader of their poems to feel that they were in conversation with someone like themselves. In our analyses of Larkin's poems, in Part I of this book, we have seen how successfully he developed just such a natural style. The reader should not feel that he or she is in the presence of an overwhelming ego, showing off his mesmerising verbal virtuosity. Neither should the reader feel intimidated and excluded by an élite, learned, 'arty' expert, experimenting for the sake of it. Both of these kinds of poem struck the new writers as pretentious. In his article naming 'The Movement', J. D. Scott wrote: 'The Movement, as well as being anti-phoney, is anti-wet; sceptical, robust, ironic, prepared to be as comfortable as possible in a wicked, commercial, threatened world …'.[19] In the Introduction to his anthology *New Lines*, in which a number of Larkin's poems appear, Robert Conquest wrote:

> If anyone had briefly to characterize this poetry of the Fifties from its predecessors, I believe the most important general point would be that it submits to no great systems of theoretical constructs nor agglomerations of unconscious commands. It is free from both mystical and logical compulsions and – like modern philosophy – is empirical in its attitude to all that comes. This reverence for the real person or event is, indeed, a part of the general intellectual ambiance of our time.[20]

Following the publication of *The Less Deceived*, Larkin was fully identified as a Movement poet in the eyes of reviewers and the public. The *Times Educational Supplement* hailed his poems as 'a poetic monument that marks the triumph of clarity over the formless mystifications of the last twenty years'.[21] Although he always insisted that he did not belong to a formal group with a 'plan', Larkin was not displeased to be identified with the Movement's supposed aims – accessible language, strict form and clarity, an ironic and sceptical attitude toward life and a hatred of pretentiousness often showing as a barbed sense of humour.

The origins and achievements of the Movement is a far bigger subject than we have space for in the present chapter; but the above statements – particularly that from the *TES* – do convey the sense that it was seen as an important, radically new kind of writing, and that there was a real conflict with the Modernists and the romantics who came before. The Movement attacked a London literary 'Establishment' as surely as the Modernists had attacked an Edwardian 'Establishment', and generated considerable hostility on both sides.

It is ironic that, during his Oxford years, Larkin felt admiration for Dylan Thomas and recognised imitation of Thomas's style in his own poems. In 1943 Vernon Watkins visited the English Club at Oxford, and gave an inspirational talk about Yeats. Larkin responded by gathering and reading as much Yeats as he could find, and the musical Irish poet's influence on his own style was enormous and hard to shed: most of Larkin's poetry for the next few years was recognisably Yeatsian, and by his own account[22] he was finally and suddenly set free from his enslavement to Yeats when he began to read Thomas Hardy's poems, one day in January 1946.

As the 1950s passed into the 1960s, the Movement began its transformation into an established rather than a rebellious grouping, and simultaneously, younger poets announced fresh voices and concerns. For example, Ted Hughes published his first collection of poems *The Hawk in the Rain* in 1957; and Sylvia Plath's *Colossus* appeared in 1960, and *Ariel* in 1965. Among novels, the era of *Lucky Jim* and *Hurry on Down* passed into the time of angry working-class writers: John Braine's *Room at the Top*, and Allan Sillitoe's *Saturday Night and Sunday Morning* (1958), with their outspoken hatred of the class system, violent language and violent actions, were more aggressive than anything the Movement had produced. William Golding (*Lord of the Flies*, 1954) wrote novels considering wide-ranging social and philosophical themes, using metaphor and symbol in original ways. Simultaneously, as Larkin remarks in 'Homage to a Government' and 'Going, Going',

Britain was in decline and shedding its empire. Several colonial writers began to speak about Englishness in the voices of outsiders: both Doris Lessing (*The Grass is Singing*, 1951) and V. S. Naipaul (*The Mystic Masseur*, 1957) established their reputations at this time. British theatre also displayed an increasingly political anger against social division, the class system and alienation: the plays of John Osborne (*Look Back in Anger*, 1956) and other dramatists such as Arnold Wesker and Shelagh Delaney, were overtly concerned with a fractured society. Where Movement writers had showed weary scepticism and genteel, if ironic fatalism, the new writers of the later 1950s and 1960s called out for change. The experiments of Modernism also returned to the theatre: Samuel Beckett's absurdist plays *Waiting for Godot* (1952) and *Endgame* (1958) were performed during the Movement's heyday, and created the climate for Harold Pinter's work. His first play *The Room* opened in 1957, followed by *The Birthday Party* in 1958.

We have noted Andrew Motion's comment that '*High Windows* turned [Larkin] into a national monument' when the collection came out, in 1974. This could be taken in one sense as a literary epitaph. The controversy his work provoked in the 1950s was past: the Movement group of writers had done their work and become established and middle-aged. As his fame grew, Larkin cultivated the image of a gloomy provincial librarian, truculently English and reactionary in his opinions. In 1972 John Betjeman, another ironic versifier with a waspish wit, whose radio and television broadcasts cultivated his image of genteel Englishness, became Poet Laureate. When he died in 1984, the Laureateship was offered to Larkin as the obvious successor: a 'national monument' indeed, with a suitably caricatural public image of Englishness. Meanwhile, Britain was awash with many varieties of new literary works, including many with specific agendas; and the world of academia spawned new 'schools' of criticism such as Structuralism, Psychoanalytical critics, Feminism, Marxism and so on. Against this volatile and exciting background, Larkin continued to concentrate on his anecdotes and opinions on ordinary life. This was only occasionally varied by a brief regretful foray into public affairs, such as those in 'Homage to a Government' or 'Going, Going'.

In this discussion, we have looked back towards the literary climate Larkin inherited and became aware of during his teens and early twenties, considered the so-called 'Movement' with which he was identified, and briefly noted some of the literary developments that occurred during the final twenty years of the poet's life. Before leaving 'The Literary Context', we should mention a longer view as well, as several Movement writers considered their role in this way.

In his *Purity of Diction in English Verse*, Donald Davie argued that the Romantic poets (Coleridge, Wordsworth, Keats, Byron, Shelley) arrogated the importance of private, personal experience, and that this caused a breach in the relationship between poet and reader that had previously been stable and secure:

> In the Elizabethan, the Caroline and the Augustan age, the poet moved in a society more or less stable and more or less in agreement about social propriety ... Presumably, the violent dislocation of English society at the end of the eighteenth century (the Industrial Revolution) had destroyed the established codes of social behaviour.[23]

Davie's claim echoed a theory of literary history that was being developed in the criticism of F. R. Leavis and Q. D. Leavis, leading lights in the development of literary criticism during the 1930s and the succeeding two decades,[24] academics who exerted a considerable influence over Movement thinking. This theory held that there had been a poetic readership able to respond with taste and intelligence, up until the advent of the Romantics. Then, these reading habits were lost to adolescent self-indulgence, and sentimentality, during the nineteenth century. Blake Morrison explains:

> The conditions which are said to have prevailed up until the end of the eighteenth century are resurrected as an ideal. In the mid-1950s, several critics dubbed the Movement poets 'Augustans' or 'New Augustans', and, in relation to this idealizing of the eighteenth-century audience, the description seems apposite.[25]

So, Larkin and his contemporaries not only reacted to the literary climate of their immediate predecessors, preferring their understated, ironic and conversational language to the excesses and arcane oddities of late 1930s romantics and early-century Modernists. They also felt

that their work would restore the poet to his audience, as if they
intended to repair damage done to the English poetic tradition from
the time of Wordsworth and Coleridge and on throughout the
nineteenth century. Morrison develops his argument to point out that
many of the Movement's poets wrote for an educated and cultured
audience – an audience of academics, automatically interested in
poetry and trained in its appreciation. He makes an exception for
Larkin, the one poet to 'write pleasurable and "accessible" poetry that
might reach a wide audience'.[26] Larkin wrote that 'at bottom poetry,
like all art, is inextricably bound up with giving pleasure, and if a poet
loses his pleasure-seeking audience he has lost the only audience worth
having, for which the dutiful mob that signs on every September is no
substitute'.[27] The 'dutiful mob' are the students Larkin watched arriving at Hull University every September, eager to join the academic
world. The 'pleasure-seeking audience', in his view, is the only audience worth writing for, and is made up of ordinary people who have
not 'had his [the poet's] experience or education or travel grant'.[28]

The grand claims of Movement poets to be returning poetry to its
tradition, supported by a theory of English poetry stretching back over
four centuries, are breathtaking in their range. It is arguable that Larkin
was the only one of the group who actually succeeded in reaching the
wider audience of which they spoke. It is equally arguable that the
eighteenth-century audience was never such an ideal, anyway, consist-
ing almost entirely of the literate middle and upper classes. In the next
chapter, we will consider Larkin's appeal in relation to the social and
educational changes that followed the Second World War. Whether his
achievement re-established a poet–reader rapport last known in
Augustan times is far more debatable.

8

The Historical Context

Philip Larkin became 8 years old in 1930, and 18 in 1940. He had been born into the period of change and turbulence in Britain that followed the Great War. Labour disputes and trade unionism at the start of the 1920s took on revolutionary overtones that frightened the British ruling 'upper' class. Conditions for coal-miners were appalling, and the employers wanted to engineer increased productivity at the same time as cutting wages. The General Strike of 1926 brought the country to a standstill for twelve days. The mines, factories, shipyards, railways all stopped as around four million workers walked out, and Britain was paralysed. On the other hand, the leadership of the Trades Union Congress remained anxious to be seen as reasonable, to avoid any suggestion of Bolshevism or class war; and Prime Minister Baldwin was also careful to avoid inflammatory moves like those of his more bellicose junior colleague Churchill. Eventually, following secret negotiations, an agreement was reached which represented a humiliating climb-down for the unions; and the world was astonished that such an enormous class confrontation had been managed without loss of life.

However, the relative decline of British industry, and the economic pressures of a currency pegged too high by the return to the gold standard, continued to cause strikes, closures and unemployment. Poverty and hardship endured. Then, in 1929, the world repercussions of the Wall Street crash, or 'Black Tuesday', dropped Britain into the Great Depression. The Labour government, under Ramsay MacDonald, failed; this was followed by a National government charged with leading the country out of crisis, and Britain left the gold standard. What all of these events show is that, while Larkin's own childhood was comparatively comfortable, the country as a whole remained terribly mutilated after the Great War and through the Depression, its industry and society fracturing. Large sectors of British industry were devastated and many industrial areas resembled waste-lands. Although a man in Sydney Larkin's position, with a secure job and comfortable salary, saw his standard of living rise steadily through the 1930s, there remained strong evidence of the failures of capitalism, and the failure of British upper-class patricians and politicians. Unemployment remained stubbornly high, production in key industries such as coal and shipbuilding continued to shrink, and poverty was highly visible. As late as 1936 *The Times* acknowledged that half the population was 'living on a diet insufficient or ill-designed to maintain health'. By contrast, Germany seemed to recover from the First War and the Depression much more strongly and rapidly.

These reflections may go some way towards explaining how a strict man like Sydney Larkin, with his predilection for efficiency, might develop an admiration for the Nazi government and a comparatively low opinion of patchy and laissez-faire British efforts at recovery. He was not alone. The English fascist party, led by Sir Oswald Mosley, numbered some 50,000 members at its high point in 1934. However, it was in that year that public opinion began to turn against the Hitler regime, with news of the massacre known as the 'Night of the Long Knives', and increasingly frequent stories from Germany of the persecution of Jews, other oppressions and brutal violence. As the 1930s drew to an end, German expansionism and aggression became increasingly apparent with the Austrian *Anschluss* and occupation of the Sudetenland, in 1938; and Prime Minister Neville Chamberlain's policy of appeasement became ever more ludicrous even in the eyes of ordinary members of the public.

In our account of Larkin's life, we have already speculated that his father's continuing public admiration for Germany through the later 1930s and even during the war, may have been an excruciating embarrassment for the teenager. Such wounds may never have healed: we noted that it was Noel Hughes's reference to Sydney Larkin's

Nazism in his essay for *Larkin at Sixty* that infuriated the poet and caused the breach in their long friendship, even a world war and thirty years later. Certainly, the history of that period may explain Larkin's unwillingness to think about the war, and the careful ironic scepticism about all politics that he maintained until later in his life.

War was declared in September 1939. Larkin affected to take no notice of it. For example, in 1945 he wrote to Sutton: 'There is a lot in the paper today about what Russia, America, Russia, England, Russia, America and Russia are going to do with Germany ... I haven't bothered to read it'.[1] In terms of his day-to-day life, however, the war had a considerable effect. He took part in fire-watching duties first at school and then in Oxford, had some ARP duties and cadet-training both at school and at Oxford, and in the late autumn of 1940 he went home to Coventry to search for his parents after the town was blitzed. Coventry was bombed heavily, and Larkin witnessed his shattered home-town the morning after the raids. Everywhere was affected by the war, and Oxford was no exception. Most of the younger dons were drafted into the services or other war work, undergraduates were called to medicals and sent into the army, food and drink were more diffi-cult to come by, and army lorries and uniforms were everywhere. The war was also, of course, a constant topic of conversation. Larkin wrote to Sutton that 'I gain the impression of being at the end of an epoch'.[2] How did the war change English society?

The answer is, considerably. The long struggle of organised labour, against the old stratified class system and towards a more equal distri-bution of wealth and more equal society, had fractured into economic turmoil during the 1920s and 1930s, in general strikes, the Great Depression and huge numbers of unemployed in areas where core industries were in decline; but this struggle continued, and socialist ideals survived. During the war years Britain had a coalition government with Winston Churchill as Prime Minister, and the country, to an extent, set aside other divisions while it devoted its efforts and economy to the war. The war years were extraordinary, however, and – as during the First World War – in such unusual conditions the normal rules of society seemed to be in abeyance. Men in the services, and women in factories, in the WRENS or on Land Work, became determined that things should not return to the prewar status quo once the great conflict and all the sacrifices were over. The result of the 1945 General Election, which brought a Labour Government to power under Clement Attlee, confirmed this. Even before VE day, in 1944, a far-reaching social reform had been enacted in R. A. Butler's Education Act. This provided state-funded free education for all, and organised secondary education into a tripartite system of Grammar, Secondary Modern and Technical Schools. The Butler Act was a fundamental move towards social equality, for two reasons. First, that every child could be educated without payment; and secondly, that in the Grammar Schools, bright children from poor families could receive an education every bit as good as (and often better than) that provided to the paying privileged in a Public School. This was a significant move in the direction of equal opportunities.

The Attlee government of 1945–51 was arguably the most radical government of the twentieth century. It established a 'cradle to grave' Welfare State, including the creation of the tax-funded National Health Service under Aneurin Bevan, in 1948; and most core industries and utilities, including coal, iron and steel, the railways, electricity and gas, were taken into public ownership. These changes did not abolish privilege and inequality from British society; but they did provide an enormous swathe of secure public service employment in large areas of the economy, and improve security and the standard of living for millions of ordinary people. The measures on education, from Butler's 1944 Act, and health brought a radical improvement in quality of life for all, and there was a considerable blurring of the class barriers that had previously stratified English society.

The Welfare State, and public ownership of core industries, was thenceforth a *fait accompli*, a pattern accepted by both Conservative and Labour governments, and remained unchanged until Mrs Thatcher's Conservative government was elected in 1979 and, in the 1980s, began to reverse the process by privatising the industries Attlee's Labour government had nationalised. Larkin lived to see violent confrontations between government and trades unions during the Miners' Strike of 1983, but not the full range of privatisations that followed in the later 1980s and the 1990s. So, nationalised utilities and the welfare state were the background to Larkin's life from his mid-twenties and for the rest of his life.

Blake Morrison describes the effect of the postwar settlement as particularly enhancing the appeal of Larkin's poetic 'personae' and the Movement writers in general. Movement writers were identified as provincial schoolteachers or university lecturers from lower middle-class backgrounds, who had won their way to Oxford and Cambridge by scholarships:

> They were identified with a spirit of change in post-war British society, and were felt to be representative of shifts in power and social structure ... [there was] the emergence of a 'lower-middle-class' literary group and the re-distribution of income and status, 'gentle though real', in the newly-created Welfare State ... [Movement writers had] the advantage of seeming to represent a newly empowered class, and it helped them to define themselves in opposition to the 'haut-bourgeois' 1930s generation ...'[3]

Larkin's bicycle-clip-removing visitor to a country church, in 'Church Going', or his speakers in 'Mr Bleaney' or 'Toads', as well as his conversational openings, are typical of the social figure described by Morrison.

In 1956, the Suez fiasco not only revealed embarrassing misjudgements and mistakes by the Conservative Prime Minister of the day, Sir Anthony Eden; it also trumpeted loud and clear the fact that Britain was no longer in the first rank of world powers. In truth, the British empire and Britain's international influence had been declining for a long time; but the process accelerated after the war. India and Pakistan gained independence in August 1947; and between 1957 and 1963, Ghana, Malaya, Cyprus, Nigeria, Somalia, Sierra Leone, Jamaica, Tanganyika, Uganda, Kenya and Gambia became independent. Rhodesia declared UDI (Unilateral Declaration of Independence) in 1965 and, after a protracted civil war, became independent in 1978. In short, the story of the British empire between 1945 and Larkin's death in 1985 is one of a long, steady decline as colony after colony was shed, and British military power shrunk and shrunk back across the world, as recorded in Larkin's poem 'Homage to a Government'. A couple of years before his death, Larkin was somewhat surprised and cheered when Mrs Thatcher's Conservative government projected power to the South Atlantic, and fought and won the Falklands War. 'Well,' Larkin wrote to Gunner, 'so we have the Argies on the run. Thank God we didn't cock it up'.[4]

Domestic politics between 1956 and 1979 was humdrum enough to breed cynicism in the observer. Conservative governments led by Prime Ministers Harold Macmillan, Alec Douglas-Home and Edward Heath alternated with Labour administrations under Harold Wilson and James Callaghan. There were events, such as Edward Heath's three-day week – an attempt to face down trade union power that failed – and Callaghan's 'winter of discontent', another attempt to ride out public-sector strikes. Chancellor of the Exchequer Denis Healey had to ask the IMF (International Monetary Fund) for financial aid, which came with humiliating strings attached, in the late 1970s. In 1973, Edward Heath took Britain into the European Community. Harold Wilson talked of 'the white heat' of new technologies reviving British prosperity. Unemployment kept on rising, inexorably. As far as the economy was concerned (and this determined such matters as inflation, tax rates, the level of rent or the value of properties, and unemployment, all the matters of most immediate concern to ordinary people), it did not seem to matter very much which of the two major parties was in charge. Neither party made a very good job of managing the British economy during these two decades; and at the same time, neither party quite toppled over the edge into absolute economic catastrophe. Politically, the main decades of Larkin's adult life were good times to be disengaged, sceptical and ironically gloomy. Unfortunately, Larkin did not pre- serve himself separate from politics; and he aired some intolerant right-wing opinions, including contempt for the student protests of the 1960s, and racism.

When we look at cultural change, however, the picture is very different. We have already commented, in the preceding chapter, that there was a growing number of new and exciting departures in British literature and drama, in the period from the 1950s onward. This was also true of society in general, which was radically transformed during the 1960s and 1970s; and of consumerism and the commercial media, which expanded at a rate comparable to an explosion during the same period. Larkin wrote famously about the sexual revolution, in 'Annus

Mirabilis' and 'High Windows'. This had two interrelated ingredients: widely available contraception, and the growth (and commercial encouragement) of a culture of youth. The 'swinging sixties' appeared to begin – as Larkin remarked – with 'the end of the *Chatterley* ban / And the Beatles' first LP'; but in fact these were simply influential moments in a process that had begun much earlier, with the American Beat generation and the evolution of rock 'n' roll out of jazz and blues perhaps, or earlier still.[5] Like most things, the 'swinging sixties' simply expanded on cultural elements that were already in place. Society became permissive; the advertising, television and broadcast media, and industry, boomed selling fashionable clothing, make-up, records and gramophones; the older generation tutted loudly in shock; homo-sexuality was legalized; and the decade ended with the phenomenon of hippies withdrawing from conventional society, 'dropping out' and attempting communal forms of living away from the commercial econ-omy. In the last years of the decade the younger generation developed more challenging traits: there were peace protests, demonstrations, and sit-ins at universities; and a thriving recreational drug culture blossomed. At its most idealistic, however, the hippy movement was purist: these enemies of capitalism eschewed drugs and other toxins, loved nature and believed that their peaceful, anti-competitive lifestyle and behaviour, or 'love', would eventually shame and overcome those still dominated by the fear and envy generated by a corrupt economic system. Gradually, the idealistic believed, all the poor frightened capitalists, and greedy politicians, would be set free from their mental shackles, and the world would live at peace.

Many in the older generation reacted to the burgeoning youth movement with aggression. Larkin was angry when he found himself caught up in student protests at Hull University, in 1968 and 1969. Motion writes that he 'kept up a barrage of complaints about the demonstrating students to anyone who would listen'.[6]

In the 1970s, youth movements lost their 'peace and love' appeal and, with the onset of punks and others, became openly abusive and aggressive. Clothing and hair became increasingly bizarre and sinister, much of it deliberately clumsy or ugly. On the other hand, once the bubble of the genuinely idealistic hippy subsided, succeeding 'move-ments' among the young seemed increasingly unimportant, and many were tarnished with the suspicion that they had been founded by advertising and public relations executives, not spontaneously produced by the young at all.

This observation brings us conveniently around to the triumph of consumerism in British society, a topic fully explored in several of Larkin's poems. Broadly speaking, every saleable product adopted the techniques of the fast-growing advertising industry, and adapted production in order intensively to maximise production and therefore sales. To understand this, consider the phrase 'built-in obsolescence': a washing machine is manufactured to last five years, by which time there is a more advanced model available, in new styling, at a higher price. In this way, a company that was making a machine to last ten years and selling one machine to each customer in every decade could sell two machines to each customer in the same period instead. Furthermore, advertising exerted pressure on consumers to discard their goods with increasing frequency, on the grounds that those goods were obsolete or out of fashion, or that a new and better model was now available. Additionally, supermarkets and shopping centres adopted psychological techniques to encourage shoppers to buy more goods than they needed, or even wanted.[7]

Broadly speaking, such practices were comparatively new just after the war, but by the 1980s they had become universal, intensive and difficult to escape from or resist. Larkin explored the exploding phenomenon of wall-to-wall consumerism, with its characteristics of tackiness, sexual titillation and magical but cheap fantasy, in poems such as 'The Large Cool Store', 'Sunny Prestatyn' and 'Essential Beauty'. The mass production of a flood of cheap, temporary material goods became ever more unedifying, irrational and wasteful. Britain was becoming a 'throwaway' consumer society.

The postwar expansion of universities was, to an extent, analogous to the growth of commercial consumerism. In the 1950s several provincial 'university colleges' offered degrees to small numbers of students, as external colleges of the older centres such as London and Birmingham. Larkin worked in one such college in Leicester. These colleges were gradually granted their own charters as independent universities, money was poured into them and they expanded rapidly. Larkin arrived at Hull in 1955, a year after it became an university in its own right. In 1945 there were 174 students at the college. In 1980 there were over 5,000. In Chapter 7 we recorded Larkin's conscientious, dedicated work in planning and building the two stages of the Brynmor Jones Library, which was part of this rapid expansion in higher education and of which he was proud. On the other hand, he certainly felt that bringing the masses into universities brought similar evils to the coterminous explosion in mass-produced goods. Larkin was increasingly contemptuous of the students, that 'dutiful mob that signs on every September', and wrote in a letter to Barbara Pym that 'The universities must now be changed to fit the kind of people we took in: exams made easier, places made like a factory ...'.[8] During the 1960s, the expansion of higher education continued with the building and opening of several new universities, such as those at Sussex, Warwick and Essex. One result of this sudden expansion was that the academic world became more commercialised. Lecturers and departments participated in an industry of publications; depended on research grants; and universities became large institutions with huge budgets, administered in a way that increasingly imitated the management of a large business. Larkin deplored what he saw as the sacrifice of quality at the altar of quantity, and his revulsion against the intrusion of business practices into academic life is clear from poems such as 'Posterity' and 'Naturally the Foundation will Bear your Expenses'. It is noticeable in 'Posterity' that Larkin associates the deplorable commercialisation of academic life with America.

One other factor among the social changes of the postwar years deserves mention here: the growth of a multicultural society. From 1948 onwards, large numbers of West Indians, Indians, Pakistanis and Bangladeshis, and smaller numbers of East Asians, Maltese and Cypriots came to settle in Britain. From being an almost exclusively white society, Britain has become a mix of many different ethnic groups. This is particularly true of London and the major industrial cities of the Midlands and the North. There were reactions against this immigration, sometimes violent; and the process of assimilation has not always been smooth. In 1968 the Conservative MP for Wolverhampton, Enoch Powell, caused a furore when he made a speech warning that 'rivers of blood' would flow as black and white fought against each other for space and economic survival. Mr Powell was expelled from the Conservative Party for this speech, although there were many who privately agreed with his prophecy. We have to record that Philip Larkin took a prewar attitude towards black immigrants. In private correspondence he was increasingly intolerant of what he saw as Britain's decline: he derided Wilson's government as 'nigger-mad', saw a 'rising tide of niggers', and thought that the 'black folks ... from the house over the way' from Eva Larkin's house, were causing his mother's 'grade' to go down.[9]

So far, we have taken a whistle-stop tour of British politics and society during the period between the Second World War and Larkin's death in 1985. However, there remains one incalculably influential fact about the history of those years that we have not yet mentioned: the atom bomb, and the subsequent nuclear arms race during the Cold War. The Americans dropped two atom bombs, on the Japanese cities of Hiroshima and Nagasaki, on 6 and 9 August 1945. Each of these bombs destroyed an entire city, and a quarter of a million people died from incineration or radiation. This changed the world: put simply, mankind now had a weapon powerful enough to obliterate an entire city, powerful enough to wipe out a whole population in one go. Suddenly there was a weapon so powerful that it terrified every citizen of the world, and for the first time a weapon existed that even frightened the politicians who were in a position to use it. For four years, America held a monopoly of nuclear weapons; but in 1949 the Soviet Union successfully tested an atom bomb, and the Cold War arms race began.

During the 1950s, with regular atom tests and the development of hydrogen bombs, more became known about the dangers and after-effects of nuclear explosions; and as megatonnage (the measure of a nuclear weapon's power) increased, so the potential extinction of the human race became more likely. Already, in 1955, the science fiction novelist John Wyndham had published *The Chrysalids*, a fantasy in which small groups of survivors lived in a society thrown back to medieval conditions following a nuclear war. By the 1970s, America and Russia owned arsenals of missiles capable of wiping out human life on earth several times over. The entire period was punctuated by complex wrangles over ineffective disarmament negotiations at US–Soviet 'summit meetings', and periodic crises such as the Berlin crisis in

1958–60, which led to the building of a wall and watchtowers through the middle of the city, sealing off West German and communist GDR zones from each other; and the Cuban missile crisis of October 1962 which took the US and the Soviet Union to the brink of war.

In Britain, the Campaign for Nuclear Disarmament (CND) was founded in 1958, and its annual marches from the nuclear facility at Aldermaston to rallies in the centre of London became enormous demonstrations of protest against the horror of a nuclear arms race, calling for unilateral disarmament. CND was an unusual protest movement in that it was not dominated by one social class, occupation or age-group. Demonstrators came from all social classes and all walks of life, and joined together into 'the largest spontaneous popular movement in postwar Britain'.[10]

Larkin affected to ignore the dropping of an atom bomb on Hiroshima in 1945, and we can only speculate on the effect upon him personally of living in a world capable of self-annihilation. As we have seen from our study of his poetry, he grew up unnaturally preoccupied with the absence of faith in a now empty universe, facing a sky 'that shows / Nothing, and is nowhere, and is endless', and continuously aware of 'unresting death', the 'black-/ Sailed unfamiliar' of the early poem 'Next, Please'. It is reasonable to suppose that his anxiety about life's futility, as well as his lack of trust in the future, and mankind's ability to preserve beauty or goodness, may have been intensified by living against a backdrop of potential destruction on a planetary scale.

This chapter has been able only to skim the surface of the period within which Philip Larkin lived, and has tried to focus on historical themes in their relation to his life and preoccupations. The hope is that this 'sketch' will lead you to look into the history of the twentieth century in greater detail; and to this end there are suggestions to follow up in Further Reading, after the next chapter.

9

A Sample of Critical Views

A large number of books and articles have been written about Philip Larkin by academic critics, and many more are published each year. They are often written in a kind of specialised jargon, or in an over-complicated style: academics are just as fond of showing off as anybody else. It is important to remember that you have read and studied Larkin's poems, so your ideas are valuable. It is also worth remembering that Larkin is an elusive writer: his poems, as we have noted, leave unresolved alternative interpretations alive, and therefore resist many of the attempts at critical resolution. Your attempt to grasp a 'whole' out of Larkin's poetry, is likely to be as coherent as anyone else's; and is likely to reflect your particular interests – whether in the social and historical context, or in Larkin's psychology and personality, or in poetic form and effect – just as the professional critics' responses often reflect their predilections.

You will also find moments of illumination: reading a critic, you may come across a remark that sends you back to the poems, where you discover a whole new perspective. It is almost as if the poems have changed since you read them for the first time. Because most of Larkin's poems are structured to be insoluble, they are particularly susceptible to this effect. With or without a critic's opinion to spur you, you will find that the poems continually 'change' on rereading, as one of Larkin's voices speaks more loudly to your mood, and another, that you heard loud and clear on first reading, is comparatively muted.

Always be sceptical in approaching the critics' ideas: you are not under an obligation to agree with them. Your mind can be stimulated by discussing the text with your teachers and lecturers, or in a class. Treat the critics in the same way: it is stimulating to debate Larkin by reading critical books and articles, challenging your ideas and theirs. This is the spirit in which you should read 'the critics'.

In this chapter we look at four different critics' reactions to the poems, but without any pretence that they are 'representative'. Those who are interested in the varieties of critical theory and approach should go on to read from the suggestions in Further Reading following this chapter, and make use of further bibliographies in the critical works themselves to pursue their research. Such reading will reveal that there are several very different strands of each of feminist, psychoanalytical, marxist/cultural, structuralist and historicist criticisms, as well as a wealth of other critics who have no single theoretical approach but borrow their concerns and techniques eclectically. The virtue of the four critics we discuss here, then, is simply that they are stimulating, and different from each other. Before summarising our four chosen critics' arguments, we will briefly consider where Larkin criticism stands at the time of writing.

The Progress of Larkin Criticism

During most of Philip Larkin's writing life, critics tended to accept his work in relation to the public image he cultivated: that of a quiet and withdrawn man, sceptical and ironic. An unexciting library drudge, he presented himself as an ordinary chap using the language of casual chat in an English pub. The critics, broadly complicit in this presentation, agreed to focus on Larkin's 'Englishness', and they divided simply on the question of whether they liked his 'Englishness' or not. For example, Charles Tomlinson complained of Larkin's 'narrowness' and saw the poems as 'The joke which hesitates just on this side of nihilism', commenting that these 'stepped-down' characteristics are 'national vices'.[1] Donald Davie defended Larkin: comparing him to Hardy, Davie asserted that 'The England in his poems is the England we have inhabited'.[2] The consensus on Larkin's 'Englishness', and his retiring, parochial personality, was not seriously challenged for a long time, which may seem surprising when we read the forthright

opinions and depth of confident reflection apparent in *Required Writing*.
Views such as Tomlinson's and Davie's – a complaint that the poetry
was narrow and therefore trivial, answered by a defence based on a
perceived English tradition – more or less set the terms of debate
about Larkin until the mid 1970s.

Stephen Regan[3] sets the date of a change at 1975, when
J. R. Watson wrote 'The Other Larkin', an article which noticed deeper
layers of emotion, and spiritual longings in the poems.[4] Certainly,
from the mid-1970s on, a variety of critics began to approach Larkin's
poetry in new ways, reflecting the growth at that time of literary
'theories', each developing its own predilections and methods, and
each applying its theory to a re-evaluation of texts. Seamus Heaney's
view[5] emphasised the affirmative elements in Larkin, finding a
visionary, transcendental quality he likened to the Modernism of
Yeats and Joyce. Heaney detects 'an escape from the ... disillusioned
intelligence' in 'a realm beyond the social and historical'. Such
moments express 'the deepest strata of Larkin's poetic self' that could
be called 'Elysian'. Heaney's essay was one part of a rethinking about
Larkin that continued past the poet's death through the 1980s.
Andrew Motion and Barbara Everett contributed to symbolist readings of Larkin; David Lodge contributed a structuralist analysis; and
many others made influential contributions during this period. Blake
Morrison, in his 1980 study of the Movement, points out that Larkin
only shares some characteristics with the others in the group; and that
the Movement dissolved, each writer following 'Divergent Lines',
after 1956.[6] We are not able to follow the development of and arguments between symbolist, structuralist, feminist, historicist and other
readings in this chapter: we simply do not have the space. However,
we can draw one conclusion: that the narratives about Larkin that
had been unquestioned until the mid-1970s, could no longer be sustained. There were three 'narratives'. First, that Larkin was an ordinary and very English chap writing only about everyday trivial
experiences. Secondly, that Larkin was somehow very literal, and not
influenced by Modernists such as Yeats and Joyce, or by foreign
poetry such as the French symbolists. Finally, that Larkin was a
Movement poet limited to clarity, intelligibility and ironic scepticism.
Suddenly, when the poems themselves were reread with these three

mythical assumptions out of the way, a far wider variety of discourse became apparent.

The critical reaction to Larkin then received a nasty jolt, which reset the entire agenda: Anthony Thwaite's edition of *The Collected Poems* (1988) doubled the amount of poetry available for study and included unfinished poems and juvenilia, providing new ground for criticism. Then, with the publication of Thwaite's *Selected Letters of Philip Larkin, 1940–1985* (1992) and Andrew Motion's biography *Philip Larkin: A Writer's Life* (1993), the storm broke. The letters and the biography revealed Larkin's misogyny, racism and right-wing, even neo-fascist, opinions. Even worse, the poet was revealed as habitually using abusive and obscene language, and as a collector and user of pornography. Germaine Greer, in her review of the *Collected Poems*, was one of the first to attack, saying that the poems express attitudes 'anti-intellectual, racist, sexist, and rotten with class-consciousness'.[7] When the letters and biography were added to the melting-pot, many reacted like Lisa Jardine: writing in *The Guardian* in December 1992, she pointed out that the letters are 'a steady stream of casual obscenity, throwaway derogatory remarks about women, and arrogant disdain for those of different skin colour or nationality', and commented that Larkin was no longer taught at her college. When Alan Bennett read Motion's biography, he felt that he had 'lost a friend', and that he was 'not wanting to believe that Larkin was really like this'. Bennett felt the pressure to transfer his revulsion from the man to his reading of the poetry: 'Reading it [*A Writer's Life*] I could not see how [the poems] would emerge unscathed. But I have read them again and they do …'.[8] The mass of biographical material that suddenly appeared in 1992–3 has received further additions since, and it is these controversial revelations about Larkin the man that have driven debates about the nature and value of his poetry since then. Battle-lines have been drawn between those, like Jardine, whose first instinct is to censor; and those like Bennett, who still find pleasure in the poetry, even if that is at the expense of setting aside what they know of the author.

Where is Larkin criticism now? The full answer to this question is far too long and complicated for the present chapter. The simple answer is that the entire project is far from settled. What we have are the multiple different approaches to literature generated by the various different schools of criticism; but in the case of Larkin the landscape is further complicated by a simmering argument about the man. This argument is virulently pursued, and has been grafted onto the top of the long-running argument about whether Larkin is a major poet or a trivial pretender. As James Booth writes in his introduction to *New Larkins for Old*, 'it seems ... impossible to detect a common critical or theoretical thread uniting the fifteen essays collected here'.[9] No: Larkin criticism is very far from settled, and we must proceed to our sample with no pretence that these critics are or could be 'representative'.

Tom Paulin

Tom Paulin wrote his essay as a review of Janice Rossen's *Philip Larkin: His Life's Work*, in which she contends that the poet's range and sympathies are limited by his neuroses, and in particular by his difficulties with women and sex.[10] Paulin begins by asserting that the timeless and sad lyricism of Larkin's 'Afternoons' reminds us of medieval English lyrics, but this encourages us to respond emotionally to the 'universal' image of a season, and miss the poem's real theme, which is 'national decline' (p. 160). The 'something' pushing mothers 'To the side of their own lives' is a metaphor for 'fading imperial power'. Paulin therefore believes that 'Afternoons' is 'a subtly disguised public poem, for it comments on a social experience' (p. 161). In his view, Larkin was an English Protestant whose royalist patriotism was intensified by his experiences in Ireland.

Having stated his thesis, Paulin then elaborates with references to 'The March Past', 'Going, Going' and 'The Whitsun Weddings', seeing in all of these a theme of post-imperial decline subtly and obliquely injected by Larkin under the guise of his image as a gloomy, private man. This trick 'is another form of concealment, for it enables him to issue public statements disguised as lyric poems' (p. 162). Paulin's suggestion is that much of the 'universal' symbolic imagery of nature and the seasons in Larkin's poems is not primarily a nostalgic English pastoral, but instead presents a coded message about the nation's decline in Larkin's present. So Paulin proceeds to an interpretation of

'At Grass'. He sees the horses as emblems of heroism and victory in a past described in the third stanza, while in the first stanza:

> The phrase 'cold shade', like 'distresses', is classical – this is the under-world of dreary shades that move through the waste dominions of the dead in the *Aeneid*. The horses are heroic ancestors – famous generals, perhaps, who can now 'stand at ease' but who are also vulnerable, anony-mous and largely neglected. Only the groom and his boy tend them now. Like the last vestiges of traditional hierarchy, these servants 'with bridles in the evening come' – the closing line's elegiac, slightly archaic cadencing beautifully imparts a strange sense of threat. (p. 163)

Paulin comments that although Larkin celebrates England, these celebrations are 'shot through with an intense loathing of his own insularity'; and this feeling's bleakness and closed or restricted quality is codified in the poems under the guise of Larkin's concern about 'the autonomous self' (p. 164).

Having made a connection between the condition of national decline, and Larkin's recurrent concerns about his autonomy, Paulin then develops a further link by suggesting that Larkin's long-troubled argument with himself about marriage, is 'like a public agonising about national sovereignty' (p. 164). The various attics, rooms and flats that figure in poems like 'Mr Bleaney', 'Counting' and 'Poetry of Departures' are all attempts to achieve autonomy, and therefore to exclude the 'other' (which is represented by women in many of the poems) with varying success:

> Thus Larkin's favourite romantic value, 'solitude', designates the con-sciousness of the autonomous English male professional. It refers not to physical isolation, but to a consciousness which has been moulded by up-bringing and education to manage and govern. Such personali-ties, with their committee skills, power lusts and filing-cabinet voices, are seldom attractive, but what is so lovable about Larkin's persona is the evident discomfort he feels with the shape of the personality he has been given. Angry at not being allowed to show emotion, he writhes with anxiety inside that sealed bunker which is the English ethic of privacy. He journeys into the interior, into the unknown heart – the maybe missing centre – of Englishness. (pp. 166–7)

Paulin proceeds to analyse the character Robin from *A Girl in Winter*, and the foreign Katherine's inability to understand his repressed English personality, and then discusses Larkin's love of black American jazz. In *All What Jazz* Larkin argued that jazz lost its edge 'when the Negro stopped wanting to entertain the white man', and Paulin comments on this as an example of Larkin's deep-seated need to be in control and to submit everything to rationality, but his simultaneous 'desperate attraction to something which is apparently other than that power' (p. 169). Paulin describes Larkin's love of jazz as his use of 'mechanically reproduced emotion – emotion that can be switched off and on at will and so be controlled in the way that trees in a high wind and personal relationships cannot be' (pp. 169–70).

Picking up the thread of the rooms in Larkin's poems, Paulin suggests that they set up opposites: a warm place with light or a fire inside, and emptiness or cold outside. In 'High Windows' Larkin sets the windows of his top-floor flat against the 'paradise' of youth and permissive sexuality. This leads Paulin on to expound his idea that Larkin had a 'secret' idea of the poet, opposite to the argument he frequently put forward in his critical prose that the poet should have a 'direct relationship' with the reader by being 'normal': poetry is 'an affair of sanity, of seeing things as they are'. This idea seems humble and low-key, but Paulin asserts that 'he has an altogether more ambitious concept of the poet that Milton, Shelley and Yeats would have approved' (p. 171).

To clarify this point, Paulin picks out the images of 'a flattened cube of light' of 'By day, a lifted study-storehouse' (*CP*, 220), the 'air-sharpened blade' of the moon in 'Vers de Société', and finally the poem 'Livings II' about a lighthouse-keeper, and 'Friday Night in the Royal Station Hotel'. The hotel is like a 'fort' and Paulin finds that the 'bold deployment of *ostranenye* [defamiliarisation] which transforms the Victorian hotel into a place of mystery and danger is essentially colonial, rather than European' (pp. 173–4). He then suggests that these images are analogous to Yeats's tower or Milton's star-gazing Platonist, although what Larkin sees from his tower is not the same. Paulin ends his essay by reminding us that Larkin often seems to speak for the England of Norman Tebbit, the right-wing Conservative politician, 'and for that gnarled and angry puritanism which is so deeply ingrained in the culture'. Recognising this:

> Larkin called himself 'one of nature's Orangemen', adopting the mask of an Ulster Protestant, a sort of Belfast Dirk Dogstoerd,[11] in order to ironise his own philistinism. Yet that attitude was itself a strategy because it enabled him to conceal the knowledge that he had created many outstandingly beautiful poems. In that distinctively embarrassed English manner he had to bury his pride in his artistic creations under several sackfuls of ugly prejudices.   (pp. 175–6)

Paulin signs off by describing 'the very cunning and very wounded personality of a poet whose sometimes rancid prejudices are part of his condition, part of the wound' (p. 176).

Tom Paulin's essay, then, begins with an assertion that the poems are coded comments on post-imperial Britain, but this is only a preamble. What he is most interested in is the psychology of a repressed Englishman, unable to express emotion and brought up to insist on power, in order to control his life and surroundings: the 'autonomous English male professional'. From there, Paulin's essay develops suggestions about Larkin's careful concealments and the strategies by which he manages to dissemble himself, as it were. The conclusion seems balanced between Larkin's character and his works. Paulin is clear that there was something psychologically wrong with Larkin, but sees the poems as 'outstandingly beautiful'.

James Booth

Booth begins by declaring that many critics (including Paulin) have examined Larkin's poems as products of history and his time, rather than aesthetically as lyrics.[12] He then promises to consider Larkin's 'Englishness' from three points of view: first, with an analysis of the lighthouse-keeper's poem, 'Livings II'; secondly by comparing Larkin's and Alice Walker's treatments of masturbation; and finally by discussing Larkin's racism in connection with his enthusiasm for black jazz.

Booth's analysis of 'Livings II' begins by pointing out that the three men who figure in the three 'Livings' poems are simply random

choices, from different times. All they have in common is 'simply that
they are "living" '. Larkin returns to an earlier style, using extravagant
symbolism, in 'Livings II', although 'the rich evocativeness of his
early style has been replaced by a mannered, elliptical terseness
reminiscent of Imagism' (p. 191). Booth analyses a virtuoso poetic
performance, describing the effects Larkin achieves with his use of
metre and imagery, and praising his success in combining 'Elaborate'
technique with 'the impression of a real person speaking spontaneously' (p. 192). Larkin uses the surprising image of the radio as a
cricket rubbing its legs together to introduce a startling paradox: he
chooses the 'traditional cosy retreat in a warm inn' as the contrast to
the speaker's solitude. This makes the concept of solitude uncompro-
mising: 'The lighthouse-keeper exults in the storm, in the swerving
snow and the "Leather-black waters" which confirm his immunity
from human intrusion. His retreat is no warm sociable inn; it is a
fiercely anti-social cell of solitude' (p. 192). Booth suggests that the
desire for solitude, to escape from human company, expressed in
'Livings II', is more akin to Andrew Marvell's in 'The Garden', than
to Yeats's Platonist in his tower, since Larkin's character is simply
earning his living by looking after the lighthouse, not embarking on
a spiritual quest as in Yeats's poem. There may be a sense in which
Larkin's and Marvell's 'witty projections of their private worlds place
them in a distinctly English tradition' (p. 193), and this thought
raises the ideological debate again: should we follow up this thought
by seeking a political interpretation of the poem?

James Booth launches himself back into the debate with gusto.
He is a persuasive writer, particularly in the common-sensical mode
he adopts for demolishing Paulin. Having summarised part of
Paulin's argument, Booth then points out that the problem is the
argument's ethical claim:

> No doubt the author of 'Livings II' is, as Paulin says, English, he is
> male, he belongs to the professional classes, and he has a strong sense
> of privacy. He might also be said to have a 'wounded personality'.
> But the same could be said for innumerable other men of Larkin's
> generation who wrote no poetry or bad poetry. The *poetry* cannot be
> explained by this analysis. And Larkin is a poet, not a propagandist.

He quite lacks the ideological assertiveness which Paulin attributes to him. (pp. 194–5)

Booth points out that, in lyric poetry, the writer uses his form and style to reduce the specifics of time and place, or ideological influence, not to conceal or expand them. The lyric characteristically seeks to express a universal theme such as time or death, and 'Livings II' is no exception: 'Larkin has not cast the poem in this highly-wrought symbolic mode in order to conceal or mystify his own "real" ideological concerns, but in order to transcend them' (p. 195).

Booth is scathing about Paulin's interpretations of 'At Grass' and 'Afternoons' as political allegory; instead, he sees these straightforwardly as lyrics evoking the universal themes of time and ageing, themes relevant to all of us and to the poet. This is what lyric poems do, according to Booth:

> Larkin's Englishness may be intense, but it is not a matter of coherent ideology. His poems present lyric universals with an English accent. This is why his work is so popular abroad. In Paulin's hands Larkin's beautiful, static, depersonalised lyrics are perversely returned to the parochial kinetics from which they have been so artistically disengaged – as though the critic's duty were to uncover what Larkin's poetry would have been like had he *not* been a great poet. (pp. 196–7)

On the question of 'At Grass' and 'Afternoons' I find myself on Booth's side of the argument: Paulin's 'real' coded message does seem to be simple assertion, reading meaning into the poem with no evidence that such a meaning is there. On the other hand, some of Paulin's remarks on Larkin's 'secret' concept of the isolated poet and the motifs of towers, forts and windows, and his analysis of Larkin's need to 'control' a too wild reality, chime with what we have found in our analyses in Part I. Later in this chapter we will summarise yet another – and again completely different – reading of 'At Grass', from Stephen Cooper. The two critics we have sampled so far are instructive as they show how widely disagreement yawns between opposed views, and Booth shows how forcefully critics can write about each other: his response to Paulin's essay could be called – in Larkinesque English vernacular – a 'trashing'.

However, we will stay with James Booth to sample another portion of his argument, this time from his 1992 book *Philip Larkin: Writer*. In the final chapter of this work, Booth develops his view that lyric poems aim to 'transcend' the parochial, and that Larkin's poetry is of this kind, by suggesting that his poems differ from previous lyrics in one essential: that he achieves what Booth calls a 'diction of negative sublimity'.[13] Booth points to the poem 'Here' as a successful example of this effect. The journey through Hull 'progresses from detachment into deeper detachment' (p. 164) because it is not a journey to Hull at all, only a journey passing through the bustling town, while the speaker remains separate from the life of the place, observing and slightly patronising. The true aim of the journey is in fact the seashore at the end of the Holderness peninsula, where 'the poet finds the more sublime detachment at which he has been aiming' (p. 164). Booth notes the repeated prefix 'un-' in the final lines, and asks two questions: does the poet enjoy his seclusion and his safety because he is 'out of reach' of others? Or, is he excluded, 'selflessly contemplating an unfenced existence, which is by definition "out of reach", even of himself?' (p. 165).

Booth feels that this sort of speculation might lead us to think there is a religious element in Larkin's poems, and notes that this has been suggested by other critics. However, he then turns to 'Water', 'Solar' and 'High Windows' as a means of clarifying the question. These poems, he says, treat natural elements with a 'distinctive light-textured lyricism'. In 'Water', there is a joke pagan religion which sets water and light in the place of God, and these are 'totally unhuman elements ... with no spiritual, moral or emotional content, quite unrelated to human values' (p. 166). Booth eventually turns to 'High Windows' and notes how starkly, and without warning, the poem moves from Larkin's coarser manner to the opposite, lyrical style. Booth comments:

> The poem repeats in more succinct form the pattern of 'Here'. The poet moves from unsatisfactory social exclusion into the absolution of beautiful emptiness. In this poem however the elements of Larkin's negative sublime take even purer forms. The 'deep blue air' of 'High Windows' is more abstract than the 'bluish neutral distance' of the

Holderness peninsula, and the air here is not 'Luminously-peopled', even by midges. Rather, it 'shows / Nothing ...'. (pp. 167–8)

Booth points out that this sudden emptiness also silences the poet: it comes 'rather than words', and so removes his poetic function. In conclusion, Booth explains that:

> His rhetoric contrives a sublime emotional elevation out of negatives. It is essential to the effect, for instance, that 'endless' comes emphatically last in the sequence of three adjectives. In actual fact there is 'nothing' to be endlessly prolonged and 'nowhere' to prolong it. None the less 'endless' inevitably carries the force of transcendence, of eternity. The poet dispels his sordid and embarrassing social resentments by the extreme expedient of absenting himself rhetorically from the poem. Once again it is the contemplation of his own absence which most thrills him. (p. 168)

Booth then follows up his analysis of Larkin as a lyric poet concerned with the timeless themes of lyric poetry, with this suggestion that Larkin's means of transcending the parochial is paradoxically to seek, and poetically achieve, self-erasure.

This is an interesting argument, and certainly expresses something of the extraordinary effects Larkin achieves in the finales to 'Here' and 'High Windows'. Although we may accept that Booth is striving to express the inexpressible, with his paradoxical poet writing about an absence of words, and writing himself into nothingness, there is no question about the sudden power with which nothingness is evoked in these two finales.

Steve Clark

Steve Clark takes up the argument between the aesthetic reading of Larkin and a historicist reading.[14] He rehearses the views of James Booth and Stephen Regan, and takes issue with them via his own interpretation of 'If, My Darling', which reads it as an allegory of Britain's altered status in the postwar period. Clark comments that

'This would be supported by the now fairly traditional reading of Larkin's writing in terms of internalized political elegy' (p. 167), but contends that things are really more complicated than has previously been acknowledged, because the poem's tone is anger rather than the mood of resignation you would expect; and because the objects signifying empire are located 'in my head' and are not real. This is the point that gives Clark his title, as all that has been 'lost' in this poem were always illusions, or 'displays'. This point answers the criticism that Larkin ignored the financial motives of the empire (in poems such as 'Homage to a Government'), since the insubstantial illusion of empire he conveys was actually an economic bluff for a hundred years, according to recent historiography: Britain did not profit from holding an empire after the mid nineteenth century, so the 'essentially chimerical nature' of the empire accords well with Larkin's chimerical 'Pure marchings, pure apparitions' (*CP*, 55).

Clark then digresses to disagree with Paulin's reading of 'Afternoons' and 'At Grass', partly on the grounds that losing an empire is not, historically, necessarily coterminous with decline: it can bring greater prosperity. He then puts forward the revisionist historical view that the Suez debacle was, effectively, a ruthless *coup d'état* in which America got rid of a disobedient British premier, and states his main contention: 'that issues of empire in the postwar period necessarily involve issues of Anglo-American relations, more specifically the displacement of an older empire by a newly ascendant power' (p. 170). Clark notes the convergence of views between those who wish to remove Larkin from his place in English studies, and those who defend the poems as 'the beautiful flowers … growing … out of pretty dismal ground',[15] as both presuppose a connection between Larkin's nostalgia and Britain's postwar decline. Clark, on the other hand, questions this assumption. To do so, he begins by picking up from Seamus Heaney's remark that poets of colonial nations once suffered from a 'peculiar affliction' because they were not English but spoke and wrote in English. Heaney throws off the idea that 'The poets of the mother culture, I feel, are now possessed of that defensive love of their territory which was once shared only by those poets whom we might call colonial'. Clark takes up this 'peculiar affliction' of post-imperial writers and applies the idea to Larkin. He points out that the idea of nostalgia for communal Englishness is very un-Larkin-like: 'the prospect of "sharing" in any form tends to be regarded by Larkin with an utter lack of enthusiasm' (p. 172). 'I Remember, I Remember' 'refuses any sentimental idealization of the "forgotten boredom" of childhood, and, by implication, any nationalist myth of organic continuity' (pp. 172–3).

There is a new perspective on 'tradition' among social historians, who are now more likely to emphasise how traditions are invented and projected back into the past, as convenient myths to underlie the present; and recent work has highlighted how many English 'traditions' were concocted in the late nineteenth century. Clark then adds a further ingredient to his argument, suggesting that the real conflict was never between past power and present decline: instead, it was a battle in the present against American hegemony, both in poetry and in terms of world power. This can be seen in Larkin's edition of *The Oxford Book of Twentieth Century English Verse*, where the purpose of his selection was to explore whether the Georgians could be said to be an English tradition submerged by the 'double impact of the Great War and the Irish-American-continental properties of both Eliot and Yeats';[16] and the threat can be seen in A. Alvarez's introduction to *The New Poetry* in 1962, which attacked Larkin and championed Lowell, Berryman, Plath and Sexton for dramatizing 'disintegration and breakdown' and therefore representing a 'large step forward'. Clark concludes that Larkin's criticism was intended to invent a tradition in order to fend off the incursions of American Modernism.

The crucial poem, according to Clark, is 'MCMXIV', and he quotes a number of critics who have complained that this poem presents a series of distant images, while the poet remains cut off and the past is like a 'stage set'. Clark agrees with these observations about the poem, but adds that the poem 'offers a commemoration of the dead that brings them back to life as a conscious fiction' (p. 175). He explains that the disconnected list of impressions the poem provides is deliberately like a slide show, highlighting its artificiality, and that the silence of the departing men ('Without a word') 'allows Larkin to comment obliquely on the process of mythicization that the poem itself performs' (p. 176). Quoting Larkin's letter to Sutton about not bothering to read the newspapers, and struggling to write *A Girl in Winter* instead, Clark concludes that Larkin's anti-political pose may be thought defensive rather than neutral, 'as a form of intervention against an emergent American hegemony during this period' (p. 177).

Larkin's consistently hostile attitude towards America underlines this point, and Clark quotes from various letters, including a small verse regretting that Amis, Conquest and Wain all went to America, and asserting that Larkin would put up with 'gassy beer, / The trolley-bus at ten past nine' and be 'staying here'.[17] Clark's argument here seems to be turning around previous assumptions about Larkin's relation to post-imperial Britain. Larkin is not writing from a past 'centre' of imperial power, and nostalgic about its decline, because he recognizes such a so-called 'tradition' as an artificial fiction in any case. Instead, Larkin is defending from the 'periphery' of a new, American sphere of influence, like a colonial writer in the days of Britain's hegemony. Jake Balokowsky, in 'Posterity', is the representative enemy in this battle.

Clark's article ends by pointing out that Larkin carried on this battle to preserve 'his own territory' from American economic and cultural invasion, in his professional life as a librarian: witness his long campaign to keep manuscript collections of British writers in the country, and his resentment of the massive buying power of American universities. In *Required Writing* Larkin complained that 'A meeting of British national and university librarians to discuss modern literary manuscripts resembles an annual convention of stable-door lockers'.[18]

Clark's article is wide-ranging as it builds its argument, and there are some doubtful moments where he adduces evidence that may not be material. We may question in particular his reference to recent historiographers and social historians who are revising our interpretations of the Suez crisis and of manufactured 'traditions': would Larkin have viewed current events in this 'recent' light? On the other hand, his analysis of 'MCMXIV' is persuasive, and his article certainly helps to elucidate the contradiction that was always apparent, between a Larkin who recoiled from sharing or joining in, and the assertion that he felt nostalgia for a traditional community. Clark certainly succeeds in questioning an oversimplified view of Larkin; and his suggestion that the poet was engaged in post-colonial defence of his territory from the periphery of a new American empire, and fighting a contemporary battle, not one lost in the past, can help us with some elements in the poetry that have previously seemed anomalous.

Stephen Cooper

Stephen Cooper's recent book tackles the accusations against Larkin of racism, sexism and reactionary views, by arguing that he was ultimately a subversive writer.[19] Cooper spends most of his book discussing Larkin's two novels *Jill* and *A Girl in Winter*, and a wealth of recently available biographical material relating to Larkin's friendship with Jim Sutton, and Sutton's aesthetic as a painter. Cooper turns to the poems in the final chapter of his book. We will look at his analysis of 'Deceptions', then quote his conclusion in full to see how he faces the problem Alan Bennett described when he wrote, 'Reading it [*A Writer's Life*] I could not see how [the poems] would emerge unscathed'.

'Deceptions' is a poem central to the debate about Larkin's misogyny. Janice Rossen argued that 'Larkin almost exploits the scene by evoking the girl's words and her misery and then turning to the criminal's point of view. It appears almost frighteningly detached'.[20] She concludes about 'Deceptions' that 'the callousness which it exhibits and the sadism which it in part condones ought at the least to be seen as problematic – and as a limitation in Larkin's art'.[21] Cooper responds to this charge as part of his argument that Larkin's major poems are 'performative' and highly conscious and deliberate in the impression they create, due to their many dramatized voices, and he 'combines theatrical and novelistic ploys with a colloquial idiom in order to probe settled attitudes in the 1950s' (p. 124).

'Deceptions', Cooper argues, follows a conventional moral response to the Victorian anecdote, and allows this voice full play: Larkin's sympathy for the victim is fully expressed. However, the poem as a whole does not follow the conventional moral line, but instead the blunt fifth line of the second stanza wrecks the metre, and signals a break with 'pat conventional attitudes'. The controversial final lines which suggest that the rapist is more deluded than his victim actually conflate both experiences: 'Just as the girl was physically trapped, the rapist is also caught in the caverns of predatory male sex-uality' (p. 133). He stresses, also, that Larkin has separated his remarks about deception, from his empathy for the female victim, by acknowledging that she 'would not care', so that the poet's sense of her suffering is not diminished by his reflections about the rapist. The poem 'expresses a greater empathy for the rape victim' (p. 133) than some critics have allowed. Cooper appears to be arguing that this poem is a critical comment on gendered behaviour; that the poet, implicitly, is calling for liberation of both sexes from the imprisonment and suffering of exploitative behaviour.

Cooper then turns to 'At Grass'. He rehearses previous critics' interpretations of this poem, including Paulin and Booth who are represented in the present chapter: some, he says, have seen an alle-gory of past glory, while others see the horses' retirement as akin to the 'oblivion' longed for elsewhere in Larkin's work. Cooper brings in a dream about horses from among the dreams Larkin recorded under the influence of Jung, while he was at Oxford in 1942, and then enters on a skilful analysis of the poem. The opening empha-sises the horses' oneness with nature ('the eye can hardly pick them out') and casts doubt on the human observer's status in the scene: they are 'seeming to look on', but the poet cannot know the reason for their pose. He 'imposes purpose and strategy on what is simply instinctual behaviour' (p. 137). Similarly, their 'names were artificed' exposes human interference, as conventional labels are imposed on oppressed subjects. In Cooper's view, the poem is a criticism of exploitation: 'The animals have been used simply as a means of perpetuating a highly profitable human activity ... An ardent supporter of animal rights, Larkin chafed at such manipulative treatment of innocent beasts' (p. 138). Cooper notes that, although there is some relief from exploitation because 'they have slipped their names' and thus shed their imposed identity, the final line cuts against any idealistic reading, for the 'bridles' still represent human ownership and control.

The argument that Cooper builds is, essentially, that Larkin under-cuts, by means of parody, contrast and interplay of 'performative' voices, or implicit attack, any and all oppressions and restrictive structures that appear in his poems; and that the aesthetic he and

Sutton developed, and to which he remained true, demanded that no clichéd narrative could remain unsubverted. Larkin calls on the reader to deplore both forms of sexual oppression in 'Deceptions', and the exploitation as well as the false projection of human motives onto instinctual beasts, in 'At Grass'. Cooper concludes:

> There are, it seems, two Larkins: one is the idealistic rebel deconstructing the dogmas of the other entrenched conformist persona, unwriting or parodying the vindictive tirades expressed in the letters. Such aspects of Larkin cannot be ignored. But these 'limitations' are mapped onto the geography of the poems, where they are ridiculed, taunted and rejected so that – aesthetically transformed – they become enlisted in Larkin's career-long campaign against clichéd narratives.   (p. 182)

Stephen Cooper's study of Larkin's and Sutton's jointly developed aesthetic, and his consequent reinterpretation of the poems, is in deliberate response to Stephen Regan's expectation, that the availability of ever more biographical and personal material about Larkin will lead to a re-evaluation. Predicting the future direction of Larkin studies, Regan wrote in 1992: 'it seems likely that many readers will come to regard the poetry of Philip Larkin as an imaginative declaration of resistance and solidarity against the aggressive and demeaning self-interest that has characterised the final decades of the twentieth century'.[22]

This might be an appropriate thought with which to conclude our sample of critics if it were not for the fragmented, unsettled state of Larkin studies: there are other directions in which criticism may develop in the future, and in which it is developing at present, which are different from the kind of re-evaluation Regan and Cooper envisage. For example, John Osborne's 'PostModernism and Postcolonialism in the Poetry of Philip Larkin' discusses the poetry as developing beyond existentialism and, with its recurrent preoccupation with 'decidability', preparing the way for an English 'postModernism': Larkin was 'post Modernist' but not 'postmodern'.[23] Clearly, Osborne is engaged upon a different project from Regan and Cooper; and his line of enquiry is different again from that of James Booth which we sampled above, although there is more common ground in that direction. V. Penelope Pelizzon, on the other hand, shares some perceptions with Cooper: her application of ideas about Carnival from Bakhtin to Larkin's poetry echoes Cooper's emphasis on dramatic performance as well as subversion.[24]

We are unable to predict the course of future Larkin criticism, then; but in this chapter we have met some variety, and mentioned some of the major controversies along the way. We pointed out at the start of the chapter that our sample cannot pretend to be representative, but at least the variety has enabled us to present the argumentative nature of current professional criticism written about Larkin.

I am, inevitably, regretful that this chapter could not present the views of Seamus Heaney, Stephen Regan, John Osborne, Barbara Everett, David Lodge, Stan Smith, Andrew Swarbrick, and V. Penelope Pelizzon, to name only a few. I can only urge you to read more widely among Larkin critics, using the suggestions for further reading that follow this chapter, as a starting-point. There are so many different points of view and ongoing critical projects, you are sure to find some which provoke, challenge or stimulate you, and send you back to the poetry seeking fresh readings and insights.

Notes

Chapter 1: Hearing Larkin's Voices

1 *Philip Larkin: Collected Poems*, ed. Anthony Thwaite (London, 1988), p. xv. References to Larkin's poems will be to this edition (identified as *CP*), followed by the page number.

2 Philip Larkin, in D. J. Enright (ed.), *Poets of the 1950s* (Tokyo, 1956).

3 Andrew Motion, *Philip Larkin: A Writer's Life* (London, 1993), p. 129. Hereafter *A Writer's Life*.

Chapter 2: 'Solitaire, Solidaire'

1 *Solidaire, Solitaire* is the choice between the reclusive and the gregarious life that the artist cannot resolve, in Albert Camus's short story *Jonas, où l'artiste au travail*.

2 'If, My Darling' (*CP*, 41).

3 See 'Vers de Société'.

4 See Chapter 3 for a detailed discussion of this poem.

5 See *A Writer's Life*, pp. 288–9.

6 'If, My Darling' (*CP*, 41), l. 21.

7 'It is an aged mother and the thought of marriage, just as much as the prospect of drinking "washing sherry" and talking drivel, that threaten the time he would prefer to spend "under a lamp" ' (*A Writer's Life*, p. 412).

8 Letter from Ruth Bowman to Philip Larkin, 22 September 1950, quoted in *A Writer's Life*, p. 194.

9   See, for example, James Booth's view (summarised in Chapter
     9): 'The lighthouse-keeper exults in the storm, in the swerving
     snow and the "Leather-black waters" which confirm his immu-
     nity from human intrusion. His retreat is no warm sociable inn;
     it is a fiercely anti-social cell of solitude' (James Booth, 'Philip
     Larkin: Lyricism, Englishness and Postcoloniality', in
     Stephen Regan (ed.), *New Casebooks: Philip Larkin* (Basingstoke,
     1997), p. 192).
10   We will return to this particular line in Chapter 5.

Chapter 3: Weddings and Work

1   Quoted in *A Writer's Life*, pp. 287–8.
2   See *The General Prologue* to *The Canterbury Tales*, ll. 208–69.
     The quotation is from line 264.
3   *Shorter Oxford English Dictionary* (*SOED*), 1975.
4   *SOED*, 1975.
5   See, for example, Auden's 'On this Island', or Sylvia Plath's
     'Blackberrying' which was published in 1971, the year before
     Larkin completed 'The Building'. Larkin's own 'Next, Please' (*CP*,
     52) implicitly employs the same figure: people stand on the shore
     watching the approach of the 'black-sailed unfamiliar' ship of
     death; and the final stanza of 'Here' could be another analogous
     seashore.
6   'Ambulances' (*CP*, 132–3), ll. 13–14.
7   Stan Smith, for example, feels 'a little uncomfortable' and notes
     that Larkin must be a motorist himself to be in the M1 café, in
     order to observe the other patrons. He comments: 'Tourists
     always complain that the tourists are spoiling the view' (S.
     Smith, *Inviolable Voice: History and Twentieth-Century Poetry*,
     Dublin, 1982).
8   'Posterity' (*CP*, 170).
9   *Selected Letters of Philip Larkin, 1940–1985*, ed. Anthony
     Thwaite (London, 1992). References to this work will
     appear in the text identified as *Letters*, followed by the page
     number.

10 *Jane Austen's Letters*, ed. R. W. Chapman, 2nd edn (London, 1952), p. 401.

11 You may also wish to look at Steve Clark, ' "Get Out as Early As You Can": Larkin's Sexual Politics', and Janice Rossen, 'Difficulties with Girls', both in Regan (ed.), *New Casebooks: Philip Larkin*, pp. 94–159. These two articles will give you a start in looking at the critical arguments.

Chapter 4: 'Tilting a blind face to the sky'

1 Andrew Motion, 'Philip Larkin and Symbolism', in Regan (ed.), *New Casebooks: Philip Larkin*, p. 33.

2 David Lodge, 'Philip Larkin: The Metonymic Muse', in Regan (ed.), *New Casebooks: Philip Larkin*, p. 79.

3 For example, 'Lines on a Young Lady's Photograph Album' and 'Wild Oats'.

4 *A Writer's Life*, p. 468.

5 *Thomas Hardy: The Complete Poems*, ed. James Gibson (London, 1976), p. 81.

6 Ibid., p. 346.

7 In this chapter there is no space to pursue such philosophic elements in Larkin's poems further. An interesting discussion of Larkin's place in the development of twentieth-century thought and aesthetics can be found in John Osborne's 'Post Modernism and Postcolonialism in the Poetry of Philip Larkin', in James Booth (ed.), *New Larkins For Old: Critical Essays* (Basingstoke, 2000), pp. 144–65.

8 See, for example, 'The Life with a Hole in It', which was composed in 1974 (*CP*, 202).

Chapter 5: Travel, Skies and Observation

1 Winifred Arnott, a young library colleague in Belfast with whom Larkin carried on an 'almost-affair' in the early 1950s before she left to marry her long-term admirer, in 1953.

2 *Younger British Poets of Today*, BBC radio broadcast, 20 August 1958.

3   Sigmund Freud, *The Complete Introductory Lectures on Psychoanalysis*, trans. James Strachey (Oxford, 1971), pp. 376–7.
4   See, for example, Janice Rossen's view that the poem is 'a limitation in Larkin's art' because it exhibits 'callousness' and partly condones 'sadism' (Rossen, 'Difficulties with Girls', in Regan (ed.), *New Casebooks: Philip Larkin*, p. 154).

Chapter 7: Larkin's Life and the Literary Context

1   Molly Bateman, quoted in *A Writer's Life*, p. 152.
2   Ibid., p. 391.
3   Quoted ibid., p. 475.
4   Maeve Brennan, *The Philip Larkin I Knew* (Manchester, 2002).
5   Ibid., p. 51.
6   *A Writer's Life*, p. 453.
7   Brennan, *The Philip Larkin I Knew*, p. 132.
8   Ibid.
9   Maeve Brennan in a letter to Andrew Motion, quoted in *A Writer's Life*, p. 447.
10 Brennan, *The Philip Larkin I Knew*, p. 133.
11 'Annus Mirabilis', *CP*, 167.
12 D. H. Lawrence, 'Pornography and Obscenity', *Selected Literary Criticism*, ed. Anthony Beal (London, 1967), pp. 32–51. Lawrence's theory is that Victorian prudishness encouraged the habit of masturbation, and a masturbatory, 'pornographic' and exploitative attitude towards sexual love. Lawrence believed that English men grow up unnaturally perverted by the influence of the Victorian century and its 'dirty little secret' of masturbation. As a result, he suggests, English men are unable to achieve love in a sexual relationship.
13 'Alas! Deceived', in Regan (ed.), *New Casebooks: Philip Larkin*, p. 248.
14 *A Writer's Life*, p. 446.
15 For example, Amis's reviews of *A Girl in Winter* and *All What Jazz* were complimentary.

16   *A Writer's Life*, p. 523.
17   Virginia Woolf, *A Woman's Essays: Selected Essays*, vol. 1, ed. Rachel Bowlby (London, 1992), p. 84.
18   Stefan Zweig, *The World of Yesterday* (London, 1949).
19   *The Spectator* (1 October 1954), p. 400.
20   Robert Conquest (ed.), *New Lines* (London, 1956), pp. xiv–xv.
21   *TES* (13 June 1956).
22   In the Introduction to the reissued *The North Ship*, 1965. Larkin's account can be found in *Required Writing: Miscellaneous Pieces, 1955–1982* (London, 1983), p. 29, where he tells us that 'When reaction [against Yeats's influence] came, it was undramatic, complete and permanent'.
23   Donald Davie, *Purity of Diction in English Verse* (London, 1952), pp. 138–9.
24   F. R. Leavis's *New Bearings in English Poetry* came out in 1932, and his *The Common Pursuit* in 1952, for example.
25   Blake Morrison, *The Movement: English Poetry and Fiction of the 1950s* (Oxford, 1980), pp. 112–13.
26   Ibid., p. 126.
27   Philip Larkin, 'The Pleasure Principle', in *Required Writing*, pp. 81–2.
28   Ibid., p. 82.

Chapter 8: The Historical Context

1   Quoted in *A Writer's Life*, p. 33.
2   Philip Larkin to Jim Sutton, 21 May 1941.
3   Morrison, *The Movement*, pp. 57–8.
4   Philip Larkin to Colin Gunner, 15 June 1982.
5   Such searches for original cause are fruitless: consider the 'roaring twenties', or the *fin de siècle*, or even the Regency beaus. Generational rebellions have a long pedigree!
6   *A Writer's Life*, p. 377.
7   An exposé of postwar psychological selling techniques can be found in Vance Packard's *The Hidden Persuaders* (1957).

8   Quoted in *A Writer's Life*, p. 377.
9   Quoted ibid., pp. 409–10.
10 David Reynolds, *One World Divisible: A Global History Since 1945* (London and New York, 2000), p. 133.

Chapter 9: A Sample of Critical Views

1   C. Tomlinson, 'The Middlebrow Muse', *Essays in Criticism, 7* (1957), pp. 208–17.
2   D. Davie, 'Landscapes of Larkin', in *Thomas Hardy and British Poetry* (London, 1973), p. 64.
3   Regan (ed.), *New Casebooks: Philip Larkin*, p. 7.
4   J. R. Watson, 'The Other Larkin', *Critical Quarterly*, 17 (1975).
5   S. Heaney, 'The Main of Light', *The Government of the Tongue* (London, 1988), repr. in Regan (ed.), *New Casebooks: Philip Larkin*, pp. 23–31.
6   Morrison, *The Movement*.
7   *The Guardian*, 14 October 1988.
8   A. Bennett, 'Alas! Deceived' (1993), repr. in Regan (ed.), *New Casebooks: Philip Larkin*, p. 248.
9   James Booth (ed.), *New Larkins for Old: Critical Essays* (London and New York, 2000), p. 1.
10 The summary and quotations from Tom Paulin are drawn from 'Into the Heart of Englishness' (1990), repr. in Regan (ed.), *New Casebooks: Philip Larkin*, pp. 160–77. Page references to this work are given in parentheses in the text.
11 A comic name for a Dutch painter from Larkin's poem 'The Card-Players' (*CP*, 177).
12 The summary and quotations from James Booth are drawn from 'Philip Larkin: Lyricism, Englishness and Postcoloniality' (1994), repr. in Regan (ed.), *New Casebooks: Philip Larkin*, pp. 187–210. Page references to this work are given in parentheses in the text.
13 Booth, *Philip Larkin: Writer* (Hemel Hempstead, 1992), p. 164. Page references to this work will appear in parentheses in the text for the remainder of the section.

14 The summary and quotations from Steve Clark are drawn from ' "The Lost Displays": Larkin and Empire', in Booth (ed.), *New Larkins for Old*, pp. 166–81. Page references to this work are given in parentheses in the text.

15 *A Writer's Life*, p. xx.

16 *Letters*, 380.

17 Ibid., 307.

18 Larkin, *Required Writing*, p. 100.

19 The summary and quotations from Stephen Cooper are drawn from *Philip Larkin: Subversive Writer* (Brighton, 2004). Page references to this work are given in parentheses in the text.

20 Rossen, 'Difficulties with Girls', in Regan (ed.), *New Casebook: Philip Larkin*, p. 153.

21 Ibid., p. 154.

22 Stephen Regan, *Philip Larkin*, Critics Debate series (Basingstoke, 1992), pp. 141–2.

23 Osborne, 'Post Modernism and Postcolonialism in the Poetry of Philip Larkin', in Booth (ed.), *New Larkins for Old*, pp. 145–65.

24 V. P. Pelizzon, 'Native Carnival: Philip Larkin's Puppet-Theatre of Ritual', in Booth (ed.), *New Larkins for Old*, pp. 213–23.

Further Reading

Your first job is to study the text. There is no substitute for the work of detailed analysis: that is how you gain the close familiarity with the text, and the fully developed understanding of its content, which make the essays you write both personal and convincing. For this reason it is a good general rule not to read other books around or about the text you are studying until you have finished reading it for yourself. You can easily lose this crucial first response if you go to the professional interpreters too soon.

Once you are familiar with the text, you may wish to read around and about it. This brief chapter is intended only to set you off: there are many relevant books and articles, and we can mention only a few; but most critical works have suggestions for further reading or a bibliography of their own. Once you have begun to read beyond your text, you can use these and a good library to follow up your particular interests. This chapter is divided into 'Reading around the Text', which lists Larkin's works, and a few suggestions from the same period; 'Biography and Context'; and 'Criticism', which contains a small selection of titles that will introduce you to some of the varieties of opinion among professional critics.

Reading Around the Text

Larkin's Works

Larkin's poems are available as *Philip Larkin: Collected Poems*, edited and with an Introduction by Anthony Thwaite (London and Boston, 1988 and 1990). This is the edition recommended for use in Part I, rather

224

than the individual collections *The Less Deceived, The Whitsun Weddings* and *High Windows*, although these are still available separately.

Larkin published two novels during his lifetime: *Jill* (1946) and *A Girl in Winter* (1947). At least one of these should be on the reading list of the serious student of Larkin. He collected jazz reviews in *All What Jazz: A Record Diary* (London, 1970), and other prose writing and journalism in *Required Writing: Miscellaneous Pieces, 1955–1982* (London and Boston, 1983). Since his death, Larkin's early unpublished schoolgirl novels together with two unfinished novel-fragments have been published as *Trouble at Willow Gables and Other Fiction* (London, 2002); and a further collection of other prose has appeared as *Further Requirements, 1952–1985* (London and Boston, 2001). A large number of Larkin's letters have been published, edited by Anthony Thwaite, as *Selected Letters of Philip Larkin, 1940–1985* (London and Boston, 1992). In addition to these published books, there is a large amount of further material in the Larkin archive at the Brynmor Jones Library of the University of Hull, and scholars and critics are gradually mining the still unpublished letters, pieces and notebooks held there.

It is worthwhile for the student of Larkin's poetry to have some familiarity with other poetry from the same period, and with predecessors who may have influenced Larkin. The poets mentioned are all frequently anthologised, or separate editions of selected and collected poems are widely available. It is worthwhile to read one or two poems by each of them. This does not amount to studying them, but it will give a flavour of their preoccupations and first-hand experience of their style. Modernist or romantic poets Larkin reacted against include T. S. Eliot, Ezra Pound, e. e. cummings, D. H. Lawrence and Dylan Thomas. Predecessors he admired, and to whom he may owe a debt, include Thomas Hardy, W. B. Yeats, W. H. Auden and Robert Graves, as well as John Betjeman whose poetry is often closely linked to Larkin's own. From that period it is also worth looking at Stephen Spender and Louis MacNeice. Among his fellow Movement writers, it may be worth reading poems by Kingsley Amis, Robert Conquest and Elizabeth Jennings as well as Thom Gunn, whose later work develops away from Movement precepts. Then, read poems by

Ted Hughes, Sylvia Plath, Charles Causley and Seamus Heaney. This list could go on (for example, we have not mentioned the 'Liverpool Poets' of the 1960s such as Roger McGough; or continuing 'English' comic verse such as that of Pam Ayres!); but the above will certainly provide a flavour of the relevant periods and styles.

It may be worthwhile to read some fiction, particularly that which belongs to the postwar period. Kingsley Amis's *Lucky Jim* (1954), in which there is a character based on Philip Larkin, has been available in Penguin since the 1960s, and you should be able to find John Wain's *Hurry On Down* either online or in libraries. The hard-hitting working-class novels *Room at the Top*, by John Braine, and Alan Sillitoe's *Saturday Night and Sunday Morning* (1958) are also worth looking at.

Biography and Context

I have already mentioned Anthony Thwaite's selection of Larkin's letters. You should also read at least some passages from Andrew Motion's biography *Philip Larkin: A Writer's Life* (London, 1993), and it is worth looking at the essays and tributes in *Larkin at Sixty*, edited by Anthony Thwaite (London, 1982). Out of the memoirs that have appeared, I suggest two: Jean Hartley's autobiography *Philip Larkin, the Marvell Press and Me* (Manchester, 1989) gives an intelligent and readable account of her friendship with Larkin, and of his personality; and *The Philip Larkin I Knew*, by Maeve Brennan (Manchester, 2002), is almost as interesting for revealing how Larkin kept one kind of romance separate from another, and how Brennan deals with discovering his compartmentalised life, as it is for a plain and readable account of their affair and, particularly, of Larkin's work and colleagues in the library at Hull.

Criticism

The critical works sampled in Chapter 9 are: Tom Paulin, 'Into the Heart of Englishness', in Stephen Regan (ed.), *New Casebooks: Philip Larkin* (Basingstoke, 1997), pp. 160–77; James Booth, 'Philip

Larkin: Lyricism, Englishness and Postcoloniality', in Regan (ed.), *New Casebooks: Philip Larkin*, pp. 187–210; James Booth, *Philip Larkin: Writer* (Hemel Hempstead, 1992); Steve Clark, ' "The Lost Displays": Larkin and Empire', in James Booth (ed.), *New Larkins for Old: Critical Essays* (Basingstoke, 2000), pp. 166–81; and Stephen Cooper, *Philip Larkin: Subversive Writer* (Brighton, 2004).

Anthologies of critical essays and articles are a good way to sample a wider variety of critical views. You can then go on to read the full-length books written by those critics whose ideas and approaches you find stimulating. The *New Casebooks* series (general editors John Peck and Martin Coyle), published by Macmillan, collects a variety of critical articles together, and provides an introduction which discusses the critical history of the text. The volume on *Philip Larkin* is edited by Stephen Regan and includes the essays by Tom Paulin and James Booth we sampled in Chapter 9. Other collections which contain important critical views include Linda Cookson and Brian Loughrey (eds), *Critical Essays on Philip Larkin: The Poems* (Harlow, 1989); and James Booth (ed.), *New Larkins for Old: Critical Essays* (Basingstoke, 2000).

The following full-length works are some of the more significant contributions to Larkin studies (but do not forget James Booth and Stephen Cooper, who have already been mentioned): Stephen Regan, *Philip Larkin* (Critics Debate series, Basingstoke, 1992); Andrew Swarbrick, *Out of Reach: The Poetry of Philip Larkin* (Basingstoke, 1995); Janice Rossen, *Philip Larkin: His Life's Work* (Hemel Hempstead, 1989); and A. T. Tolley, *My Proper Ground: A Study of the Work of Philip Larkin and its Development* (Edinburgh, 1991).

These are only a few suggestions, intended to provide a first step towards the variety of Larkin criticism. Use the bibliographies and 'further reading' lists in the books mentioned here to lead you in pursuit of different views, or in pursuit of your particular interest.

It is worth remembering that discussions of Larkin are also found in works which are not solely concerned with him. One such work is Blake Morrison's *The Movement: English Poetry and Fiction of the 1950s* (Oxford, 1980), which contains a great deal of information about Larkin's friendships with Amis, Wain and others, as well as interesting consideration of his poetry. Also, as examples, it may be worth your while to look at discussions of Larkin in John Lucas's

Modern English Poetry from Hardy to Hughes (London, 1986); or in Geoffrey Thurley's *The Ironic Harvest: English Poetry in the Twentieth Century* (London, 1974). When you are in a library, use the catalogue system resourcefully. There are numerous books which appear to be on different subjects – Modern Poetry, Postwar Culture, and so on. Many of these contain chapters, passages or essays about Larkin which may bring an illuminating angle to bear upon his writing.

Index